AMBIVALENT EMBRACE

Recent Titles in
Contributions to the Study of World History

AMBIVALENT
_____ EMBRACE

America's Troubled Relations with
Spain from the Revolutionary War
to the Cold War

RODRIGO BOTERO

Contributions to the Study of World History,
Number 78

GREENWOOD PRESS
Westport, Connecticut • London

Library of Congress Cataloging-in-Publication Data

Botero, Rodrigo.
    Ambivalent embrace : America's troubled relations with Spain from the
Revolutionary War to the Cold War / by Rodrigo Botero.
        p.   cm.—(Contributions to the study of world history, ISSN 0885–9159 ; no. 78)
    Includes bibliographical references (p.   ) and index.
    ISBN 0–313–31570–1 (alk. paper)
    1. United States—Relations—Spain.   2. Spain—Relations—United States.   I. Title.
    II.   Series.
    E183.8.S7B68   2001
    303.48'273046—dc21   00–035356

British Library Cataloguing in Publication Data is available.

Library of Congress Catalog Card Number: 00–035356
ISBN: 0–313–31570–1
ISSN: 0885–9159

First published in 2001

Greenwood Press, 88 Post Road West, Westport, CT 06881
An imprint of Greenwood Publishing Group, Inc.
www.greenwood.com

Printed in the United States of America

The paper used in this book complies with the
Permanent Paper Standard issued by the National
Information Standards Organization (Z39.48–1984).

10 9 8 7 6 5 4 3 2 1

For Louise

and, In Memoriam
Jaime Botero Londoño
Fabiola Montoya de Botero

Contents

The author shaking hands with Francisco Franco. At center is Misael Pastrana, Ambassador to Washington at the time, later President (1970–1974).

Introduction

Significant differences in the historical trajectories of Spain and the United States have shaped the peculiar character of their bilateral relations for two centuries. From the start of the North American Revolutionary War in the 1770s, until the consolidation of constitutional democracy in post-Franco Spain during the 1970s, the pattern of relations between Spain and the United States could be described as consisting of long periods of disinterest and estrangement, interrupted by short bursts of mutual interaction, usually of an adversarial nature. It is only in the last two decades that the bilateral relationship has come to resemble the prevailing norm between advanced Western democratic societies, which is one of close ties and friendly cooperation in the economic, political, cultural, and military spheres.

Spain has been a leading protagonist of world-historical events on three occasions: first and foremost, during the ascendancy of the Hapsburgs, when an American colonial empire was established; in modern times during the struggle against the Napoleonic invasion, and again during the Spanish civil war of 1936–1939. For the United States, the Revolutionary War, the adoption of the Constitution, the expansion to continental dimensions and the Civil War were events of world–historical significance, as was its emergence as a major industrial and military power at the end of the nineteenth century. During several of these stages the colonial interests of Spain came into conflict with the interests of the United States as an expanding power. In the process of territorial expansion and consolidation of its role as the preeminent power in the Western Hemisphere, policy makers in the United States regarded Spain as a rival and an obstacle to the fulfillment of the national destiny. Likewise, Spanish officials regarded the emergence of a sovereign nation in North America as a potential threat to the metropolitan trade monopoly, and eventually to the security of the Spanish American colonies.

From the early stages of the bilateral relationship, North American and Spanish policy makers became aware of the potential for conflict in their respective perceptions of the national interest. Some of these differences were of a zero-sum nature and constituted legitimate grounds for antagonism. The settlement of these differences could have been facilitated by an environment of preexisting mutual trust and goodwill. The prevailing cultural and religious prejudices of both sides, however, had the opposite effect.

The bilateral relationship was characterized not only by mutually perceived conflicting national interests but also by an asymmetry of power. From 1775 to 1783, before the recognition of independence, the United States was the relatively weaker partner, requesting and obtaining assistance from Spain in the war with Great Britain. Subsequently, a growing and assertive United States, provided by the Constitution with a strong executive branch, was able to negotiate from a position of strength with a weak and fragmented Spain that was caught in the upheavals resulting from the French Revolution. The two settlements of bilateral territorial disputes of 1795 and 1819 (Pinckney's Treaty and Adams-Onís Treaty, respectively), overwhelmingly favorable to the demands of the United States, reflect the changes that had taken place in the correlation of power between the two parties. This asymmetry was most dramatically illustrated with the brief hostilities of 1898 and the definitive loss of the Spanish colonial empire.

During the first three decades of the twentieth century, official dealings between Spain and the United States were relatively uneventful. Policy makers in Madrid and Washington coincided in assigning a low priority to the bilateral relationship.

The Spanish civil war (1936–1939) became a matter of concern for the administration of President Franklin D. Roosevelt for fear that it could aggravate a rapidly deteriorating international situation. During World War II, exchanges between Spain and the United States took place within an unfavorable context.

The war in Spain ended with the defeat of the Republic by a military uprising that had received significant support from Nazi Germany and Fascist Italy. The regime that emerged from the conflict was a right-wing dictatorship led by General Francisco Franco, a regime that did not conceal its contempt for the Western democracies, and—at least in the early years of the world war—openly proclaimed its pro-Axis sympathies, notwithstanding Spain's status as a neutral country.

Once the United States entered the war against the Axis powers, governmental attitudes towards Spain acquired an adversarial character on account of the origins, the antidemocratic nature, and the behavior of the Franco regime.

Washington's hostility to Franco was tempered principally by the tactical objective of keeping Spain from entering the war on Germany's side, an objective that was strongly supported by Great Britain. This restraining element disappeared after the defeat of Germany in 1945.

In the early postwar years, Franco's Spain was denounced for its pro-Axis sympathies, excluded from the United Nations, and isolated diplomatically. Between 1945 and 1947 the State Department adopted a policy of ostracism of the Franco regime in the hope that it would bring about a peaceful governmental change in Spain. From 1947 to 1951 this policy was abandoned, in part due to Spanish diplomatic endeavors, but primarily because of the international tensions that gave rise to the cold war. The climate of confrontation between Western democracies and the Soviet Union and its allies provided the impetus for the change that took place in Washington's policy towards the Spanish regime, from antagonism to cooperation. The cooperation began primarily in the military sphere, but eventually extended to the economic and diplomatic spheres as well. The improved bilateral relations with the United States opened the way for Spain's reincorporation into the international community and the gradual normalization of its relations with the countries of Western Europe.

This work studies the vicissitudes of the bilateral relationship from the emergence of the United States as an independent nation to the period after World War II, when the United States and Spain reached an agreement on military cooperation as part of the overall defense of Western Europe. Chapters 1 and 2 discuss the relations between the two countries from the beginning of the Revolutionary War to the signing of the Adams-Onís Treaty of 1819 that formalized Spain's withdrawal from North America. Chapter 3 describes the commencement of hispanic studies in the United States, and the divergent trajectories followed by the two countries during the nineteenth century. Chapter 4 discusses the deterioration of the bilateral relationship brought about by Cuba's struggle for independence from Spain, and the brief but decisive Spanish-American War of 1898, which resulted in the loss of the Philippines and of Spain's remaining possessions in the Caribbean.

Chapters 5 and 6 study the bilateral relations during the first half of the twentieth century, with emphasis on the period 1942 to 1951, when the two countries dealt with each other under adverse external circumstances, initially as quasi adversaries, and eventually as de facto allies.

Chapter 1 ———————————————————

Cobelligerents, but
Not Allies

EARLY BILATERAL RELATIONS, 1775–1783

Two factors contributed to shape the parameters of the bilateral relationship as the United States appeared on the world scene as an independent actor. Throughout the eighteenth century, with the installation of the Bourbon dynasty in Madrid, Spain and France had become close commercial and diplomatic partners. The two Bourbon monarchies had formalized this relationship in a mutual defense alliance known as the Family Compact. The counterpart to this relationship was Spain's long standing hostility towards England, aggravated by the loss of Gibraltar in 1713, and the territorial losses in North America—Florida and possessions east of the Mississippi—resulting from the settlement of the Seven Years' War in 1763.

The mutual distrust and enmity that characterized relations between Spain and England since the sixteenth century, periodically erupting into open warfare, contributed to shape the attitudes of both parties as the emissaries of North America began negotiations with the representatives of Carlos III. The educated elite of the North American colonies inherited from England the image of Spain as the traditional enemy, reinforced by anti-Catholic sentiments and Anglo-Dutch contributions to Hispanophobic literature and propaganda. In addition to these preconceived points of view, Enlightenment intellectuals had popularized the notion of Span-

General Franco and President Eisenhower at Torrejon Air Force Base on December 22, 1959. Eisenhower's visit to Madrid, which signaled the end of the international isolation of the Spanish dictatorship was perceived as a major diplomatic triumph for Franco. Used by permission of Agencia EFE.

ish decadence, which they attributed to a system of oppression, obscurantism, and backwardness. Spanish officials in turn, regarded the
colonists as Englishmen, that is as hereditary adversaries, and as Protestants.

From within the political culture of an absolute monarchy, the concept
of a legitimate right of armed resistance to royal power was repugnant
in itself and particularly troubling as a precedent in the New World.
From the recurring episodes of Anglo-Spanish hostilities in the eighteenth century, two considerations are particularly noteworthy because
of their implications for the relations between Spain and the United
States. The first is the priority assigned by Spain to the recovery of Gibraltar. This objective was to impinge on the negotiations leading to the
settlement of the North American War of Independence. The second is
the cession—made by Louis XV of France to Carlos III of Spain—of Louisiana in 1763 in compensation for the loss of Florida in the Seven Years'
War. With this transfer, the navigation of the Mississippi River and access to the Gulf of Mexico became issues that concerned both Spain and
the United States.

As the differences between the North American colonies and the metropolis moved towards military hostilities, the leaders of the resistance
to Great Britain began to seek external sources of support for the approaching struggle. France and Spain were likely candidates, since the
two European powers were opposed to Great Britain's commercial and
colonial expansion. Furthermore, given their close ties, it could be expected that cooperation from one of these powers would bring about a
similar response from the other.

The colonies were also in need of commercial partners, given the trade
embargo imposed upon them by Parliament in December 1775, of military supplies and personnel, and of financial and diplomatic assistance.
In November 1775 the Continental Congress created a Committee of Secret Correspondence entrusted with handling external relations. This
body, which carried out the functions of a foreign office, included among
its most influential members Benjamin Franklin and John Jay.

In March 1776, the committee decided to send an agent to the Court
of France to obtain approval for the purchase of supplies on credit and
to enquire about the possibilities of French political and military support
in the impending war with Great Britain. The person chosen for this
task—the first foreign mission of the United States—was Silas Deane, a
delegate from Connecticut who arrived in Paris on July 7, 1776.

The French foreign minister, Count Charles Gravier de Vergennes, received Deane cordially, and informed him of his government's decision to keep its ports open to both North American and British shipping, a tacit recognition of belligerency. For the purchase of munitions, he referred Deane to his agent Caron de Beaumarchais in London. The latter organized a cover for the channelling of supplies to the colonies under the name of Roderigue Hortalez & Co.

The success of Deane's mission was assured by decisions that had already been made in Madrid and in Versailles. Several months before his arrival in Paris, the governments of France and Spain had agreed to provide secret financial contributions in support of the insurrection of the colonies.

On March 1, 1776, Vergennes wrote to his Spanish colleague, Jerónimo the marquis of Grimaldi, inquiring if Spain would be willing to join France in giving covert assistance to the colonies. Grimaldi's reply of March 14 marks the beginning of Spain's participation in the North American Revolutionary War. His letter outlines his government's policy on the matter, which coincided in part with that of the French government notwithstanding differences in objectives and in perspectives. Grimaldi agreed in the usefulness of encouraging the revolt as a means of weakening Great Britain and repaying her for similar actions against Spain: "Right and interest should persuade us to help the English Colonials."

Taking into account that the means of providing covert assistance were easier to find in France than in Spain, his royal master, Carlos III, left the decision to proceed and the form of carrying it out to Louis XVI and his ministry, and agreed to share the expenses to the best of his ability. Grimaldi pointed out that "nobody has asked us to help the Colonies in revolt," thereby dispelling Vergenne's impression, based on information provided to Beaumarchais, his London-based agent, by the colonial representative Arthur Lee. With respect to the desirable outcome of the conflict, he stated: "It is certainly to our advantage that the revolt of these people is sustained. And we should desire that they and the English exhaust themselves reciprocally."[1]

This document foreshadows some of the features of the emerging relationship between the United States, France, and Spain during the Revolutionary War. The early diplomatic initiatives of the United States assigned preeminence to relations with France. Although the two Bourbon monarchies were expected to join forces against Great Britain at the opportune time, it was tacitly understood that France would play a leading military and diplomatic role. While Spanish policy makers concurred in the goal of weakening Great Britain, the achievement of independence on the part of the North American colonies was not regarded as a high-priority objective.

On the latter issue, the policy of the Spanish monarchy was clearly at odds with that of its Bourbon ally. For the French ministry, the revolt of the colonies was seen as the opportunity to reverse the advantages gained by Great Britain by the Treaty of Paris as a result of the Seven Years' War, altering thereby the balance of power in France's favor. This policy, which was originally adopted by Étienne-François de Choiseul, the foreign minister under Louis XV from 1758 to 1770, and continued by Vergennes, his successor, specifically contemplated encouragement and support of colonial separation from Great Britain. Independence of the North American colonies, with the subsequent military and economic weakening of the metropolis, was therefore a French policy objective that to the detriment of Great Britain, held the possibility of commercial advantages. Therefore, when France entered the war as an ally of the United States in 1778, Vergennes formally committed his government not to lay down its arms until the independence of the United States had been secured.

The Spanish government, however, was unwilling to accept this objective. It specifically excluded it from the terms of the secret Franco-Spanish Convention of Aranjuez in accordance to which it entered the war in 1779 after its offer of mediation had been rejected by Great Britain. Spain entered the war as an ally of France, but only as a cobelligerent of the United States whose independence it refused to recognize before it had been acknowledged by Great Britain.

Furthermore, the Convention of Aranjuez bound France to continue the war until Gibraltar had been recovered by its ally, which was Spain's foremost policy objective. When Britain refused to return Gibraltar and Minorca as the price for her mediation, José Moñino y Redondo, the count of Floridablanca, Grimaldi's successor as foreign minister, decided to pursue the same goal by other means. He insisted on this objective as the condition for Spain's agreement to join the war, which was the price that Vergennes was willing to pay. As a result, France bound itself by separate treaties to Spain and the United States, treaties whose terms contained potentially conflicting war objectives between its two allies. Gibraltar was of negligible concern to the United States, and North American independence was of no particular interest to Spain. Each party was willing to forsake the primary war objective of the other, for the sake of its own.

After the exchange of correspondence between the French and Spanish ministers of March 1776, Vergennes obtained approval in May from the Royal Council for an initial subsidy of one million livres to the colonies, a sum that was matched by the Spanish government. With that decision, the first step towards intervention in the conflict between Great Britain and the colonies was taken by the two Bourbon monarchies, a step that would in time bring them into war with Great Britain.

During 1776 and 1777, the two Bourbon allies contemplated the possibility of provoking Great Britain into war, but were unable to agree on the timing or the circumstances. Portugal was one source of disagreement. Some Spanish officials favored invading Portugal and annexing it to Spain in retaliation for Portuguese encroachment in the Plata region of South America. Vergennes was reluctant to commit France to war for such an objective, which he feared would further complicate European matters. In his view, it was in France's interest to avoid disrupting the peace on the Continent so as to be able to pursue a maritime war against Great Britain. According to this strategy, the major part of the military effort would take place in North America and on the seas. Spanish policy makers, on the other hand, felt that Spain had much more at risk in the New World than her ally. This vulnerability argued for a more European-oriented strategy. Unable to come to terms on a mutually acceptable plan of action, the two courts agreed to increase their military preparations, to continue to provide secret subsidies to the colonies, and to wait for the appropriate time and circumstances for a joint enterprise.

Major General John Burgoyne's surrender at Saratoga on October 17, 1777, the news of which reached France in December, signaled to Vergennes that the moment of decision had arrived. Fearing that a generous British offer, short of actual independence, might appear attractive to the colonies, which lacked significant external recognition and support, Vergennes informed the North American commissioners (Franklin, Deane, and Lee) of France's willingness—pending consultation with Spain—to extend recognition and to sign a treaty of friendship and commerce with the United States. The Spanish reaction to this initiative was not favorable. Carlos III was inclined towards remaining at peace with Great Britain. Floridablanca was unwilling to recognize the independence of the United States, and he was irritated by French policy on this question, which he considered hasty and imprudent. He complained to the Spanish ambassador at Versailles, Pedro Pablo Abarca de Bolea, the count of Aranda, of the way in which the French ministry was handling relations with the North American commissioners:

To call those Deputies, inform them of the decision taken by the Christian King and to add that His Catholic Majesty would be notified in view of the existing ties of friendship and kinship. Thereby, in addition to getting us into a conflict that may not be convenient for us, that Court has tried to reap all the credit for our consent, if it were given, or to heap upon us the mistrust and hatred of the Americans if we did not join the scheme immediately.[2]

Spain's disagreement notwithstanding, Vergennes decided that, if necessary, France would proceed alone even though such a step would be contrary to the spirit of the Family Compact.

On February 6, 1778, the plenipotentiaries of France and the United States signed a treaty of amity and commerce and a treaty of alliance for the purpose of securing the independence of the United States. The treaty of alliance included a separate and secret provision reserving the right of the king of Spain to adhere to both treaties. Louis XVI formalized the recognition of sovereignty by receiving the representatives of Congress at Versailles on March 20, 1778. Hostilities between France and Great Britain began in June of the same year.

Vergennes's violation of the Family Compact left the cautious Floridablanca at liberty to follow an independent policy towards the Anglo-American conflict guided by what were perceived as Spain's particular interests. The decision taken was to refrain from entering the war, but to increase military preparedness as a precaution against aggression. Great Britain was informed that Spain did not want war but did not fear it. The good offices of Carlos III were offered to mediate between the parties in conflict and to bring about a negotiated settlement of the war. After several offers of mediation were rejected, a final offer of terms— in the form of an ultimatum—was sent by Floridablanca to Great Britain in April 1779. The offer was refused by the British government. In accordance with plans previously negotiated with France for joint military operations, Spain declared war on Great Britain on June 21, 1779.

Spain's belligerence was welcome news to both the United States and France. The winter of 1778–1779 and the following spring were among the most unfavorable periods of the Revolutionary War. The Continental army was confronting adversity at Valley Forge, and on the seas, the British were using to advantage their superiority in ships and armament over the French fleet.

As General George Washington wrote to Gouverneur Morris on October 4, 1778, "If the Spaniards would but join their fleets to France and commence hostilities, my doubts would all subside. Without it, I fear the British navy has too much in its power to counteract the schemes of France."[3] In effect, the incorporation of Spain into the ranks of her adversaries compelled Britain to modify the deployment of the navy in order to protect Gibraltar and the West Indies as well as a precaution against the threat of invasion of England, which the combined French and Spanish fleets now made possible. Thanks to this dispersal of British naval forces, a French squadron under Admiral François-Joseph-Paul de Grasse sailed into the Chesapeake Bay on August 31, 1781, acquired effective control of those waters, and played a decisive role in the Yorktown campaign.

Spain concentrated her war efforts in the pursuit of European objectives. Minorca was taken and Gibraltar was besieged, without success. In North America, Spanish forces under the command of Bernardo de Gálvez captured West Florida. Also, from Spanish posts on the west bank of the Mississippi, expeditions were sent across the river against British held positions. These operations gave rise to Spanish claims on the east bank of the Mississippi, above and below the Ohio River, as territory taken from Britain.

Spain's gains in North America highlighted areas of eventual disagreement with the United States on the question of boundaries. On August 14, 1779, Congress defined terms for peace negotiations, which were to be entrusted to John Adams. The following objectives were declared sine qua non conditions for an acceptable peace settlement: (1) independence, and (2) the Mississippi River as the western boundary of the United States and the line 31 degrees north latitude as the southern boundary on the West Florida frontier.[4] Even as they looked forward to the favorable outcome of the war against a common enemy, it was becoming apparent to policy makers in Spain and the United States that the two nations were destined to share a disputed border that separated sparsely settled territories and that constituted a potential source of conflict.

From the beginning of the Revolutionary War, regular exchanges of a semiofficial nature took place between representatives of the North American colonies and Spanish officials, to handle matters of mutual interest. After making the initial contribution of one million livres to launch Beaumarchais's scheme of subsidies disguised as commerce, Spain secretly provided money to Lee and other North American agents in Europe, without the use of French intermediaries. The funds were managed by Don Diego de Gardoqui, an official in the Ministry of Finance, and channelled through his father's firm, the house of Gardoqui and Sons of Bilbao.[5] Through this mechanism, military supplies were made available to the Continental army at Havana and New Orleans. In January 1778, Don Juan de Miralles, a Cuban merchant and slave trader arrived in Charleston, South Carolina, following instructions from José Gálvez, Spanish minister of the Indies. His function was to act as an observer without diplomatic status, reporting to Gálvez via the governor of Havana. His orders were to inform Gálvez on the progress of the war and on any danger to Spanish and French possessions as well as to dissuade the colonies from negotiating a settlement with Britain, without the protection of France and Spain. Miralles, his lack of official accreditation notwithstanding, was received as a minister and remained in the United States until his death at General Washington's camp in April 1780. He was succeeded by his secretary Francisco Rendón, whose functions continued until the end of the war.

In the early stages of the war, Congress assigned the task of establishing relations between the United States and Spain to the commissioners at the Court of Versailles, Franklin, Deane, and Lee. In January 1777 Congress invested Franklin with full powers to negotiate a treaty of alliance and mutual defense with duly authorized representatives of the Spanish Crown. Franklin's interlocutor for the first official exchanges between the two governments was Aranda, the Spanish ambassador to France and a prominent Aragonese statesman who had previously occupied the position of chief minister to Carlos III, as president of the Council of Castile. After Spain entered the war, Congress appointed Jay as its representative to Carlos III's Court. Jay remained in Spain from January 1780 until May 1782, when he departed for Paris to participate in the peace negotiations. From the time of his departure until 1783, Jay was succeeded by his secretary William Carmichael. In 1783, Carmichael was recognized by the Spanish Court as the official representative of the United States.

Jay arrived in Spain with instructions to obtain from the Court of Madrid acknowledgement of independence, a treaty of alliance, recognition of the western and southern boundaries determined by Congress, navigation rights on the Mississippi to the sea below the 31st degree north latitude line, a port of entry into Spanish territory below that line, and a loan or subsidy of five million dollars—an ambitious set of objectives for which the United States had little to offer Spain in reciprocity. His mission failed. Floridablanca received him cordially, listened to his proposals, and provided him with modest financial support, but declined any formal commitments. The Spanish ministry's refusal to recognize the independence of the United States before Britain precluded the possibility of concluding a treaty before the end of the war. Spanish officials regarded the North American representatives as insurgents rather than as agents of a sovereign nation. This distinction was made explicit with characteristic Spanish punctilio. Aranda received Franklin and his fellow commissioners in Paris in his private capacity as a Spanish nobleman rather than as ambassador. Floridablanca in turn, extended an invitation to Jay to attend his table as an American gentleman of distinction, an invitation that Jay declined as improper for a representative of an independent nation. For similar reasons he declined being presented at court as a foreigner of distinction.[6] Jay's predicament, of being accredited to a government that did not recognize his official status, would be replicated a few decades later, this time by a Spanish minister to the United States.[7]

The failure of Jay's mission to Madrid illustrates the shift in the mood of influential North American statesmen towards Spain from one of high hopes and friendship, to one of disillusionment, resentment, and mistrust. Spain's entry into the war was received in North America with high expectations, for military as well as financial reasons. Thus, in a letter to Jay, Robert Morris, the newly appointed superintendent of finance of the United States, referred to "the derangement of our money affairs, the enormity of our public expenditures, the confusion in all our departments" and added:

> While we have neither credit nor means at home, it is idle to expect much from individuals abroad. . . . We must then turn our eyes to Spain, and we must ask either loans or subsidies to a very considerable amount. Small sums are not worth the acceptance. They have the air of obligation without affording relief. A small sum therefore, is not an object to the United States, for they do not mean to beg gratuities but to make rational requests.[8]

The importance attached by Congress to a treaty of alliance with Spain may be judged by the price it was willing to pay to bring about such a treaty. By resolution of February 15, 1781, Congress, responding to an unfavorable military situation, modified its previous instructions to Jay, and empowered him to forego navigation rights on the Mississippi from the 31st degree line to the sea, in exchange for Spain's accession to the alliance between France and the United States. Neither Franklin nor Jay were favorably inclined to offer such a concession to Spain.[9]

Notwithstanding his personal reservations, Jay transmitted to Floridablanca the offer, as instructed by Congress, but made it contingent upon Spain's signing a treaty of alliance before the negotiation of a peace settlement.[10] Jay's negotiating capacity on the major issues of bilateral interest was hindered by his need to periodically request funds from the Spanish ministry, for his own support and to cover drafts that Congress drew on him.[11]

Jay was willing to acknowledge the asymmetry in the power relationship between the two parties. He drafted a letter to Floridablanca urging a prompt reply to his proposal for a treaty of alliance that contained the following passage: "I am sensible that Spain possesses a higher degree on the scale of national importance than the United States and I can readily admit that the friendship of this court is of more immediate consequence to America than that of America to the Spanish Empire."[12]

At a conjuncture where Spain held the advantage of a strong bargaining position, and where entering into an alliance would have secured the foundation of a friendly relationship with the United States, Floridablanca adopted a policy of procrastination. Through systematic delays and evasions, he let it be understood that the Spanish Court was not prepared to acknowledge a sovereign American nation, the issue on which all else depended. With the end of the war in sight, and in view of the need to begin preparations for a settlement, Jay departed from Spain in May 1782, in order to participate in the peace negotiations in Paris.

The disappointing outcome of Congress's bid for a Spanish alliance during the war of independence contributed to shape the emerging context of bilateral relations as policy makers in the United States looked ahead to settling the issues of boundaries and commerce of the new nation.

Irrespective of its objective justification, this impression of unrequited friendship formed during the Revolutionary War, would carry over into the world-view of the North American nation, and shape public attitudes as well as government policies toward Spain in the following decades. The resentment of Spain's aloofness on the part of North American statesmen during this period can be attributed at least in part to overly optimistic expectations as to the enthusiasm with which an established imperial power would be willing to support an insurrection against European rule over the North American continent. While the representatives of the North American colonies were pursuing the unequivocal, overriding objective of achieving independence, the officials of the Spanish Crown were operating within the restraints and complexities of the European power structure.

Franklin manifested his displeasure at the meager results of Jay's endeavors in Madrid by stating:

> I am much surprised at the dilatory and reserved conduct of your court. I know not to what amount you have obtained aids from it, but if they are not considerable it were to be wished you had never been sent there, as the slight they have put upon our offered friendship is very disreputable to us, and, of course, hurtful to our affairs elsewhere. I think they are shortsighted, and do not look very far into futurity, or they would seize with avidity so excellent an opportunity of securing a neighbor's friendship, which may hereafter be of great consequence to their American affairs.[13]

In a letter to Congress, Jay reflected upon his experience in dealing with the representatives of Carlos III in the following manner: "It is natural as well as just that Congress should be dissatisfied with the conduct of this court; they certainly have much reason; and yet a distinction may be made between the ministry and the nation, the latter being more to be pitied than blamed."[14] Expressions of North American disenchantment, caused by unfulfilled expectations of Spanish support were not restricted to the diplomatic representatives directly concerned.[15]

Floridablanca's ambivalence towards the Revolutionary War can be attributed to his personal caution and to his perception of Spain's shortcomings vis-à-vis the major European powers. The reluctance of Spanish officials to embrace the cause of North American independence also reflected the limitations inherent to a system of absolute monarchy, even an enlightened one.[16]

Whatever reasons may have weighed more heavily in the decision of the Spanish ministry to reject the proposed alliance with the United States, obscurantism and religious bigotry were not among them. The reign of Carlos III (1759–1788) was a period of administrative, commercial, and intellectual improvement promoted by outstanding reform-minded statesmen such as Gaspar Melchor de Jovellanos; Pedro Rodríguez Campomanes y Pérez, the count of Campomanes; Aranda; and Floridablanca with the encouragement and backing of the king. These men were familiar with the ideas of the philosophes and shared many of the Enlightenment assumptions about the desirability of progress and the advancement of science. They also shared some of the Enlightenment aversion to traditional religion, which manifested itself in anticlericalism and in resentment of the obstacle that the church represented to the assertion of royal sovereignty. During this period the role of the Inquisition was restricted, the number of religious orders was curtailed, the Jesuits were expelled from the realm, and royal authority over the Spanish church was firmly established to the detriment of the Papacy.[17]

Measures were taken to promote manufacturing, to reduce obstacles to commerce, to encourage science, and to improve the quality of education.[18] A typical manifestation of the Spanish Enlightenment spirit was the establishment, under royal patronage, of patriotic associations for the promotion of learning and technical innovation, the societies of Amigos del Pais (Friends of the Country).

Despite these well-intentioned reforms, the Spain of las luces still lagged—economically, scientifically, and militarily—far behind the most advanced European nations. This was particularly so with respect to Great Britain, which by the 1770s had acquired the technological, economic, and institutional preconditions for the onset of the Industrial Revolution. Although Spain made remarkable progress under Carlos III, several decades of enlightened government were not sufficient to compensate for the lead that her principal rivals had established during a century and a half of Iberian economic and intellectual stagnation. Spain's economic development at this time was still severely hampered by monopolistic practices, an archaic fiscal system, widespread aristocratic and ecclesiastic entail, and an entrenched antibusiness mentality. The timing and the nature of some of the reforms are illustrative of the handicaps under which the Spanish economy operated. It was only in 1778 when absolute freedom of trade between Spain and her colonies was established and the unwieldy system of transatlantic fleets abolished. Adequate sources of domestic credit were nonexistent, given the rudimentary nature of the financial institutions. To correct this state of affairs, the Bank of San Carlos—predecessor of Spain's central bank—was founded in 1782 at the suggestion of a Frenchman, Count François de Cabarrus. (The Bank of England—by comparison—was incorporated by an act of Parliament in 1694.) It was not until 1783 that "gentlemen" were permitted to engage in "base and vile" activities without losing their status, and the practice of all trades henceforward declared to be honest and honorable. (The 1783 provisions were not extended to the

American colonies of Spain until 1811, by an act of the Cortes.) The governmental decision-making process, highly centralized and traditionally ponderous, was rendered even more cumbersome by the court's itinerancy.[19]

Furthermore, with few exceptions, the major works of the Enlightenment that were transforming the way in which Western societies thought about government, religion, science, and human rights—Montesquieu's *Spirit of the Laws*, the writings of Voltaire and Jean-Jacques Rousseau, the *Encyclopédie*, Cesare Bonesana Beccaria's *On Crimes and Punishments*—were placed by the Inquisition in the *Index of Forbidden Books*.[20]

Aside from the constraints imposed by these systemic weaknesses, considerations of a practical nature limited the policy options of the Spanish ministry towards the North American colonies during the Revolutionary War. In contrast to France, the prospects of commercial gain suggested by North American negotiators offered little attraction to Spain.[21] Spain's industrial output was incapable of supplying both the home market and the needs of the colonies. To Spanish officials, eventual trade between the United States and Spanish America was regarded as a threat to the colonial trade monopoly rather than as an outcome to be encouraged.[22] Opportunities for significant trade flows between Spain and the United States were modest. Trade, therefore, was not a decisive consideration. The government of Carlos III regarded the consequences of North American independence primarily from the viewpoint of the security of the Spanish colonies, the outlook for which did not appear promising. In 1780, Peru was convulsed by the rebellion of Tupac Amarú. Even more ominously, in 1781 popular protests in New Granada against tax increases caused by the war with Great Britain led to the uprising of the Comuneros.

Considerations of a different nature tended to reinforce the inhibitions arising from pragmatic, Realpolitik reasons. Reform-minded statesmen of the age of Enlightened Despotism were dedicated to the principles of absolute monarchy. To question this system was not considered part of their agenda. On the contrary, their intention was to strengthen it and to make it perform more efficiently. Enlightenment Spain was a nation of estates and privilege, a land of lords and vassals, an Old Regime society where throne and altar upheld and legitimized a traditional social structure. North Americans and Spaniards of this period held radically different assumptions about government, society, and economic organization. In the world-view of Spanish statesmen, the Revolutionary War established three precedents that were particularly troublesome: (1) it challenged Europe's right to rule on the North American continent; (2) it proclaimed the legitimacy of armed resistance to royal authority; and (3) it fixed popular sovereignty as the source of governmental authority. Mutual awareness of these differences helped to define the parameters of the bilateral relationship as Spain and the United States moved from the shared objective of waging war with Great Britain to settling the contentious issues of territorial boundaries and navigation rights.

NOTES

1. Grimaldi to Vergennes, March 14, 1776, in Henri Doniol, *Histoire de la participation de la France à l'établissement des États Unis d'Amérique. Correspondence diplomatique et documents. Complément du tome V* (Paris: Imprimerie Nationale, 1899), 1:370.

2. Floridablanca to Aranda, January 13, 1778, cited in Juan Francisco Yela Utrilla, *España Ante la Independencia de los Estados Unidos*, 2nd ed. (Madrid: Ediciones Istmo, 1988), 1:285.

3. "Washington's Writings," cited in Francis Wharton, ed., *The Revolutionary Diplomatic Correspondence of the United States* (Washington, D.C.: Government Printing Office, 1889), 4:360.

4. Journals of the Continental Congress, September 27, 1779, cited in Samuel Flagg Bemis, *The Diplomacy of the American Revolution* (New York: D. Appleton-Century, 1935), 1991.

5. Diego de Gardoqui later became Spain's first diplomatic representative to the United States with the title of encargado de negocios (1785–1789).

6. Jay to Livingston, April 28, 1782, in Wharton, op. cit., 5:376–377.

7. Don Luis de Onís, negotiator of the 1819 Adams-Onís Treaty. For a period of six years (1809–1815), he represented the Regency in the United States during the uprising against the rule of Joseph Bonaparte. The U.S. government abstained from recognizing either one of the claimants to legitimacy.

8. Morris to Jay, July 4, 1781, in Wharton, op. cit. 4:531ff.

9. "But I hope and am confident that court will be wiser than to take advantage of our distress and insist on our making sacrifices by an agreement which the circumstances of such distress would hereafter weaken, and the very proposition can only give disgust at present. Poor as we are, yet as I know we shall be rich, I would rather agree with them to buy at a great price the whole of their right on the Mississippi than sell a drop of its waters. A neighbor might as well ask me to sell my street door." Franklin to Jay, October 2, 1780, in Wharton, op. cit., 4:74–75.

"But Spain being now at war with Great Britain to gain her own objects, she doubtless will prosecute it full as vigorously as if she fought for our objects. There was and is little reason to suppose that such a cession would render her exertions more vigorous or her aids to us much more liberal. The effect which an alliance between Spain and America would have on Britain and other nations would certainly be in our favor, but whether more so than the free navigation of the Mississippi is less certain. The cessation of this navigation will, in my opinion, render a future war with Spain unavoidable, and I shall look upon my subscribing to the one as fixing the certainty of the other." Jay to the President of Congress, October 3, 1781, in Wharton, op. cit., 4:738ff.

10. Propositions submitted to the Count of Floridablanca, September 22, 1781, transcribed in Jay to the President of Congress, October 3, 1781, in Wharton, op. cit., 4:738ff.

11. ". . . nothing could be clearly established with Jay in several conversations Don Bernardo del Campo and I held with him because his two principal points were: Spain, recognize our independence and Spain, give us money." Florida-blanca to Aranda, September 20, 1782, in Yela Utrilla, op. cit., 2:364–365.

12. Jay showed the draft of the letter to the French ambassador to Spain, Armand Marc, comte de Montmorin, who dissuaded him from sending it to avoid giving offense by the reference to Spanish dilatoriness. The text of the letter is included in Jay to the President of Congress, October 3, 1781, in Wharton, op. cit., 4:755.

13. Franklin to Jay, January 19, 1782, in Wharton, op. cit., 5:354.

14. Jay to Livingston, April 28, 1782, in Wharton, op. cit., 5:374–375.

15. Robert Livingston, from the Office of Foreign Affairs wrote: "This letter goes by too hazardous a conveyance to admit of my entering into many of those causes of complaint which daily administer food to distrusts and jealousies between Spain and the people of this country. The Havana trade, notwithstanding the important advantages it affords to Spain, meets with the most unjustifiable interruptions. . . . These transactions, together with the delays and slights you meet with, cannot but have a mischievous effect upon that harmony and confidence which it is the mutual interests of Spain and America to cultivate with each other. It seems a little singular to this country that the United Provinces who never gave us the least reason to suppose that they were well inclined towards us, should precede Spain in acknowledging our rights. But we are a plain people; courts value themselves on refinements which are unknown to us. When a sovereign calls us friends, we are simple enough to expect unequivocal proofs of his friendship." Livingston to Jay, June 23, 1782, in Wharton, op. cit., 5:502.

John Adams, commissioner to the peace negotiations, referring to the principle of unconditional acknowledgement of North American independence stated: "Mr. Jay has acted on the same principle with Spain and with Great Britain. The dignity of the United States being thus supported, has prevailed in Holland and Great Britain; not indeed as yet in Spain, but we are in a better situation in relation to her than we should have been if the principle had been departed from." Adams to Livingston, November 6, 1782, in Wharton, op. cit., 5:584.

16. Aranda dissented from official policy on this question. Although he foresaw difficulties in dealing with the new nation, he thought it was in Spain's self-interest to provide active support to North American independence: "To conserve our own possessions in America we need to safeguard them from the example of the British Colonies, should they become disappointed in our lack of support. Likewise, we need to dissuade the latter from providing any assistance to the former. To achieve this it is in Spain's interest to reach a binding agreement

with this new American power by means of a solemn treaty, and to do so when the British Colonies are in urgent need of help and we will receive credit for providing it." Aranda to Grimaldi, January 13, 1777, in Yela Utrilla, op. cit., 2:43.

17. The Spanish Crown also exerted diplomatic pressure on Pope Clement XIV to bring about the abolition of the Company of Jesus (1773), an initiative in which Floridablanca was an active participant as Spanish ambassador to Rome.

18. Promotion of reform from above in the context of eighteenth-century absolutism also took place under Catherine the Great of Russia, Frederick the Great of Prussia, Leopold of Tuscany, and Joseph II of Austria. This phenomenon has been described as Enlightened Despotism, a term coined by Diderot in the 1760s. Carlos III ranks as one of its most successful practitioners as well as one of Spain's most capable rulers since Isabel.

19. "This place is the dearest in Europe. The court is never stationary, passing part of the year in no less than five different places, viz: Madrid, Pardo, Aranjuez, San Idelfonso and the Escorial; hence considerable expenses arise." Jay to the President of Congress, May 28, 1780, Wharton, op. cit., 3:732.

20. A comprehensive description of censorship of publications as well as prevailing intellectual currents of this period can be found in Richard Herr, *The Eighteenth-Century Revolution in Spain* (Princeton: Princeton University Press, 1958).

21. "Our commerce with Spain is also in itself a very considerable object. At this moment we take from her wine, oil, fruit, silk, cloth etc. And after the conclusion of the war our remittances of wheat, corn, fish and naval stores will be of very great consequence to the commerce of that country." Morris to Jay, July 4, 1781, in Wharton, op. cit., 4:537.

22. "The Americans propose only friendship and reciprocal trade. But if that is sufficient for France it could not be adopted by Spain without specifying that such trade refers exclusively to the realm in Europe. To extend the concession to her American dominions would destroy the nation's commerce." Aranda to Grimaldi, January 13, 1777, in Yela Utrilla, op. cit., 2:42.

Chapter 2

Unfriendly Neighbors

The period between the end of the North American War of Independence (1783) and the proclamation of the Monroe Doctrine (1823) witnessed the initiation of formal relations between Spain and the United States, against a background of international upheaval, rapid economic and social change, and significant transformations in the domestic circumstances of both countries. The French Revolution as well as the Industrial Revolution and their consequences, combined to set in motion those trends—industrialization, secularism, liberalism, nationalism, and romanticism—that mark the beginning of the modern age. Within the span of those four decades there occurred a reversal of roles between the two countries, as the United States, benefitting from the turmoil in Europe, expanded territorially into the remnants of Spain's North American possessions and emerged as the leading hemispheric power. The Napoleonic Wars also brought about a shift in European diplomatic practice, from the traditional balance of power approach to the multilateral framework agreed upon by the Congress of Vienna, known as the Concert of Europe. The wars of independence in Spanish America brought about a realignment in hemispheric trade patterns, with Great Britain and the United States emerging as the principal beneficiaries of the disappearance of Spain's trading monopoly. These wars also became an irritant in the relations between the two countries, as Spain attempted to dissuade the

United States from recognizing the independence of the new American nations.

These developments conditioned the outcome of the prolonged negotiations preceding the treaties of 1795 and 1819 that settled boundary differences and enabled the transcontinental expansion of U.S. territory.

During this period, both countries assigned a high priority to their bilateral relationship. The settlement of mutual differences required the attention of the principal North American and Spanish policy makers. However, events taking place at this time in the two great powers—France and Great Britain—gave rise to an international conflagration from whose consequences neither Spain nor the United States was able to emerge unscathed. Relations between Spain and the United States were, therefore, overshadowed as well as influenced by the relations of each to France and to Great Britain. The drawn out pace of the bilateral negotiations can thus be understood within the context of external turmoil and domestic political unrest. These factors also help to explain a much more favorable outcome for the United States of the final agreements than could have been predicted solely on the basis of the relative economic and military strength of the two parties.

John Jay's departure to Paris in May 1782, an unrecognized minister to the Court of Madrid, signalled not only the conclusion of an unsuccessful mission but also a shift in North American priorities. With the termination of hostilities in sight, the diplomatic efforts of Congress were concentrated on securing satisfactory terms with Great Britain, as part of the general peace settlement. Therefore, the elusive pursuit of an alliance with Spain ceased to be strategically meaningful. In fact, the war objectives of the United States and Spain had by then diverged to the point of becoming contradictory. After the decisive victory at Yorktown, in October 1781, and the subsequent fall of Lord North's ministry in March 1782, the outcome of the North American War of Independence ceased to be in doubt. Having de facto obtained the war objective by force of arms, the North American colonies were anxious to confirm by treaty what had been resolved on the battlefield. Consequently, they were not inclined to prolong the hostilities against Great Britain on behalf of strictly intra-European rivalries.

Spanish officials viewed matters differently. Spain's principal war objective was to recover Gibraltar, either militarily or as part of the peace settlement. Vergennes had committed France by treaty to support this claim. In order for Spain to relinquish this claim, given British reluctance to part with Gibraltar after its spirited defense, it became necessary to provide Spain with adequate compensation. (Great Britain eventually agreed, therefore, to cede the two Floridas to Spain as part of the general settlement.) Furthermore, the threat that a victorious Britain could have implied for Spanish America was now replaced with the prospect of an expansion-minded republic on the North American continent.

The war approached its final stage in 1782 with Admiral George Rodney's naval victory over Admiral de Grasse in the West Indies and the failure of the combined French and Spanish assault on Gibraltar. As negotiations began between the different participants on the terms of an eventual peace settlement, the conflicting nature of the territorial claims of Spain and the United States became apparent. It was Floridablanca's aim to keep the western boundary of the new nation as far east of the Mississippi River as possible, an objective that was incompatible with the instructions given by Congress to the North American delegates. Upon Jay's departure, Floridablanca had requested Aranda to continue the negotiations with him in Paris, informally, that is, not in his capacity as ambassador to France but as a Spanish nobleman. These preliminary boundary discussions between Jay and Aranda, which included occasional attempts at mediation by the French ministry, highlighted the irreconcilable nature of their differences. They also contributed to accentuate, in Spain as well as in the United States, preexisting feelings of apprehensiveness and mistrust. By the end of the war, the two cobelligerents were beginning to regard each other as potential adversaries. As Franklin reported to Congress,

> Mr. Jay will acquaint you with what passes between him and the Spanish ambassador respecting the proposed treaty with Spain. I will only mention that my conjecture of that court's design to coop us up within the Allegheny Mountains is now manifested. I hope Congress will insist on the Mississippi as the boundary, and the free navigation of the river, from which they could entirely exclude us.[1]

Aranda in turn expressed his fears in a letter to the king:

> This federal republic is born a pigmy. A day will come when it will be a giant, even a colossus, formidable in these countries. Liberty of conscience, the facility for establishing a new population on immense lands, as well as the advantages of the new government, will draw thither farmers and artizans from all the nations. In a

few years we shall watch with grief the tyrannical existence of this
same colossus.[2]

On November 30, 1782, preliminary Anglo-American articles of peace
were signed that included territorial concessions far beyond what Spain
and—to a lesser degree—France considered justified. The Mississippi
River was acknowledged as the western boundary of the United States,
and unrestricted freedom of navigation in the same from its sources to
the ocean was guaranteed to the nationals of both countries. The 31st
degree north latitude was acknowledged as the southern boundary. A
secret article was added, stating that in the eventuality that West Florida
should be British by the end of the war, its boundary should be the
latitude of the mouth of the Yazoo River (about 32 degrees 28 minutes
north latitude), that is, approximately a hundred miles to the north of
the 31st degree line. Although this article was dropped from the definitive treaty (signed in Paris, September 3, 1783), the discovery of its existence as a concession to Great Britain would serve a few years later to
reinforce Spanish claims to the Yazoo line as the boundary for West
Florida.

Preliminary Anglo-French and Anglo-Spanish articles of peace were
signed in Paris on January 20, 1783. After the exchange of ratifications
and providing time for transatlantic communications, hostilities ceased
in April of the same year. On August 6, 1783, George III issued a proclamation accepting the provisional Anglo-American articles of November
30, 1782, thereby formalizing British recognition of the independence of
the United States.[3] A few weeks later, on August 23 Spain did likewise.
On that date, Carlos III received William Carmichael at court, in his
capacity as chargé d'affaires of the United States.[4] The general peace
settlement was confirmed on September 3, 1783, by the definitive signature in Paris of the Anglo-American treaty, and in Versailles of the
Anglo-French and Anglo-Spanish treaties.

The unresolved issues of trade and navigation between Spain and the
United States as well as the new ones originating in the British cession
of the two Floridas to Spain and in Spanish claims east of the Mississippi
below the Ohio River were left for the two countries to settle through
bilateral negotiations. On September 24, 1784, Carlos III designated Don
Diego de Gardoqui as his plenipotentiary to the Congress of the United
States with the title of encargado de negocios and with full powers to
carry out and complete the negotiation of a treaty between the two countries.[5]

The postwar relations between Spain and the United States were shaped not only by prevailing diplomatic practice but by the reciprocal impressions acquired during the war by the principal decision makers as well as by their respective world-views.

Eighteenth-century European diplomacy reflected and institutionalized the contemporary practice of power politics. Rulers sought territorial expansion and commercial advantage as means of increasing the influence and prestige of their states.[6] Rank and reputation, the attributes of power, were jealously protected. The first North American representatives during the Revolutionary War and the subsequent postwar negotiations had ample opportunity to become familiarized with the relentless, undisguised pursuit of national advantage that characterized European diplomacy. These experiences were particularly relevant for the initial formulation of U.S. foreign policy, given the prominent positions that the early diplomats would occupy in the society and the government of the new nation. Franklin, after completing his diplomatic mission, became an influential elder statesman and a delegate to the Constitutional Convention. Jay became secretary of foreign affairs and the first chief justice of the Supreme Court. Thomas Jefferson became the first secretary of state, and president. John Adams became the first minister to the Court of Saint James and president. Their firsthand acquaintance with the complexity and the intensity of inter-European rivalries, in addition to their original set of values, would eventually be incorporated into specific attitudes and guidelines in external affairs: the determination to disassociate the Republic from Europe's conflicts, a preference for commercial rather than political treaties, a belief in the legitimacy of territorial expansion, and the dislike of royal courts and aristocratic privilege.[7] Adams, for example, was concerned by the end of the war about the need "to defend ourselves from the wiles of Europe" and to protect republican virtue from the depravity of courts.[8]

These reactions to European politics and the attitudes they contributed to shape brought about a heightened awareness of the unique circumstances of the United States and of the differences that separated North American conditions from the traditions of the Old World. These attitudes were not necessarily or specifically anti-Spanish in character. However, the incorporation of these convictions into the practices and policies of the U.S. government during the first few decades of national existence was bound to come into conflict with Spanish imperial interests and with the objectives of the Spanish Crown with respect to its possessions in North America.

THE TREATY OF 1795 (TREATY OF SAN LORENZO)

The negotiation of the first treaty between Spain and the United States took place in two stages under considerably different circumstances: (1) from 1785 to 1788 when Congress was the responsible policy maker on the North American side, and (2) from 1790 to 1795 when the recently created Department of State became the interlocutor of the Spanish ministry. The convening of the Constitutional Convention in Philadelphia and the French Revolution were the events that transformed the context of the negotiations between the two periods.

The initial negotiations were carried out in New York by Diego de Gardoqui, Spain's chargé d'affaires, and Jay in his capacity as secretary of foreign affairs for the Continental Congress. Despite their best efforts to reach a mutually acceptable compromise, these negotiations failed to resolve the differences on the question of the navigation of the Mississippi. Given their unsuccessful outcome, these deliberations may be described briefly.

By the acquisition of the two Floridas from Great Britain, Spain controlled the entire Gulf of Mexico. As a result, contiguous Spanish territory surrounded the United States stretching from the mouth of the St. Mary River in the south (on the present day border between Georgia and Florida) to the source of the Mississippi River in the west. Spain controlled both banks of the lower Mississippi from its confluence with the Yazoo River to the sea. According to international practice at the time, the power that dominated the mouth of a navigable river (the Sheldt by the Netherlands, the Tagus by Portugal) was in full control of that part of the waterway. The upstream riparian states had no navigation rights to the river in question below their respective boundaries. Spain maintained, not unreasonably, that this situation could not be altered by the terms of the Anglo-American Peace Treaty of 1783 and that therefore, no foreign craft could navigate the lower Mississippi through Spanish territory without her permission. Spain's claim to exclusive navigation rights on the lower Mississippi was supported not only by accepted international practice but also by the 1781 offer made by Jay to Floridablanca to accept Spanish cloture of the river in exchange for a treaty of alliance, following instructions from Congress. With respect to the mouth of the Yazoo River as the boundary of West Florida, Spain invoked legal precedent: the same boundary had applied when West Florida was under British rule. Furthermore, Spain enjoyed possession of the territory.

As an inducement to accept the cloture of the river, an issue on which Gardoqui refused to make concessions, Spain offered a thirty-year treaty of commerce and alliance that would establish commercial reciprocity between the United States and the peninsular domains of the kingdom as well as the Canary Islands. (Trade with Spanish America would continue to be excluded.) These provisions were of particular interest to the states of the East Coast that exported fish, grain, flour, and rice to Spain, and received payment in cash specie, a scarce and highly valued commodity at the time. Spain also agreed to purchase every year, in cash, a quantity of hard wood for building purposes at competitive prices and quality, and to mediate between the United States and Britain for the recovery of the strategic posts on the northern frontier and if necessary, to provide military support to achieve that purpose. Each party would guarantee the territory of the other in America as it would be determined by treaty against attack by a third party. (Spain's possessions in Europe were excluded from this guarantee.) Jay was negotiating ad referendum by Congress and his instructions specifically prohibited yielding on the issue of North American navigation rights on the Mississippi.[9] His request that Congress remove this restriction in order to conclude the negotiations in an amicable way brought the issue of the Mississippi into national prominence and revealed a sharp difference of opinion along regional lines, with the northern states in favor, and the southern states opposed to the modification. (A two-thirds majority being necessary to approve an eventual treaty, the opposition of the five southern states was sufficient to guarantee the failure of the negotiations.)

The terms of the preliminary Jay-Gardoqui understanding provide an indication of the relative strength of the two negotiating parties. The following concessions reveal a significant effort to accommodate Spanish concerns on the part of the United States: (1) willingness to forbear the exercise of navigation rights in the lower Mississippi River for twenty-five years, (2) willingness to compromise on the boundary of West Florida, (3) acceptance of an alliance with Spain, and (4) the commitment to a territorial guarantee of Spain's American possessions. (None of these features appeared in the 1795 Treaty of San Lorenzo, which was negotiated under entirely different circumstances.)

During this period, Spain was harvesting the fruits of Carlos III's commercial and administrative reforms. Floridablanca, the principal minister, was one of the ablest statesmen of his time. In addition to enjoying favorable economic conditions, Spain had rebuilt her maritime power, had emerged victorious from the war with Great Britain, and remained in control of a vast colonial empire. The United States, on the other hand, was severely hindered during the early postwar years by the weakness of the federal government originating in the Articles of Confederation.

The national finances were in disarray, due to the inability of the central government to levy taxes on its citizens.[10] The public debt, domestic as well as foreign, was in arrears. Each one of the thirteen states had the power to regulate commerce and to issue paper money. There was no uniform external tariff and no single national currency. Territorial disputes between states (Connecticut and Pennsylvania over the Wyoming Valley, New York and New Hampshire over the Green Mountains) and incidents such as Shay's Rebellion in Massachusetts and the besieging of Congress in Philadelphia by unpaid troops, were raising the specter of domestic unrest and national disunity.[11]

This state of affairs did not help the diplomatic initiatives of the United States. It was difficult both to obtain foreign credits because of the arrears on existing debts, and to negotiate treaties of commerce in the absence of a single trade policy.[12] In retaliation for the inability of Congress to enforce compliance with the articles of the Peace Treaty concerning debts to British merchants and the treatment of North American Loyalists, Great Britain refused to fulfill her obligation to evacuate the northern posts.

The apparent drift towards anarchy during the first years of self-government was creating doubts about the viability of the republican experiment and the eventual unity of the thirteen states.[13] The irreconcilable differences on the question of the Mississippi between the northern and the southern states doomed the Jay-Gardoqui negotiations and provided further impetus to the movement in favor of a Constitutional Convention. In one of its final actions, in September 1788, the Continental Congress resolved to put an end to the negotiations with Spain, and to refer the matter to the future federal government. In October of the following year, Don Diego de Gardoqui returned to Spain.

A reversal of fortunes occurred between 1789 and 1795, as the United States inaugurated a period of stable, competent governance while Spain was afflicted with political instability and vacillating leadership at a time of unprecedented external challenges. With the completion of the process of elaboration and ratification of the Constitution (1788–1789), the United States acquired the necessary institutional framework for the establishment of an effective national government. Furthermore, the leadership of the incipient federal government was exercised by a group of statesmen of outstanding ability and experience: George Washington, president; John Adams, vice president; Alexander Hamilton, secretary of the treasury; and Thomas Jefferson, secretary of state, among others.

On December 14, 1788, Carlos III died. The best, and the most successful Spanish monarch since Isabel, left a legacy of enlightened reforms, prudent government, as well as scientific, intellectual, and economic progress. He was succeeded by his son, Carlos IV, an amiable but incompetent ruler who inherited from his father the love of hunting, but none of his diligence or wisdom. In addition to the chase, Carlos IV occupied himself with such pursuits as the care of his collection of clocks and watches, carpentry and leatherworking, playing the violin, and the game of cards. He was deeply devoted to his spouse, the frivolous and domineering Maria Luisa of Parma, who habitually interfered with the business of government. One of her interests was the acquisition of Italian principalities for the advancement of her children. Both Carlos and Maria Luisa developed an unusual attachment to the royal favorite, or válido, Manual Godoy, a controversial figure also known by two of the several titles they conferred on him: duke of Alcudia and prince of peace. The inanity of Carlos IV, the Italian dynastic ambitions of Maria Luisa, and the unconventional relationship with Godoy became relevant to Spain's relations with the United States in two ways: (1) They contributed to discredit the monarchy, weaken the government, and divide the society at a time of national crisis, thereby reducing Spain's margin for maneuver in international affairs. (2) The pursuit of an Italian principality for one of the queen's daughters resulted in the eventual cession of Louisiana to France and its subsequent purchase by the United States. The titles, wealth, and power that Godoy accumulated as a result of royal favor provoked the jealousy and the enmity of the heir to the Crown, Fernando, prince of Asturias. Fernando's conspiracy against his parents and their favorite sparked a chain of events that helped bring about the collapse of the monarchy.

The French Revolution and the Napoleonic era posed a dire threat to the survival of traditional forms of government and social organization in Old Regime Europe. In this regard, Spain's troubled reaction to the momentous upheaval in France was part of a more general European phenomenon. Nevertheless, it was Spain's misfortune to confront the dual challenges of revolution in France and an assertive republic in North America burdened with a feeble monarchy, riven by court intrigue and tarnished by scandal.

A brief chronology of the early years of the reign of Carlos IV provides some background to the agreement between Spain and the United States formalized by the Treaty of San Lorenzo, also known as Pinckney's Treaty. The new king kept Floridablanca as first secretary until February 1792, replacing him with his political rival, Aranda. In November of the same year, Aranda was replaced by Manuel Godoy, a young officer of the royal guards from the lower provincial nobility. Although he lacked political experience and was unfamiliar with international affairs, Godoy was favorably inclined towards the Enlightenment reform agenda and was hardworking. His meteoric rise to power and his presumed liaison with the queen made him vulnerable to the resentment of the nobility, the clergy, and the people. Godoy was first secretary until March 1798.[14]

Floridablanca's reaction to the French Revolution was to try to protect Spain from contagion by establishing a cordon sanitaire along the Pyrenees and prohibiting the publication of any information of events in France. This attempt to enforce a news blackout was frustrated by the smuggling of revolutionary propaganda and by the first waves of French emigrés—aristocrats as well as several thousand conjuring or refractory ecclesiastics, who had refused to accept the Civil Constitution of the Clergy—that fled to Spain. Aranda relaxed the press censorship and adopted a more accommodating, less hostile attitude towards revolutionary France.[15]

This policy was also favored by Godoy, but events were moving in a different direction. Shortly after Godoy became first secretary, the trial of Louis XVI for treason by the National Convention was announced.

Carlos IV sent a personal plea to the French government interceding for the life of his royal cousin. The execution of Louis XVI horrified the court and outraged the country. The church was clamoring for war against the regicides. Godoy, resisting pressure from the court and from popular opinion, made a last, unsuccessful attempt to avoid a confrontation with France.[16] On February 19, 1793, the French ambassador was provided with his passports. On March 7 the National Convention declared war on Spain and expressed the hope that the Spanish Bourbons would lose their throne. Shortly after the commencement of hostilities, Spain concluded an alliance with Britain, the traditional enemy, an alliance that was unpopular at home. Enthusiasm for war against a people "without King, without law and without God" was not matched by military preparedness. After a promising beginning, the war against revolutionary France went badly for Spain. In 1794 French armies crossed the Pyrenees, entered the Basque provinces, and threatened Catalonia. Dissatisfaction with the British alliance and the danger of a full-scale invasion led Godoy to initiate peace negotiations with France and to terminate the military cooperation with Great Britain.[17] On July 22, 1795, the Treaty of Basel, which ended hostilities with France, was signed, much to the relief of Carlos IV, who rewarded Godoy with the title of prince of peace. Godoy then began to orchestrate a hazardous reversal of alliances, in preparation for the consequences of Britain's wrath for the conclusion of peace and the subsequent rapprochement between Spain and France. Before the operation was completed, that is, after the abandonment of the British alliance but previous to the conclusion of an alliance with France, Spain felt vulnerable, and her foreign policy reflected that perception. Under these conditions, obtaining the friendship of the United States became a desirable objective for Spain, even at a price. This was the conjuncture that provided the United States with an early opportunity to benefit from the rivalries between European powers.

From 1791 to 1795 negotiations between Spain and the United States proceeded at a leisurely pace. The most pressing foreign policy problem for the Spanish government was the disconcerting turn of events in France. Furthermore, Spanish officials viewed the westward expansion of the United States with disfavor and apprehension. Some of them supported a far-fetched conspiracy by adventurers from Kentucky to create a secessionist state along territories west of the Appalachian Mountains, a state that would be placed under the protection of the king of Spain.[18] The United States had reasons of its own to proceed slowly towards the achievement of its goals. Jefferson took up the newly created office of secretary of state after having spent six years at the Court of Versailles. His experience in France had convinced him of the fragility of the European balance of power, a state of affairs that provided opportunities to advance the interests of the United States. With respect to relations with Spain, Jefferson held two convictions that were to guide his conduct of the negotiations. Concerning the navigation of the Mississippi and boundaries, he believed that the United States could obtain its objectives by waiting for Spain to be involved in a European war.[19] For the longer run, he foresaw that the United States would acquire Spain's possessions in North America.[20]

Until the beginning of 1795, the negotiations with Spain had been carried out by William Carmichael, chargé d'affaires in Madrid, and by William Short, a former minister resident at The Hague and chargé d'affaires in France who had been Jefferson's private secretary. Godoy had assigned as their counterpart Don Diego de Gardoqui, who was now minister of finance. As a former minister to the United States, Gardoqui was well acquainted with North American issues. However, the problems originated by the war with France did not permit him to devote much time to meetings with Carmichael and Short. The opening of peace negotiations with France, and the perspective of hostilities with Great Britain provided Godoy with the incentive to come to an agreement with the United States.[21] This predicament was the opportunity for which Jefferson had been patiently waiting. Thomas Pinckney, the U.S. minister to the Court of Saint James was sent to Spain as envoy extraordinary with powers to sign a treaty of peace and friendship with Carlos IV. The treaty recognized the principal territorial claims of the United States, namely the 31st degree north latitude line as the northern boundary of West Florida and the free navigation of the Mississippi River to the sea. It also permitted the privilege of deposit in New Orleans for three years, a stipulation that eventually led to the North American attempt to purchase New Orleans, and thereby to the acquisition of Louisiana.

The Treaty of San Lorenzo (Pinckney's Treaty), signed on October 27, 1795, at San Lorenzo el Real, was an enormous diplomatic success for the United States. It was also an important first step towards the fulfillment of Jefferson's national aspiration of acquiring Spain's possessions in North America.

In addition to the fulfillment of national aspirations on boundaries and access to the lower Mississippi River, the North American delegates negotiated the first treaty with Spain in accordance with three distinctive guidelines of an incipient U.S. foreign policy:

1. a preference for commercial, rather than political agreements;
2. a rejection of foreign entanglements and European power politics; and
3. a commitment to territorial expansion on the North American continent.

The Treaty of San Lorenzo created a framework for commerce and navigation between the two nations. It provided for the reciprocal appointment of consuls and for free access by nationals of each country to the courts of justice of the other to settle disputes. It also established procedures for the identification of contraband, for boarding vessels while at sea, and for the treatment of merchant ships in wartime. In his memoirs, written in exile and published in 1842, Godoy highlights the commercial aspects of the treaty and describes it as "the first example of the adoption of modern ideas."[22] Commercial matters, however, were not Godoy's principal motive for negotiating a treaty with the United

States in 1795. He had suggested an alliance as a means of strengthening Spain's position vis-à-vis Great Britain and of safeguarding the Crown's American possessions. Pinckney declined the proposal of an alliance, even though he had received no instructions on that precise topic.[23] By that time, the U.S. policy of avoiding inter-European conflicts was firmly in place as evidenced by President Washington's Proclamation of Neutrality of April 22, 1793. Pinckney also turned down the proposal for a mutual guarantee of territorial integrity, in compliance with specific instructions previously sent by Jefferson.[24]

The preamble to the articles of the treaty, identifying the two plenipotentiaries, highlighted the stylistic contrast between a modern society, shaped by the ideals of the Enlightenment, and a traditional, ancient régime of caste and privilege. Pinckney was described by nationality and function, as "a Citizen of the United States and their Envoy Extraordinary to His Catholic Majesty," while Godoy's description came under eighteen different titles, which apparently did not exhaust the list of his honors and distinctions.[25]

Achieving peace with France and guaranteeing the friendship of the United States were intermediate steps towards the completion of Spain's reversal of alliances. Shortly after the Treaty of Basel—which reestablished peace between France and Spain—was signed, the British ambassador in Madrid advised his government that "The Treaty of Peace will be shortly followed by a Treaty of Alliance, and a Treaty of Alliance by Hostilities."[26] His assessment of the course of events proved to be prescient. The Treaty of San Idelfonso, formalizing an alliance between France and Spain was subscribed on July 27, 1796, and ratified the following month. About two months later, on October 5, Carlos IV signed the declaration of war against Great Britain. The Spanish ministry returned thereby to the traditional Bourbon foreign policy guidelines of the Family Compact, although under radically transformed governmental conditions in France. With the ratification of the Treaty of San Idelfonso, Spain's rulers made a high-stake gamble on the eventual outcome of the struggle between France and Great Britain. They also linked the fate of an enfeebled absolute monarchy to the vicissitudes of the postrevolutionary French governments, a decision based more on dynastic convenience than on Spain's national interest.

Spain's alliance with France was riven by mutual distrust. It was a disparate, acrimonious relationship that ultimately proved to be untenable. The new French elite had little knowledge and even less understanding of their transpyrenean neighbor. Their views had been shaped by distorted descriptions of Spanish society that failed to acknowledge the significant reforms and improvements introduced during the second half of the eighteenth century. In the article on Spain published in 1783 in the first volume of Charles-Joseph Panckouke's *Encyclopédie méthodique*, Nicolas Masson de Morvilliers made a scathing attack on what he regarded as Spain's backwardness, obscurantism, and bigotry. "What do we owe to Spain?" he inquired. "What has it done for Europe in the last two centuries, in the last four, or ten?" Masson's article produced an outburst of indignation among enlightened circles in Spain, while Carlos III requested and obtained an official apology from the French government.[27]

A French financier, commenting on Spain in 1804, stressed the contrast with his own country "where everything was new, customs, laws, attire, language, opinion, government" and its neighbor.

> I found myself all of a sudden transported into an old monarchy that remains immobile amidst the movement of Europe . . . Those monastic garments among the people; those massive carriages similar to the ones in which Philip V arrived, those cavalrymen equipped like the ones I had seen in paintings of the battles of Louis XIV; those Walloon guards wearing the same kind of uniforms with which their predecessors fell at Rocroy; that minute etiquette, those gothic traditions made even more rigid by Spanish gravity, all of that appeared to me as a spectacle that at first sight was somewhat imposing. It was a representation of the 17th Century, it was history in action.[28]

The Directory, and later Napoléon Bonaparte, treated the representatives of Carlos IV with arrogance and disrespect. French high-handedness and condescension were reciprocated by Spanish resentment and recalcitrance.

Napoléon had acquired an overly optimistic impression of Spain's military prowess and financial resources during the course of his Italian campaigns. These misconceptions did not provide the basis for a realistic Spanish policy.[29] When he came to power, he made use of the alliance to request troops and ships from Spain, to extract tribute from her in the guise of a financial subsidy, and to set her at war with Portugal—the War of the Oranges—in pursuit of French strategic objectives. His policy towards Spain, according to rapidly changing circumstances, shifted from intervention in internal affairs, to dismemberment, to the overthrow of the Bourbon dynasty. The obsequious acquiescence of Carlos IV to his demands and the facility with which he manipulated both the king and the crown prince, Fernando, to abdicate in his favor, led Napoléon to underestimate the capacity of the Spanish people to resist French domination. This judgement was an error that he would have reason to regret.[30]

The turbulent unravelling of this misalliance brought about—inter alia—the collapse of the monarchy, the French invasion and subsequent national uprising, and the loss of the American colonies, with political repercussions that lasted well into the nineteenth century. Much of this critical period is more properly viewed from the perspective of Franco-Spanish relations.[31] Nevertheless, Spain's relations with the United States were transformed as an unforeseen consequence of the turmoil in the Iberian Peninsula originating in the alliance with France. The issue of boundaries between Spain and the United States—which had been settled amicably in 1795—became once again part of the bilateral agenda as a result of the Louisiana Purchase. Additionally, Spain's inability to effectively control its transatlantic empire due to the European conflagration provided the United States with new opportunities to expand territorially and to increase its trade and navigation with Spanish America. These circumstances prepared the setting for the next treaty negotiation between Spain and the United States.

THE ADAMS-ONÍS TREATY OF 1819

On October 1, 1800, a second Treaty of San Idelfonso was signed by the First Secretary Mariano Luis de Urquijo and Napoléon's special envoy, General Alexandre Berthier. The second treaty provided for Spain's cession of Louisiana to France, and committed France to the creation of the Kingdom of Etruria in Tuscany for the benefit of the daughter of the Spanish royal couple, Maria Luisa Josefina, who was married to the heir apparent of the duchy of Parma. Although the justification for this transaction was strictly dynastic, Urquijo downplayed the significance of the concession made by Spain.[32] Napoléon, in turn, sold Louisiana to the United States in 1803, notwithstanding the commitment previously made to Spain to not alienate the territory that was retroceded in 1800. Furthermore, the sale of Louisiana to the United States did not specify the precise boundaries of the territory.[33] The second Treaty of San Idelfonso contained an ambiguity concerning West Florida: it was uncertain whether it had been included in the retrocession (as an integral part of

Louisiana) or whether it remained Spanish (as separate from Louisiana, by virtue of the Anglo-Spanish treaties of 1763 and 1783). The United States favored the former interpretation of the treaty, Spain the latter. This disagreement was sufficient in itself to justify the renewal of negotiations between Spain and the United States. Additionally, the importance that New Orleans had attained for the navigation of the Mississippi River and as a center for the rapidly expanding commerce of Kentucky and Tennessee, had transformed the attitude of U.S. policy makers with respect to the acquisition of both Floridas. What previously had only been a cherished regional aspiration became, in the aftermath of the Louisiana Purchase, a North American strategic objective of the highest priority.[34] This new development, and the dimensions of the Louisiana territory, required the redrawing of boundaries between the two countries, this time on a transcontinental scale.

The first two decades of the nineteenth century were a period of upheaval and discontinuity in Spanish affairs. War against Great Britain as an ally of France, from 1796 to 1802, disrupted Spain's transatlantic trade and resulted in economic and financial hardship. In the Peace of Amiens concluded between Britain, France, and Spain (March 27, 1802), Spain lost Trinidad to Britain but gained the district of Olivenze from Portugal. Spain decided to remain neutral when hostilities between France and Britain resumed in May 1803. The nation required peace in order to benefit from the recently revived colonial trade and in particular, to protect the badly needed flow of bullion from Spanish America. Also, the Spanish Court resented Napoléon's cavalier behavior with respect to Louisiana.[35] This respite, however, was short-lived. In response to British outrages against Spanish shipping, Carlos IV reluctantly announced the declaration of war on December 14, 1804. From this time until the 1820s, Spain, militarily unprepared and weakened by internal dissent, found herself at war with Britain, France, and Spanish America.

The combined Franco-Spanish 1805 maritime campaign against Britain was a disaster for Spain. The destruction by the Royal Navy of the Spanish fleet at Trafalgar on October 21, 1805, had far-reaching economic and diplomatic consequences. The subsequent inability of Spain to project effective power in the Western Hemisphere undermined her control of Spanish America and weakened the credibility of her diplomacy when confronting the United States. Likewise, the undisputed British naval supremacy in the Atlantic Ocean created lucrative opportunities for traders from Britain and the United States in the Spanish American market. Therefore, business interests in these two nations, along with influential

Spanish American merchants, acquired a strong incentive to foreclose the eventual reintroduction of Spain's commercial monopoly.

Spanish cooperation in a French expedition against Portugal, purportedly with the objective of forcing that nation into the Continental blockade (and into making territorial cessions to France and Spain), resulted in the stationing of French troops on Spanish territory. This development, and the intrigues of Crown Prince Fernando and his aristocratic followers against Carlos IV, Maria Luisa, and Godoy, provided Napoléon with the opportunity and the means to create a vacancy in the throne. On May 5, 1808, both Carlos and Fernando renounced their rights to the Crown in favor of Napoléon and began their royal exile in France as the emperor's guests and prisoners. Thereupon, Bonaparte summoned a group of Spanish notables to Bayonne to adopt a constitution and offer allegiance to his older brother Joseph, whom he appointed king of Spain and of the Indies. The popular uprising against el rey intruso—the intruder king—became Spain's War of Independence (1808–1813), also known as the Peninsular War on account of the prominent role played by British troops under the command of Arthur Wellesley, the duke of Wellington. During this period, Spain had two rival governments, with competing claims to legitimacy: that of Joseph Bonaparte, backed by French troops, and a junta, in alliance with Great Britain for the purpose of waging war on Napoléon.[36] (The alliance was signed in London on January 14, 1809.) What ensued, to settle this dispute, was a civil war as well as a war of national liberation that became part of the European-wide conflagration. Spanish America also rejected the rule of Joseph Bonaparte. Revolutionary juntas sprung up throughout the Continent proclaiming affection to the Spanish Crown, but in practice, moving towards de facto independence.

These dramatic events disrupted the normal conduct of governmental affairs, domestic as well as foreign. Their detrimental effect on Spain's diplomacy was felt even after the withdrawal of the French army and the restoration of the Bourbon monarchy. The sequence of a devastating war, aggravated by royal ineptitude, reduced Spain's international influence and severely restricted the scope of her diplomatic initiatives.[37]

In contrast, by the end of the Napoleonic Wars, the United States had become not only larger and more populous, but stronger. It had also become more prosperous thanks to a stable, competent government and an expanding economy based on agriculture, an incipient manufacturing sector, shipping, fishing, and foreign trade. The United States had proven to be a respectable adversary during an undeclared maritime war with

France (1799–1800) and full-scale war with Britain (1812–1814) in assertion of its policy regarding neutral rights. The national leadership had
become more self-confident, as manifested by a readiness to pursue the
commitment to territorial expansion by diplomacy if possible, but by
force if necessary.[38]

The outcome of the second boundary settlement between the United
States and Spain reflected the divergence of their respective national fortunes in the period between 1795 and 1819. The two antagonists were
rather unevenly matched: the former, an emerging regional power, forcefully striving to fulfill its self-assigned national destiny, the latter, a besieged, politically unsettled European nation, trying unsuccessfully to
recover its colonial empire in the Americas. Both sides were ably represented by skillful, experienced negotiators: John Quincy Adams, secretary of state during the administration of President James Monroe, and
Don Luis de Onís y González, a career diplomat who had served for
over thirty years in Spain's foreign office.[39] Onís labored diligently to
justify his government's territorial claims on legal and historical grounds.
His copiously documented arguments were not, however, an adequate
substitute for economic and military power. Spanish efforts to obtain the
backing of Britain were unsuccessful.[40] Likewise, the attempt to have the
British foreign office act as a mediator was blocked by the U.S. government, which insisted on a strictly bilateral negotiation.

Having eliminated the possibility of a joint Spanish-British démarche,
Adams then used his position of strength to drive a hard bargain. In the
pursuit of his objective, he revealed the single-minded determination and
the ruthlessness of someone who believed to be acting as the instrument
of Divine Providence.[41]

Adams even turned to advantage an unprovoked American armed
incursion into Spanish territory led by Andrew Jackson, in the spring of
1818. Jackson, who was carrying out a war of extermination against the
Native Americans of the Southeast (Seminole, Creek, Cherokee, Choc-
taw, and Chikasaw), invaded Florida and occupied St. Mark's and Pen-
sacola on the pretext of punishing the Seminole. In response to the
protest of José Pizarro, the Spanish foreign minister, Adams sent a letter
of instructions to George William Erving, the U.S. minister in Madrid, a
remarkable document for its audacity, if not for its equanimity. Adams
justified Jackson's behavior as an act of self-defense against the outrages
of "savages, negroes and banditti." Blaming the local Spanish officials
for the incident, he demanded that they be punished. Describing the
United States as the aggrieved party, he demanded payment of an in-

demnity from Spain. Instead of expressing regrets for the invasion, a threat was issued: "if the necessities of self-defense should again compel the United States to take possession of the Spanish forts and places in Florida, declare, with the frankness and candor that become us, that another unconditional restoration of them must not be expected."[42]

By the end of 1818, the Spanish government abandoned any hope for assistance in the Americas from the Holy Alliance (Russia, Prussia, Austria, and France) and proceeded to give Onís full authorization to conclude the negotiation according to the circumstances, without need for further consultation with Madrid. On his own responsibility, Onís reached an agreement with Adams that formalized—with only minor concessions to Spain—the acceptance of the terms demanded by the U.S. government: the acquisition of the two Floridas, the Sabine River as the boundary in the Southwest, and access to the Pacific Ocean in the Northwest. The Adams-Onís Treaty was signed in Washington on February 22, 1819, and ratified on February 22, 1821. The choice of a historically meaningful date for the signature of the treaty—Washington's Birthday—suggests the importance that Adams ascribed to this transaction for the future of the United States. By means of this treaty, Spain was provided with a gracefully negotiated exit from North American territories that the United States felt destined to occupy.[43]

The signing of a transcontinental treaty that for practical purposes eliminated Spain as a colonial power in North America was the crowning achievement of Adams as secretary of state. He was aware of the significance of his accomplishment, but in characteristic manner was willing to share the credit with Divine Providence, as he recorded the event in his diary:

> It was perhaps the most important day of my life. What the consequences may be of the compact this day signed with Spain is known only to the all-wise and all-beneficent disposer of events, who has brought it about in a manner utterly unexpected and by means the most extraordinary and unforeseen . . .
>
> The acknowledgement of a definite line to the South Sea forms a great epocha [sic] in our history. The first proposal of it in this negotiation was my own, and I trust it is now secured beyond the reach of revocation. It was not even among our claims by the Treaty of Independence with Great Britain. It was not among our pretensions under the purchase of Louisiana—for that gave us only the range of the Mississippi and its waters. . . . It is the only peculiar and appropriate right acquired by this treaty in the event of its

ratification. I record the first assertion of this claim for the United States as my own, because it is known to be mine perhaps only to the members of the present administration, and may perhaps never be known to the public—and, if ever known, will be soon and easily forgotten.[44]

The stage was thereby set for the westward expansion of the United States and its eventual emergence as a major power. Spain's concessions in this negotiation were part of the larger process of withdrawal from the Western Hemisphere, imposed upon her by the transformations that had taken place in the European power system.

By the end of the second decade of the nineteenth century, the imbalance between Spain's external commitments and her domestic resources had become unsustainable. The political upheavals and the warfare of the previous twenty-five years had disrupted the mechanisms that had helped to preserve a semblance of imperial stability. The disparity between Spain's claims in the New World and her capacity to enforce them was not a recent phenomenon; its origins dated back to the time of the Hapsburg dynasty. However, since the beginning of the eighteenth century, Spain had been protected from the consequences of strategic overstretch by a favorable external environment, which was the product of special circumstances.[45] As part of the settlement of the War of the Spanish Succession (1702–1714), Great Britain, France, and Spain reached an agreement with regard to Spain's transatlantic possessions. Britain acquired limited trading rights with the Spanish American colonies. The French agreed to maintain Spanish possessions separate from those of the French Crown upon the accession of Louis XIV's grandson, Philip, duke of Anjou, to the Spanish throne. Spain agreed not to alienate its colonial possessions for the benefit of a third power without the concurrence of Great Britain[46] Britain's naval supremacy combined with the laxity of Spanish colonial administration provided ample opportunity for British merchants to carry out a thriving contraband trade under the cover of the legally permitted amounts. France, in turn, derived commercial benefits in Spain and its colonies from the family ties linking the Bourbon dynasties in Madrid and Versailles. In the interest of the European balance of power system, Great Britain and France acquiesced in the continuation of Madrid's authority in Spanish America, even as both powers sought to undermine Spain's colonial trade monopoly. But it suited their reciprocal interests to accept commercial encroachment in Spanish America as an adequate substitute for major—and potentially destabilizing—territorial acquisitions. The implicit guarantee, provided by Europe's principal maritime and continental power, respectively, greatly reduced the cost to Spain of asserting its claims in the Americas. With occasional disruptions, this understanding lasted for three quarters of a century. The French Revolution, the collapse of the Old Regime, and the turbulence of the years 1793–1815 put an end to this arrangement, confronting Spain with the military and financial implications of having to defend her transatlantic possessions against all challengers. As Richard Herr observed "in a Europe overshadowed by the ambitions of Bonaparte, no nation could successfully claim half of America without fighting for the privilege of enjoying this claim."[47]

The French Revolution weakened enlightened despotism's appeal as an instrument of reform from above, and substituted the concept of popular sovereignty for the divine right of kings. The impact of these ideas in Spain fractured the elite solidarity that characterized the reign of Carlos III, creating a long-lasting political and religious confrontation between reform-minded and traditionalist elements. The Terror, anticlerical excesses, and the foreign policies of the Directory and of Napoléon undermined the political legitimacy of enlightened Spanish intellectuals, clerics, and statesmen, who were regarded as being partial to French ideology. In turn, the fears of the aristocracy and the religious orders— abetted by the French emigrés and nonjuring priests—strengthened the hand of the more conservative elements of Spanish society during the course of the struggle against domination by France. Upon the return of Fernando VII, those sectors of the Spanish elite that could have taken a less hostile view of the United States and of the independence movements in Spanish America were persecuted, driven into exile, or imprisoned. In Spanish America, French revolutionary ideology and the example of the United States destroyed the legitimacy of colonial rule. Fernando's pretension to reimpose the most obscurantist version of royal absolutism, eliminated the possibility of a negotiated settlement of the colonial revolt on the basis of a mutually acceptable compromise. The settlement of the conflict was thereby left to the test of arms, with the accompanying bitterness and ill feeling on both sides. At the time of ratification of the Adams-Onís Treaty in 1821, the independence of most of Spanish America had been de facto established, although Spain delayed its recognition of the same until the following decades.

The Spanish Court had hoped that settling the territorial dispute with the United States would contribute to the "pacification" of Spanish America, by depriving the rebellious colonists of a potential ally. A pri-

mary objective of Spanish diplomacy at this time was to forestall recognition of any of its former colonies as an independent state. Adams
made a skillful use of this issue by hinting that the United States was
prepared to take such a step if Onís failed to reach an agreement
promptly. At the final stage of the negotiation, Adams agreed to forego
recognition of independent Spanish American nations until after the conclusion of the treaty with Spain.[48]

The same logistic and financial constraints that had precluded an effective response to Jackson's incursion into Florida, also hindered the
prosecution of large-scale military operations against the Spanish American insurgents. The Napoleonic Wars had disrupted Spain's foreign
trade and exhausted the royal finances. The maritime debacles of Cape
Saint Vincent (1797) and Trafalgar (1805) had crippled the Spanish navy.
Furthermore, the prospect of waging a distant and costly war to reimpose royal absolutism on the Spanish American colonies was not popular at home. The gathering in Cadiz of an army for embarkation to the
Americas sparked a successful military revolt in the name of the constitution of 1812 by liberal officers commanded by Rafael del Riego in January 1820. Fernando summoned the Cortes and swore adhesion to the
constitution. The ensuing period of constitutional government (the Liberal Triennium) ended in the spring of 1823 when a French army, acting
in the name of the Holy Alliance, entered Spain and restored Fernando
to absolute power. By this time, however, the independence of the Spanish American colonies was a foregone conclusion. Royalist hopes for assistance from the Holy Alliance to reimpose Spanish colonial rule in the
Americas were dissipated by the confluence of British disapproval,
backed by the effective dissuading power of the Royal Navy, and the
diplomatic opposition of the United States, made explicit by the presidential message to Congress of December 2, 1823, which subsequently
became known as the Monroe Doctrine.[49]

Riego's revolution also made possible a peaceful—if not amicable—
Spanish withdrawal from North America, by ensuring the ratification of
the Adams-Onís Treaty, which was being blocked by the objections of
Fernando VII and the majority of the members of the Consejo de Estado.
A further complication arose in the form of the dispute over extensive
land grants in Florida made by Fernando to several of his favorites prior
to the signature of the treaty, grants that the United States declared
void.[50]

The king appointed a new minister to Washington for the purpose of
renegotiating the treaty. For that task he chose Major General Francisco

Dionisio Vives, who arrived in April 1820. Vives requested that the United States strengthen its neutrality laws in order to dissuade privateers from providing assistance to the insurgents, that a guarantee of territorial integrity be provided for the remaining Spanish possessions, and that the United States promise not to recognize the independence of any of the rebellious colonies. These requests were unacceptable to Adams, although he offered the government's efforts in trying to curtail the activity of the privateers. The imminent prospect of the unilateral occupation of the Floridas, for which President Monroe had requested the authorization of Congress, was averted by the political changes in Spain brought about by Riego's revolution. On March 7, 1820, Fernando accepted the constitution, which transferred sovereignty from the king to the nation and made it necessary for the Cortes to approve transfers of territory. On October 5, 1820, the Cortes approved the ratification of the treaty by the king and declared the disputed land grants null and void. On October 24 Fernando signed the ratification. The U.S. Senate approved the treaty on February 19, 1821. Three days later, on the second anniversary of its original signature, Adams and Vives exchanged ratifications of the Adams-Onís Treaty.

In contrast to the conciliatory aftermaths of the previous Anglo-American conflicts—the Revolutionary War and the War of 1812—the settlement of the territorial dispute between Spain and the United States did little to reduce the mutual dislike to which both sides were predisposed by religious and cultural differences. Notwithstanding the triumph that Adams had celebrated at the end of the negotiations, he blamed Spanish procrastination and duplicity for the vicissitudes that accompanied the ratification process. Spanish officials on their part resented the high-handed, menacing manner in which they had been treated. In the words of a diplomatic historian:

> Despite the inevitability of Florida's fate, the negotiation had its ugly aspects. Spain, to be sure, was shuffling, dilatory, and irresponsible; but the United States was rough, highhanded, and arrogant. Some writers have cited the acquisition of Florida as a case of international bullying. Others have called it Manifest Destiny— the falling of ripe fruit. Perhaps it was the manifest determination of the American people to achieve their physiographic destiny, coupled with the manifest weakness of Spain. The normal and inexorable push of the American pioneers was not to be denied. It was Spain's misfortune, as it was later Mexico's, to be in their way.[51]

The adversarial nature of this negotiation would have unfavorable consequences for inter-American harmony, as U.S. officials adopted the formula of moral righteousness accompanied by the threat of the use of force—which Adams had developed and put to advantage in his dealings with Spain—to relations with its Latin American neighbors.[52] As the Adams-Onís Treaty went into effect, and the independence of Latin America became established, Spain and the United States turned their backs on each other at the governmental level, by mutual consent. This situation lasted well into the latter part of the nineteenth century when the two nations would meet again, this time in more dramatic circumstances.

NOTES

1. Franklin to Livingston, August 12, 1782, in Francis Wharton ed., *The Revolutionary Diplomatic Correspondence of the United States* (Washington, D.C.: Government Printing Office, 1889) 5:657.

2. Cited in John Fiske, *The Critical Period of American History, 1783–1789* (Boston: Houghton Mifflin, 1888), 22.

3. The texts of the proclamation as well as of the Act of Parliament reestablishing trade and intercourse with the United States are in Wharton, op. cit., 6: 633–634.

4. The elaborate ceremonial of his presentation at court, which was made by Floridablanca himself, and repeated during several days for other members of the royal family, is described in Carmichael to Livingston, August 30, 1783, in Wharton, op. cit., 6:663ff.

5. The text of the royal commission is in Albert Bushnell Hart, *American History Told by Contemporaries* (New York: Macmillan, 1968), 3:170–171. Don Diego de Gardoqui was the same official who had handled Spanish secret subsidies to the North American colonies during the early years of the Revolutionary War. He remained in the United States from 1785 to 1789.

6. In his insightful book on the early foreign policy of the United States, *To the Farewell Address* (Princeton: Princeton University Press, 1961), Felix Gilbert refers to Frederick the Great of Prussia as someone who explicitly formulated the spirit of power politics of the age. His contemporaries, William Pitt, Vergennes, and Floridablanca were also skilled practitioners of the craft.

7. A comprehensive treatment of these concepts and their origins can be found in Gerald Stourzh, *Benjamin Franklin and American Foreign Policy* (Chicago: University of Chicago Press, 1954). Stourzh documents the evolution of Franklin's views on security, mercantilism, expansionism, and power politics. He describes Franklin as the embodiment of the Age of Enlightenment. Gilbert, op. cit., traces the aversion to foreign entanglements to the influence of Thomas Paine's *Common Sense* and to the influence of reform-minded English Whigs, such as James Burgh, the author of *Political Disquisitions*. An American edition of this book appeared in 1775.

8. "My apprehensions of the importance of our foreign affairs have been much increased by a residence of five or six years in Europe. I see so much enmity to the principle of our governments, to the purity of our morals, the simplicity of our manners, the honest integrity and sincerity of our hearts, to our contentment with poverty, our love of labour, our affection for liberty and our country; . . . You may depend upon this: the moment an American minister gives aloose [sic] to his passion for women, that moment he is undone; he is instantly at the mercy of the spies of the court and the tool of the most profligate of the human race." Adams to Gerry, September 3, 1783, in Wharton, op. cit., 6:669–670.

9. For a detailed description of the Jay-Gardoqui negotiations and the proceedings of the Continental Congress with respect to the same, see Samuel Flagg Bemis, *Pinckney's Treaty: America's Advantage from Europe's Distress, 1783–1800* (New Haven: Yale University Press, 1960), 60–108 passim.

10. "Our diplomacy had failed because our weakness had been proclaimed to the world. We were bullied by England, insulted by France and Spain, and looked askance at in Holland. The humiliating position in which our ministers were placed by the beggarly poverty of Congress was something almost beyond credence. It was by no means unusual for the superintendent of finance, when hard pushed for money, to draw upon our foreign ministers, and then sell the drafts for cash. This was not only not unusual; it was an established custom. It was done again and again, when there was not the smallest ground for supposing that the minister upon whom the draft was made would have any funds wherewith to meet it. He must go and beg the money. That was part of his duty as envoy—to solicit loans without security for a government that could not raise enough money by taxation to defray its current expenses. It was sickening work." John Fiske, op. cit., 185.

11. "Thomas Paine was sadly mistaken when, in the moment of exultation over the peace, he declared that the trying time was ended. The most trying time of all was just beginning. It is not too much to say that the period of five years following the peace of 1783 was the most critical moment in all the history of the American people." John Fiske, op. cit., 65.

"It is plain that a government which has not the power to tax its own citizens, or to enforce its own laws, or to regulate commerce, lacks the vital essentials of sovereignty; and in this condition was the United States under the Articles of Confederation." John Henry William Elson, *History of the United States of America* (New York: Macmillan, 1914), 321.

12. "I have been . . . instructed to learn from you, gentlemen, what is the real nature of the powers with which you are invested, whether you have received separate powers from the respective States . . . The apparent determination of the respective States to regulate their own separate interests, renders it absolutely necessary, towards forming a permanent system of commerce, that my Court should be informed how far the Commissioners can be duly authorized to enter into any engagements with Great Britain, which it may not be in the power of any one of the States to render totally fruitless and ineffectual." Letter from John Frederick Sackville, the Duke of Dorset, British Ambassador to France, to the

United States Commissioners, Paris, March 26, 1785, cited in Hart, op. cit., 171–172.

13. "It appears, sir, that in all the American provinces there is more or less tendency toward democracy; that in many this extreme form of government will finally prevail. The result will be that the confederation will have little stability, and that by degrees the different states will subsist in a perfect independence of each other. This revolution will not be regretted by us. We have never pretended to make of America a useful ally; we have had no other object than to deprive Great Britain of that vast continent. Therefore, we can regard with indifference both the movements which agitate certain provinces and the fermentation which prevails in Congress." Cabinet of Versailles to acting Minister Louis Guillaume Otto, August 30, 1787, cited in George Bancroft, *History of the Formation of the Constitution of the United States of America* (New York: D. Appleton, 1882), 2:438.

"Mr. Gardoqui affects the greatest indifference about these negotiations. Recognising the instability of the American governments, the weakness of congress, and the continual fluctuation of political principles, he sees no necessity of concluding a treaty which his Catholic Majesty can easily do without. He has often said to me that in spite of all the precautions of the government it would be impossible to prevent contraband trade and other disorders which the Americans would not fail to cause; that it was of infinite importance to his court not to encourage establishments on the Mississippi which might one day become neighbors so much the more dangerous for the Spanish possessions, since even in their present weakness they were already conceiving vast schemes for the conquest of the western bank of the river; that the savages would always form the best barrier between the two nations; and that nothing better could be done than to leave matters on their present footing." Otto to Vergennes, September 10, 1786, cited in Bancroft, op. cit., 2:391–392.

14. Godoy continued to exercise influence at court and political power until 1808. After the abdication of Carlos IV in favor of Napoléon Bonaparte, Godoy went into exile with the royal couple and never returned to Spain. Godoy was despised while in office and barely escaped with his life when he fell from power in 1808. The hatred of his contemporaries and the failure of his attempt to come to terms with Napoléon have given him a consistently bad reputation in Spain and abroad. A balanced assessment of his personality and his performance as a statesman is provided by Douglas Hilt, *The Troubled Trinity: Godoy and the Spanish Monarchs* (Tuscaloosa: University of Alabama Press, 1987). Spain's relations with the French Directory are described by Emilio La Parra López, *La Alianza de Godoy con los Revolucionarios: España y Francia a fines del Siglo XVIII* (Madrid: Consejo Superior de Investigaciones Científicas, 1992).

15. An early setback to Spain's foreign policy as a result of the French Revolution was the realization that the Family Compact had disintegrated. During a confrontation with Britain concerning the Nootka Sound in the Pacific Northwest in 1790, Spain appealed for French support against William Pitt's threat of war. The National Assembly turned down the request. Spain avoided war by accepting Britain's territorial claims and providing compensation.

16. Godoy informed the French ambassador that war could be averted on two conditions: (1) that the safety of Queen Marie Antoinette and her children would

be guaranteed, and (2) that the National Convention would abstain from furthering subversion and revolution abroad. Bourgoing, although personally sympathetic, was unable to accept those conditions in his official capacity.

17. In December 1793 Admiral Samuel Hood, the commander of the British fleet, ordered the destruction of a French fleet and the firing of the naval arsenal at Toulon. In June 1794, Lord Richard Howe's naval victory crippled the French navy. These actions convinced Spain's military leaders that the real purpose of British warfare was the elimination of France as a maritime power, an objective that was contrary to the interests of Spain.

18. The instigator of this conspiracy was James Wilkinson, a disloyal military officer who had settled in Kentucky. The scheme, which received the support of Jaudenes, Spain's chargé d'affaires in Philadelphia, was the revival of an earlier attempt by Wilkinson and others to detach Kentucky from the Union, an attempt that had been countenanced by Gardoqui and by Baron Francisco Luis Hector de Carondelet, the governor of Louisiana. Although sometimes described as the "Spanish Conspiracy," this plot was actually initiated by North American frontiersmen and approved by Spanish officials.

19. "Those therefore who have influence in the new country would act wisely to endeavor to keep things quiet till the western parts of Europe shall be engaged in war." Jefferson to John Brown, Paris, May 26, 1788. *Writings*, Volume V, p. 17.

20. "But those who look into futurity farther than the present moment or age, and who combine well what is with what is to be, must see that our interests, well understood and our wishes are that Spain shall (not forever, but) very long retain her possessions in that quarter." Jefferson to William Carmichael, Paris, June 3, 1788. *Writings*, Volume V, p. 23.

21. Godoy also feared that the Treaty of Amity, Commerce and Navigation between Great Britain and the United States, signed in London on November 19, 1794, known as Jay's Treaty, constituted an alliance between the two nations, a development that would represent a grave danger to Spanish America. The treaty contained no such provision, and was actually regarded as unfavorable to North American commercial interests. It was approved by the Senate by a slim margin. Godoy's fear, although unfounded, provided an impetus to the successful conclusion of the Treaty of San Lorenzo.

22. Manuel Godoy, *Memorias del Príncipe de la Paz* (Madrid: Ediciones Atlas, 1956), 1:126.

23. Pinckney to Monroe, August 28, 1795, Pinckney Papers, Spain, 127. Cited in Bemis, op. cit., 270.

24. Jefferson to Carmichael and Short, March 23, 1793, "Gentlemen—It is intimated to us, in such a way as to attract our attention, that France means to send a strong force early this spring to offer independence to the Spanish American colonies, beginning with those on the Mississippi, and that she will not object to the receiving those on the East side into our confederation. Interesting considerations require that we should keep ourselves free to act in this case according to circumstances and consequently that you should not, by any clause of treaty, bind us to guarantee any of the Spanish colonies against their own independence. Nor indeed against any other nation. For when we thought we might guarantee Louisiana on their ceding the Floridas to us, we apprehended

it would be seized by Great Britain who would thus completely encircle us with her colonies and fleets. This danger is now removed by the concert between Great Britain and Spain: And the times will soon enough give independence, and consequently free commerce to our neighbors, without our risking the involving ourselves in a war for them." *Writings*, 1792–1794, Volume VI, p. 206.

25. "The most excellent Lord Don Manuel Godoy and Alvarez de Faria, Rios, Sanchez Zarzosa, Prince de la Paz Duke de la Alcudia Lord of the Soto de Roma and of the State of Albalá: Grandee of Spain of the first class: Perpetual Regidor of the City of Santiago: Knight of the illustrious Order of the Golden Fleece, and Great Cross of the Royal and distinguished Spanish Order of Charles the III. Commander of Valencia del Ventoso, Rivera, and Aceuchal in that of Santiago: Knight and Great Cross of the religious order of St. John: Counsellor of State: First Secretary of State and Despacho: Secretary to the Queen: Superintendent General of the Posts and High Ways: Protector of the Royal Academy of the Noble Arts, and of the Royal Societies of natural history, Botany, Chemistry, and Astronomy: Gentleman of the King's Chamber in employment: Captain General of his Armies: Inspector and Major of the Royal Corps of Body Guards etc. etc. etc." Text of the Treaty of San Lorenzo in Bemis, op. cit., 343–362.

26. Bute to Grenville, August 10, 1795. Record Office, F.O. 72, 38. Cited in André Fugier, *Napoléon et L'Espagne, 1799–1808*, Bibliothèque d'histoire contemporaine (Paris: Librairie Félix Alcan, 1930), 1:9.

27. "Espagne," *Encyclopédie méthodique ou par ordre de matières*, Series "Géographie moderne" I, pp. 554–568, cited in Richard Herr, *The Eighteenth-Century Revolution in Spain* (Princeton: Princeton University Press, 1958), 220.

28. Gabriel-Julien Ouvrard, *Memoires* I, 82, cited in Fugier, op. cit., 1:14.

29. "Of the notions that Bonaparte had about the neighbouring nation in 1800, that is to say, her Italian preoccupations, her naval power and her financial possibilities, the first one was accurate but the two others were much less so. It was a misfortune that afterwards these inexact appreciations were not rectified, that the shortcomings in knowledge were not corrected and that Napoléon ended up imagining that he knew Spain when in fact he knew almost nothing about her. As will be seen, this ignorance cannot be entirely or at least directly attributable to him. The effects of this ignorance however were thereby no less disastrous." Fugier, op. cit., 1:93.

30. "That unfortunate war of Spain was the first cause of all of France's misfortunes . . . All the circumstances of my disasters are linked to that fatal knot; it destroyed my morale in Europe, complicated my difficulties, opened a school for English soldiers . . . That unfortunate war was my perdition." Las Cases, *Memorial de Sainte-Hélène*, ed. 1842, I, 547, 693. Cited in Fugier, op. cit., 2:454.

31. Contemporary accounts of these troubled decades can be found in Andrés Muriel's *Historia de Carlos IV* (Madrid: Atlas, 1959) and Manuel Godoy's *Memorias*. For relations between Spain and France in that period, see Emilio La Parra López's *La Alianza de Godoy con los Revolucionarios* (Madrid: Consejo Superior de Investigaciones Científicas, 1992), Fugier's *Napoléon et L'Espagne*, and Miguel Artola's *Los Afrancesados* (Madrid: Ediciones Turner, 1979), which focuses on the group of Spanish politicians and officials that collaborated with the regime of Joseph Bonaparte (1808–1813).

32. "Between ourselves, Louisiana costs us more than what it is worth. By giving it to France we will be inconvenienced by their bringing of contraband into Mexico. But the British are also doing it now by means of the Americans. Therefore, it is to our great benefit to place between ourselves and the ambitious projects of American conquest, a wall and a barrier by means of a nation such as France, that neither has a great colonizing spirit, nor the means to do it because of its Continental affairs." Urquijo to Muzquiz, (Spain's ambassador to France), June 22, 1800, cited in Muriel, op. cit., 3:197.

Queen Maria Luisa was quite explicit as to what had been achieved. When the duke of Parma was made king of Etruria she joyfully exclaimed "Bonaparte is in charge of providing bread to feed our children." Cited in Muriel, op. cit., 2: 199.

33. To Robert Livingston's inquiry about the boundaries of Lousiiana, Charles-Maurice de Talleyrand-Périgord replied "I can give you no direction. You have made a noble bargain for yourselves and I suppose you will make the most of it." Cited in William E. Weeks, *John Quincy Adams and American Global Empire* (Lexington: University Press of Kentucky, 1992), 23.

34. "According to the geographical situation of that region, the nature of its habitants, and in order to conserve the peace between the two nations, the Floridas should belong to the United States, and for years the Congress has taken this into consideration, and expects that Spain, in order to avoid a possible war, before exposing herself to that will concede amicably that which . . . this government claims so justly over a territory which Spain does not need, not being able to derive any advantage from it, and the maintenance of which costs more labor and expense than one could expect it to be worth." Secretary of State James Monroe to Spain's vice consul at Alexandria, Virginia, Pablo Chacón. Conference on July 15, 1812, as reported by Chacón. Cited in Philip Coolidge Brooks, *Diplomacy and the Borderlands* (Berkeley: University of California Press, 1939), 22.

35. "You have seen the trickery of the French, who have sold Louisiana to America. That reinforces our right to remain neutral, because they had given us their word that they would not sell it and they have sold it for a trifle." Carlos IV to Godoy, May 7, 1803. Cited in Fugier, op. cit., 1:196–197.

36. The Junta Central Suprema Gubernative del Reino—central supreme governing body of the realm—refused to acknowledge Fernando's renunciation of his rights and claimed to be acting in his name, under the presidency of Floridablanca. The junta was succeeded in 1810 by a Consejo de Regencia—a regency council—and the Cortes—a legislative assembly. The Junta Central first met in Aranjuez, then Seville and in 1819 took refuge from the French army in the Island of Leon in the harbor of Cadiz. In 1812, the Cortes adopted the famous Constitution of 1812, which became the touchstone of nineteenth-century liberals in Spain. The constitution was promptly suspended by Fernando VII upon his return from France to restore absolutism.

37. Fernando VII fully merited the reputation he acquired as one of Spain's worst kings. As a person, he was deceitful, bigoted, and ignorant. As a ruler he was vindictive, obscurantist, and mistrustful of his own ministers. He reestablished the Inquisition, discouraged science and education, persecuted the followers of Joseph Bonaparte as well as the liberals, and dealt harshly with dissenters.

He used the regal power to appoint reactionary bishops and to rid the Spanish church of enlightened prelates. He governed with the help of a group of influential sycophants, known as the camarilla—the small chamber—that undermined the royal officials. He attempted to eradicate not only the changes inspired by the French Revolution but also the reforms associated with the Enlightenment. He also reintroduced bullfighting, which had been abolished in 1801.

38. An illustration of a more assertive attitude in foreign affairs is the No Transfer Resolution approved by Congress in January 1811. The resolution stated that in view of its overriding interest in the territories along its southern border, the United States could not "without serious inquietude, see any part of the said territory pass into the hands of any foreign power." It authorized the president to seize East Florida in the event that "any foreign power" attempted to occupy it or any "existing local authority" proved ready to cede it. West Florida was considered to belong to the United States. Cited in Weeks, op. cit., 27–28.

39. Onís had been appointed to represent the Junta Central (and therefore the king, in whose name it acted) in the United States. He arrived in New York on October 4, 1809. President James Madison had decided not to recognize either one of Spain's two governments. As a result, Onís was not accredited until December 19, 1815, when President James Monroe received his credentials. From 1809 to 1815 he communicated through intermediaries with a government that did not officially recognize him. He was placed thereby in a situation similar to that of John Jay in Madrid during the Revolutionary War. After his rejection, Onís set up residence in Philadelphia, where he lived until 1817.

40. When José de Carvajal y Manrique, duque de San Carlos, the Spanish ambassador to London asked Robert Stewart, the viscount of Castlereagh and the British foreign secretary, for help in resisting encroachments by the United States upon the Floridas in the spring of 1818, Castlereagh replied that "the English ministry was very sorry, that they could not remedy it; that England after the expenses and sacrifices which it had incurred in the last war, could only think of its own recovery." San Carlos to Pizarro, August 1, 1818, cited in Weeks, op. cit., 116. Castlereagh's policy towards the United States was to establish cordial relations, avoiding unnecessary controversies between the two nations. To Sir Charles Bagot, the British minister in Washington, he wrote with respect to the ambitions of the United States in the Floridas: "The avowed and true policy of Great Britain being in the existing state of the world, to appease controversy, and to secure if possible for all states a long interval of repose, the first object to be desired, is a settlement of these differences upon reasonable terms." Castlereagh to Bagot, November 10, 1817, in Weeks, op. cit., 117–118.

41. "John Quincy Adams had no doubts that the United States was the agent of God's work on earth, the vehicle by which human progress could be achieved. Unless one appreciates how deeply and how sincerely this belief motivated him, much of his life is difficult to understand. His sense of purpose as an individual hinged on his perception that America had been designated by God as the redeemer nation and that he had an essential role to play in the national mission of global redemption. The founding fathers had begun this process, and the Declaration of Independence was their holy writ. Now the torch had been passed to a new generation—and Adams saw himself as the natural leader of that gener-

ation. Given his parentage and training, it was not an unreasonable assumption." Weeks, op. cit., 17.

42. Adams to Erving, November 28, 1818, *The Writings of John Quincy Adams*, ed. Worthington Chauncy Ford (New York: Macmillan, 1913), 6:501–502. The following excerpts are from the same document: "The right of the United States can as little compound with impotence as with perfidy, and that Spain must immediately make her election, either to place a force in Florida adequate at once to the protection of her territory, and to the fulfillment of her engagements, or cede to the United States a province, of which she retains nothing but the nominal possession, but which is, in fact, a derelict, open to the occupancy of every enemy, civilized or savage, of the United States, and serving no other earthly purpose than as a post of annoyance to them." Adams to Erving, op. cit., 6:488. "that the United States have a right to demand, as the President does demand, of Spain the punishment of those officers for their misconduct; and he further demands of Spain a just and reasonable indemnity to the United States for the heavy and necessary expenses which they have been compelled to incur by the failure of Spain to perform her engagement to restrain the Indians, aggravated by this demonstrated complicity of her commanding officers with them in their hostilities against the United States." Adams to Erving, ibid., 6:500.

43. "The world shall be familiarized with the idea of considering our proper domain to be the continent of North America. From the time we became an independent people it was as much a law of nature that this should become our pretension as that the Mississippi should flow to the sea." John Quincy Adams, *Memoirs*, 4:437–438, cited in Weeks, op. cit., 20.

44. February 22, 1819, *Memoirs*, 4:269, cited in Weeks, op. cit., 166.

45. The term "strategic over-stretch" was used by Paul Kennedy—in *The Rise and Fall of the Great Powers* (New York: Random House, 1987), 48—to describe the burden that, at different periods, afflicted the Hapsburg, the Ottoman, and the British empires. Although in a much different context, the Napoleonic Wars proved that this condition also applied to Spain's colonial empire in the Americas.

46. The War of the Spanish Succession was both a struggle to maintain the balance of power in Europe and a conflict over trade with Spain's colonial empire. See William Norman Hargreaves-Mawdsley, *Eighteenth Century Spain, 1700–1788* (London: Macmillan, 1979) and *Spain under the Bourbons, 1700–1833* (London: Macmillan, 1973). See also Henry Kamen, *The War of Succession in Spain, 1700–1715* (London: Weidenfeld and Nicolson, 1969).

47. Herr, op. cit., 434.

48. In fact, the process did not begin until March 8, 1822, when President Monroe sent a message to Congress declaring that five governments were entitled to recognition—La Plata (i.e., Argentina), Chile, Colombia, Mexico, and Peru—and requesting approval of the respective appropriations for that purpose. While Adams accepted the legality as well as the justice of the war for independence of Spanish America, he did not wish the United States to incur the animosity of European powers by providing active support to that struggle. In a commemoratory speech in Washington, on July 4, 1821, he asserted that the United States "goes not abroad, in search of monsters to destroy. She is the well-

wisher to the freedom and independence of all. She is the champion and vindi-cator only of her own." Adams Family Papers, cited in Weeks, op. cit., 21.

49. For Monroe and Adams, the possibility of a European expedition against the incipient republican governments of Latin America represented a serious security threat to the United States. For Great Britain, the attempt to impose a forceful return to the colonial status quo ante would have been contrary to George Canning's policy of nonintervention in domestic affairs. Furthermore, it would have been harmful to British maritime and commercial interests in Latin America. The international conjuncture as Spanish colonial rule came to an end is described by Arthur Preston Whitaker, *The United States and the Independence of Latin America, 1800–1830* (Baltimore, Md.: The John Hopkins University Press, 1941), and by J. Fred Rippy, *Rivalry of the United States and Great Britain over Latin America, 1808–1830* (New York: Octagon Books, 1972.)

50. Adams incorrectly blamed Onís for having deceived him about the dates of the land grants. Erving's dispatches from Madrid had provided the correct date of one of the grants—December 1817—a fact that had been overlooked by Adams. See Brooks, op. cit., 175–191.

51. Thomas Bailey, *Diplomatic History of the American People* (New York: Appleton-Century-Crofts, 1958), 175.

52. For an African perspective on the acquisition of Florida, and its implica-tions for hemispheric relations, see Wanjohi Waciuma, *Intervention in Spanish Floridas, 1801–1818; A Study in Jeffersonian Foreign Policy* (Boston: Branden Press, 1976).

Chapter 3

Cultural Relations and Conflict over Cuba

From the time of the implementation of the Adams-Onís Treaty until the onset of the Spanish-American War, governmental relations between Spain and the United States experienced an intermission of about seventy-five years. The nurturing of a close bilateral relationship became a low-priority item within the respective national agendas. This diplomatic hiatus registered a few brief interruptions on account of sporadic incidents related to Spain's colonial possessions in the Caribbean. The specter of Spain as a potentially hostile neighbor, that had preoccupied U.S. statesmen, disappeared with the acquisition of the Floridas and the independence of Latin America. Subsequent territorial transfers of former Spanish possessions in North America—Texas, California, and adjacent territories in the Southwest—became part of the bilateral relations between Mexico and the United States. In turn, the withdrawal from the North American continent, followed by Latin American independence motivated Spanish officials to direct their attention towards Europe, and domestically, to the urgent political and economic problems of the postwar. Along with the reduction of official intercourse between the two countries after the 1820s, this period brought about the birth of hispanic studies in the United States, as intellectual interest in Spain and to a lesser degree, in Spanish America, encouraged North American scholars, writers, and travellers to become acquainted with Spanish history, literature, and culture.

The reversal in the relative fortunes of the two nations that made possible the territorial realignment in North America in the early decades of the nineteenth century, became even more pronounced in 1898, when Spain lost her Caribbean and Asian colonies after a brief but disastrous war with the United States. This tragic encounter highlighted the diverging national trajectories of the two adversaries over the course of the century. By the 1890s, the United States was an innovative, industrially advanced, resource-rich nation that ranked as a world power in economic as well as in military terms. Spain, handicapped by political instability and economic mismanagement, lagged far behind the major European powers in terms of industrial output, technological achievement, and military potential. The immediate consequences of the Spanish-American War were neither as favorable to the victor or as catastrophic to the vanquished as it appeared to contemporaries. The former learned that the acquisition of an overseas empire carried a steep price, in material as well as in moral terms. The latter was relieved from exercising an ineffectual colonial stewardship that had become an economic liability and a political embarrassment. Nevertheless, the magnitude of the debacle of 1898 shocked Spanish public opinion and gave rise to widespread demands for social reform and national "regeneration."

The narrative about the evolving relationship between Spain and the United States proceeds as follows. A brief description of the principal developments in both countries after 1820 will illustrate the circumstances that contributed to their mutual disengagement after the ratification of the Adams-Onís Treaty. Then, reference will be made to some of the cultural aspects of the bilateral relationship, as manifested by the beginning of hispanic studies in the United States. In order to provide a background to the 1898 conflict, within an otherwise uneventful pattern of bilateral exchanges, several incidents relating to Cuba will be mentioned. Finally, a discussion about the last decade of the nineteenth century will describe the circumstances that brought about an unnecessary war.

After 1821, until the end of Fernando VII's reign in 1833, Spain turned its back on the United States as a deliberate choice. For Fernando and his circle of aristocratic and ecclesiastic confidants, there was scant reason to recommend a friendly attitude towards a transatlantic republic originating in revolution against a European monarch. To them, the United States represented the embodiment of those pernicious influences that they were committed to eradicating from Spain: constitutional government, popular sovereignty, economic liberalism, and religious tolerance.

During the subsequent decades, the nation's leaders were confronted with the task of creating an adequate institutional framework with which to replace the crumbling remnants of the Old Regime. Foreign affairs were, by necessity, relegated to a secondary role. Although the process of political and economic reform required by the advent of the modern age encountered resistance in many other European nations, in Spain the difficulties of that transition were compounded by the recalcitrance of Fernando and by the belligerent ecclesiastical opposition to any reduction in the power and privileges of the church.

Fernando's second period of absolute rule, "the ominous decade" (1823–1833), witnessed a systematic attempt to reassemble not just the political but also the social components of the Old Regime. Primogeniture was reestablished, entailed aristocratic and ecclesiastic lands that had been put up for sale were taken without compensation from the buyers and returned to their original owners, and titles of nobility were once again made a requisite for military officers. Freedom of the press was eliminated, while book publishing was severely restricted and placed under censorship. In general, intellectual activity was curtailed by an enforced subordination to a retrograde, ultramontane version of religious orthodoxy. A coincidence of events occurred in 1832 that became a symbol of Fernando's reign: the universities were closed and a School of Tauromachy was established. The advocacy of the constitution was made a crime punishable by death. The collusion of throne and altar was buttressed by clerical self-interest and by royal control over ecclesiastic appointments. Progressive priests and bishops who had been in favor of constitutional government were replaced by proponents of absolute rule. The financial obligations of the previous government were repudiated, to the detriment of Spain's credit-worthiness in the international capital markets. Fernando's vision of restored "legitimacy"—for which he hoped to obtain the support of the Holy Alliance—included the reimposition of colonial rule in Latin America and the return of Louisiana to Spain.

The harshness of official repression of dissidents and the mob violence unleashed against liberals and former government officials exceeded what Fernando's royal allies judged necessary for the restoration of the monarchy. France's King Louis XVIII—whose army had invaded Spain to overthrow constitutional rule—sent Fernando, his nephew, the following admonition in October 1823:

> A blind despotism, far from increasing royal power, weakens it. If the King's power knows no rules, if it does not recognize any laws,

it soon succumbs under the weight of its own whims; the administration is destroyed, confidence is withheld, credit is lost, and the
people, restless and tormented, rush into revolutions.[1]

Louis-Antoine de Bourbon, the duke of Angoulême—commander of
the French army of occupation that remained for several years, at Spanish expense, to protect Fernando from his own people—pleaded for re-
straint in the following terms:

> All the efforts of France would be useless if Your Majesty should
> remain bound to the system that produced the misfortunes of 1820.
> Fourteen days have elapsed since the recovery of your authority
> and the only known actions forthcoming from Your Majesty are
> arrests and arbitrary decrees. Fear, unrest and discontent are wide-
> spread. I requested Your Majesty to grant an amnesty and to offer
> your people some guarantee for the future. Your Majesty has not
> done either one of those things.[2]

Upon Fernando's death in 1833, his infant daughter was proclaimed
queen—Isabel II—and his widow, Maria Cristina of Naples, assumed
power as regent. Fernando's choice of successor produced an insurrection, the first of the Carlist Wars, by the followers of Don Carlos, brother
of the deceased king and pretender to the throne, who favored an even
more intransigent, theocratic version of absolutism. After seven years of
civil war, the government of Maria Cristina, with liberal support and
participation, prevailed over the Carlists. During this period, then
throughout the reign of Isabel II (1843–1868) until 1874, the arbiters of
Spain's political life were military leaders (Baldomero Fernández Espar-
tero, Leopoldo O'Donnell, Ramón María Narváez, Juan Prim y Prats, and
Manuel Pavía y Rodríguez, among others). However, the dismantling of
the institutional framework of the Old Regime was finally achieved, and
a gradual transition was made towards a system of limited monarchy
and constitutional government. In 1868, a military revolt brought about
the removal of Isabel II. The throne was offered to a Hohenzollern prince,
an incident that provided the pretext for the Franco-Prussian War of
1870. In 1871, Amadeus of Savoy, the duke of Aosta, became king in the
midst of political confusion and civil strife. Confronted with the recommendation that he suspend the constitution and rule autocratically,
he abdicated in 1873. An experiment with a republic (1873–1874) also
proved unsuccessful. In 1874, the monarchy was restored, with the proclamation of Isabel's son Alfonso XII (1874–1885). The Restoration insti-

tutionalized civilian rule through parliamentary government. Two parties, Liberal and Conservative, alternated periodically in power by means of a restrictive and relatively corrupt electoral system that nevertheless allowed an increase in the political franchise. The system attenuated inter-elite conflict by conciliating the demands of large landowners, business interests, the army, and the church. Notwithstanding its shortcomings, this oligarchic, pseudodemocratic arrangement provided Spain with a modicum of political stability and a modest rate of economic growth in the latter part of the nineteenth century.

The transfer of land from corporate or public jurisdiction to private ownership—which was completed by 1865—resulted in an expansion of the area under cultivation, which in turn raised agricultural production. The supply of foodstuffs kept pace with the requirements of the population, which increased from 11.5 million in 1800 to 18.6 million in 1900. During the second half of the century, private capital, foreign as well as domestic, flowed into mining and the construction of railroads. Industrial growth was led by the production of iron and steel in the Basque region and by textile manufacturing in Catalonia. Spain's economy did not experience stagnation during the course of the nineteenth century. On the contrary, consistent although modest economic growth took place. In this respect, Spain was well within the pattern of western European economic development.[3] However, the significantly higher rates of growth in France, Germany, Great Britain, and, of course, the United States created a perception of economic backwardness, as Spain's relative position deteriorated over the course of the century. While late nineteenth-century Spain could not be considered an underdeveloped country, in the contemporary sense of the term, it was a laggard, or latecomer to the process of economic modernization. By 1900, more than one half of the population was illiterate, and about two-thirds of the labor force was still in agriculture.

The challenges brought about by industrialization and the emergence of an organized working class, placed a severe strain on the political arrangements of the Restoration. However, it was a challenge of a different nature that underscored the fragility and the limitations of the political system: the movement towards Cuban independence. Spain's leaders proved incapable of providing the island with competent government, and yet were unwilling to grant it independence. They therefore drifted into a policy of heavy-handed military repression that placed the nation on a collision course with the United States.

Policy makers in the United States had reasons of their own—different

from those of their Spanish counterparts, but no less valid—to assign
the highest priority to internal affairs in the decades following the 1820s.
Between 1820 and 1900 the United States experienced spectacular territorial as well as economic growth, profound social transformation, and
a military conflict that, until 1914, was unprecedented in the Western
world for its scope and destructiveness. The incorporation of Texas, California, New Mexico, and Oregon added one million square miles to the
national territory, the largest expansion since the Louisiana Purchase. By
the end of the 1840s, the United States covered a land area that would
make it one of the largest countries in the world. The population, about
3 million at the time of the Revolutionary War, grew to 9.6 million by
1820, and had reached 31.4 million in 1860, a figure that exceeded the
number of inhabitants of Great Britain. This increase was the result of a
high rate of natural growth, complemented after the 1830s by immigration, principally from Ireland and Germany. In 1850, of a total population
of 23 million, 2.2 million were foreign-born. By 1860, some 1.5 million
Irish and about 1 million Germans had migrated to the United States.
Immigration flows became even larger in the last four decades of the
century, stimulated by lower transatlantic travel fares, labor scarcity in
the United States, and unfavorable conditions in Europe. (Spain did not
make a significant contribution to these immigration flows. Spanish
nineteenth-century transatlantic emigration was directed almost exclusively toward the nations of Latin America, Cuba, and Puerto Rico.)
Between 1860 and 1900, fourteen million Europeans migrated to the
United States, of which sixty-one percent came from three countries: Germany, Great Britain, and Ireland. By the end of the century, the United
States had a total population of seventy-six million inhabitants.

By the mid-1820s, the nation's economy was growing more rapidly
than its population. While agriculture was expanding, diversifying, and
becoming more mechanized, an industrial revolution comparable to the
one that had started in Great Britain four decades before, was taking
place. Manufacturing output doubled between 1840 and 1850, and then
doubled again in the next ten years. By 1860, the value of manufactured
goods produced in the United States was about equal to that of agricultural products.[4] Internal transportation benefitted from investments in
turnpikes in the 1820s, then in canals during the 1820s and 1830s, and
after 1840 in railroads. Railroad trackage trebled between 1840 and 1850
and then trebled again by 1860, a year at which it reached thirty thousand miles. Total railroad trackage was 93,000 miles by 1880 and 193,000
miles by the end of the century. New forms of capital accumulation were

developed in the Northeast as investment moved from commerce and shipping into industry. The growth of stock ownership, protected by the concept of limited liability, facilitated the emergence of the modern business corporation.

Economic development, particularly in the North, came about not only from increases in the factors of production—land, labor, and capital— but also from productivity gains originating in technological improvements, specialization, large-scale production, and entrepreneurship. The process of innovation accelerated: until 1860, 36,000 patents had been granted in the United States; the figure for the period 1860–1890 was 440,000.

Considerable progress was made in the effort to establish a system of universal public education. By 1861 the United States had attained the highest literacy rate of any nation in the world: ninety-two percent in the population of the North and eighty-three percent of the white population of the South (fifty-eight percent of the total population). In 1837, the first college for women was founded in Mount Holyoke, Massachusetts. Two years later the first state-supported teacher's college in the country was established by Horace Mann in Massachusetts.

Notwithstanding the conflagration of the Civil War (1861–1865) and the difficulties of the Reconstruction period in the South (1865–1877), economic growth continued during the latter part of the nineteenth century, fueled by new inventions, the beginning of mass consumption, and a widening and deepening of the financial markets. The Civil War, which was ruinous for the South, where most of the devastation occurred, contributed to accelerate the industrial development of the North. As the century came to an end, the United States had become the world's leading industrial nation. Enormous displacements of population accompanied this economic transformation in the form of immigration, the westward movement of settlers, and rural-urban migration stimulated by economic growth. The proportion of the total population residing west of the Appalachians increased from one quarter in 1830 to about one-half in 1850. By 1900, forty percent of the population lived in urban centers of twenty-five hundred inhabitants or more.

Industrialization and urbanization stimulated trade but also gave rise to new social problems and regional disparities. Unequal distribution of the benefits of economic growth created tension between regions and between social classes.

Unregulated and predatory forms of capital accumulation widened the gap between rich and poor. Industrialists mistreated workers and dealt

harshly with labor unions, monopolists profited at the expense of con-
sumers, and farmers were disadvantaged in relation to city dwellers.
There was widespread exploitation of recent immigrants, minorities,
women, and children. In 1900, ten percent of all girls and twenty percent
of all boys between the ages of ten and fifteen were in the labor force;
some 1.7 million children under age sixteen were employed in industry
and agriculture.

For blacks and Native Americans, the blessings of material progress
during the nineteenth century were elusive indeed. Until the 1860s, as
cotton production expanded in the South, slavery was actually increasing, at the time when it was being eradicated from most of the nations
in the Western world. As Reconstruction came to an end, and traditional
white elites were returned to power in the South, slavery was replaced
by different but no less effective forms of racial oppression. Poverty,
cultural deprivation, statutory discrimination, police brutality, and mob
violence kept the black population politically disenfranchised and in conditions of virtual peonage.

The wars of extermination against Native Americans and the systematic uprooting of Indian tribes during the nineteenth century belong to
the category of crimes against humanity that Bartolomé de Las Casas
had vehemently denounced three centuries earlier in his treatise, *The
Destruction of the Indies* (1552). However, while in sixteenth-century Spain
a party of humanity had registered its dissent and protest at the abuses
of the conquistadors, the outrages of the modern age were committed
with the widespread support of the white population of the United
States. Eradication of Indian communities was considered a necessary
condition for the advancement of civilization; the perpetrators of these
deeds received popular acclaim. Andrew Jackson was notorious for his
persecution of Native Americans. As governor of the newly acquired
Floridas and then as president, he carried out a policy of ethnic cleansing
that culminated in the forcible deportation of all the Indian population
of the Southeastern United States to "Indian territory" west of the Mississippi River. In due course, as white settlement advanced, the relocated
Indians were once again dispossessed, along with the other tribes of
the West.

In 1539, Francisco de Vitoria, a theologian and political scientist at the
University of Salamanca, discussed relations between Europeans and the
inhabitants of the New World and argued that the emperor could not
claim to exercise sovereignty or dominion over peoples who were outside the jurisdiction of the former Roman Empire. He concluded that

"the barbarians undoubtedly possessed as true dominion both public and private as Christians" and therefore "they could not be robbed of their property either as private citizens or as princes . . ."[5] By contrast, John Burgess, dean of the Faculty of Political Science in Columbia College in 1890, reflected on these issues and concluded that "a civilized state, pursuing its great world mission" was under no legal or moral obligation to respect the rights of a politically unorganized population that

> roves through a wilderness or camps within it . . . There is no human right to the status of barbarism. The civilized states have a claim upon the uncivilized populations, as well as a duty towards them, and that claim is that they shall become civilized; and if they cannot accomplish their own civilization, then must they submit to the powers that can do it for them. The civilized state may righteously go still further than the exercise of force in imposing organization. If the barbaric populations resist the same, a l'outrance, the civilized state may clear the territory of their presence and make it the abode of the civilized man.[6]

During the second half of the nineteenth century, the ideas of Herbert Spencer, and the application of Charles Darwin's theory of natural selection of species to social relations, provided an intellectual rationalization for the acceptance of large economic and political inequalities between classes and communities on the basis of "survival of the fittest" and racial attributes. The domination of the weak by the strong, either between classes or between nations came to be regarded as the law of nature. The remarkable economic achievements of the United States, a more assertive national self-awareness after the ordeal of the Civil War, and a growing preoccupation with the question of "race" gave rise to a sense of North American uniqueness and a belief in the special destiny of the Anglo-Saxon people. This mixture of nationalism and racism, combined with the missionary enthusiasm of a muscular Christianity, contributed to shape a distinct vision of the role that Divine Providence had assigned to Anglo-Saxons, particularly those that inhabited the United States. John Fiske, for example, foresaw the continued expansion of the English-speaking peoples until they controlled every land that was not already the seat of an old civilization.[7]

The Reverend Josiah Strong—who feared a Catholic conspiracy to dominate the United States—considered the Anglo-Saxon as the exponent of a pure spiritual Christianity, and stated that "it is chiefly to the English and American peoples that we must look for the evangelization of the world."[8] Brooks Adams—descendant of John Adams, and confidant and advisor to Theodore Roosevelt—regarded the ascendancy of capitalism and the prevalence of a business mentality as a threat to the energy of the race and the cultivation of the martial virtues (see his *Law of Civilization and Decay*, London 1895).

A university professor, John Burgess, and a naval officer, Alfred Thayer Mahan, turned their attention to international relations, and through different lines of reasoning developed arguments in favor of colonialism and imperialism. While Mahan based his recommendations on geography and the logic of sea power, Burgess invoked a manifest mission and superior political talent:

> The Teutonic nations can never regard the exercise of political power as a right of man. With them this power must be based upon capacity to discharge political duty, and they themselves are the best organs which have as yet appeared to determine when and where this capacity exists. . . . Again, another conclusion from our proposition in reference to the mission of the Teutonic nations must be that they are called to carry the political civilization of the modern world into those parts of the world inhabited by unpolitical and barbaric races; i.e. they must have a colonial policy.
>
> . . . We must conclude, from the manifest mission of the Teutonic nations, that interference in the affairs of populations not wholly barbaric, which have made some progress in state organization, but which manifest incapacity to solve the problem of political civilization with any degree of completeness, is a justifiable policy.
>
> . . . Both for the sake of the half-barbarous state and in the interest of the rest of the world, a state or states, endowed with the capacity for political organization, may righteously assume sovereignty over, and undertake to create state order for, such a politically incompetent population.
>
> . . . History and ethnology . . . teach us that the Teutonic nations are the political nations of the modern era; that, in the economy of history, the duty has fallen to them of organizing the world politically; and that if true to their mission, they must follow the line of this duty as one of their chief practical policies.[9]

Mahan regarded a strong navy as a requirement of national greatness, and as a necessary link between the domestic economy, foreign trade, a merchant marine, and colonies to provide markets and raw materials.

His three books, *The Influence of Sea Power upon History, 1660–1783* (1890), *The Influence of Sea Power upon the French Revolution and Empire, 1793–1812* (1892), and *The Interest of America in Sea Power* (1897), expounded his theories on the importance of sea power. Theodore Roosevelt was an admirer of Mahan, as was Wilhelm II, the German kaiser. The full consequences of these ideas, and the mental attitudes that they helped to shape would only become apparent in the twentieth century. The world would have the opportunity to experience manifestations of Teutonic supremacy that Burgess could not possibly have imagined. However, in 1898, Cuba's war of independence against Spain provided the United States with the opportunity to give practical application to some of these recommendations, and to acquire an empire.

During the colonial period, there was little cultural interaction between the British and Spanish settlements in the New World. Scientific and literary exchanges, in both parts of the hemisphere, took place primarily with the respective metropolis, as did trade and travel, according to well-established practices of European colonial powers. The cultural discrepancies between Great Britain and Spain, nourished by long-standing political and commercial antagonisms, were transmitted as a matter of course to their respective transatlantic possessions. These imperial rivalries occasionally erupted into actual warfare, thereby bringing the colonies of both powers into armed conflict.[10] The adversarial feelings arising from differences over commerce and territorial claims between two competing maritime empires were reinforced by the mutual antagonisms separating Puritan Protestants and Counter-Reformation Catholics.[11] These reciprocal prejudices and inherited grievances—particularly in the earlier period—conditioned the tone of the bilateral relationship between the United States and Spain, and eventually between the United States and Latin America.

At the end of the seventeenth century in New England, there was a religiously inspired attempt to overcome the language barrier that hindered communication between British Americans and Spanish Americans. Two prominent Boston Puritans, Cotton Mather, a churchman, and Samuel Sewall, merchant and member of the Council of the Massachusetts Bay Colony, studied Spanish in order to achieve the objective of Protestantizing all the Americas. This proselytizing effort produced the first book in Spanish printed in British North America. It was addressed to American Spaniards in the hope that they "will open their eyes, and be converted from darkness to light and from the dominion of Satan to God."[12]

The second Spanish book printed in North America was of a secular nature. It was a Spanish grammar, published in 1741 by Garrat Noel of New York. Noel was a bookseller, Spanish translator for the Provincial Council of the Colony of New York, and a teacher of Spanish. The title of his book was: *A Short Introduction to the Spanish language; to which is added a vocabulary of familiar words for the more speedy improvement of the Learner; with a preface shewing [sic] the usefulness of this language particularly in these parts.*

The third book, Alvaro Alonso Barba's *Arte de los Metales*, a seventeenth-century classic of Spanish American mining technology, was published in 1763 in the Pennsylvania German speaking community of Ephrata, near Philadelphia. The book was not published either in Spanish or in English, but in German, under the title *Gruendlicher Unterricht von den Metallen*. It was based on the English translation of the original made by Edward Montagu, the Earl of Sandwich, in 1699.

During the second half of the eighteenth century, manifestations of a growing North American interest in Spanish culture could be observed in New York and Pennsylvania. In 1776, the College of Philadelphia offered the first college course in Spanish grammar and literature in the United States. A greater variety of Spanish scientific and literary books became available to North American readers, initially from Great Britain, but by the end of the century directly from Spain and from Spanish America.[13] In 1792, John Logan, a Philadelphia bibliophile, endowed the first library of Hispanic and Latin American documents in the United States—the Logan Collection—with a donation of original Spanish volumes to the Philadelphia Library Company. The collection included not only editions of the history of Spain and of the conquest of Spanish America, but also representative works from Spain's golden age of literature—el siglo de oro—the sixteenth century.[14]

In the latter part of the eighteenth century, the emergence of a "republic of letters" in the cosmopolitan spirit of the Enlightenment, gave a further impetus to cultural exchanges between Spain and the United States in the form of personal relations between scholars, scientists, and statesmen by virtue of their participation in learned societies. The American Philosophical Society of Philadelphia was the first North American scientific community to include Spanish (as well as Portuguese and Latin American) scientists within its membership. Prominent Spanish members in the society before 1800 were Count Pedro Rodríguez de Campomanes y Pérez, an enlightened statesman, historian, and economic reformer during the reign of Carlos III, and two brothers from a renowned Bilbao mercantile family, Francisco de Gardoqui, auditor at Rome for the Crown of Castile and Diego de Gardoqui, Spanish minister to the United States.[15] In turn, the Real Academia de Historia of Madrid selected Benjamin Franklin in 1784 as the first of a group of North American members, that would eventually include Washington Irving, William H. Prescott, and George Ticknor, among others. By the beginning of the nineteenth century, publications about Spanish history, literature, and current affairs—Spanish as well as Spanish American—were appearing in journals such as Philadelphia's *Port Folio* and Boston's *North American Review*. Spanish was being taught regularly at Harvard College, the College of Philadelphia, and Saint Mary's College in Baltimore. Spanish and Spanish American themes appealed to a reading public attracted to romantic literature, adventure stories, accounts of discoveries, and tales of travels in exotic lands. A Spanish book trade was developed by publishing houses in Boston, Philadelphia, New York, and Charleston, South Carolina.[16] Increasing knowledge about Spain and Spanish America and greater familiarity with Spanish culture helped to undermine some of the inherited stereotypes within an articulate intellectual elite, although not in the society at large. Two distinguished and outspoken North American critics of the "black legend" were Joseph Dennie, a connoisseur of Spanish letters and an editor of the *Port Folio*, and Samuel Latham Mitchill of New York, a scientist, statesman, and ardent supporter of Latin American independence, who as a member of Congress in 1810 introduced the first congressional resolution in favor of recognition of the new Latin American nations by the United States. Under Dennie's guidance, *Port Folio* published Spanish ballads and lyric poetry, essays of Benito Jerónimo Feijoo, and samples from Miguel de Cervantes and other Spanish playwrights. It also challenged anti-Spanish prejudice vigorously:

> Nothing can be more deplorably stupid than the *vulgar* idea which has been cherished respecting the character and habits of the modern Spaniard. From simple and unprejudiced travellers we have heard so much of Castilian jealousy and Castilian laziness, of the insolence of the clergy, and of the insolence of the laity, of Inquisitorial horrors, of the broiling Philip and his gridiron Escurial. . . .
>
> Nothing is more common than to listen to very sturdy declamations against the state of letters in Spain and nothing can be more atrociously false than these *unfounded* invectives. The fact is that Learning has her temples in Spain as well as in Scotland. Literary societies and men of genius are more numerous than ever.

Publications of uncommon merit are constantly issuing from the
presses in all the cities of Spain. . . .

As at the present juncture men are particularly solicitous about
everything respecting Spain, we feel an extreme desire to make this
country better acquainted with the other. . . . [17]

His democratic convictions notwithstanding, Samuel Mitchill admired
and acknowledged the contribution made by the Spanish Crown to the
advancement of American botany. In a review of Alexander von Hum-
boldt's *New Spain* published in the New York *Medical Repository* for 1811,
Mitchill, who had been unsuccessful in his efforts for recognition of Latin
American independence, argued in favor of a better cultural appreciation
of Spanish America:

Nothing has been a more trite and erroneous subject of remark than
the ignorance of the lazy Dons. This silly cant has been imitated in
our country from the English. It has been so frequently proclaimed
and so widely repeated that many of our honest patriots sincerely
believe that the Spaniards are by a great difference their inferiors.

This is a miserable and unworthy prejudice. A moderate inquiry
will evince that New Spain has produced a full proportion of respectable observers and valuable writings. And as to public spirit
and patronage it has been manifested in the endowments of learned
institutions and in the encouragements of scientific men to an extent
of which no parallel exists in our state of society.[18]

In the first half of the nineteenth century, when foreign tourism from
the United States was still relatively rare and travel within Spain was
uncomfortable and, at times, unsafe, travel books served the purpose of
informing the North American reading public about the geography, ar-
chitecture, culture, social conventions, and institutions of a nation that
in many respects seemed both strange and fascinating. Towards the end
of the century, this literary genre that by its very nature was ephemeral,
lost part of its original appeal as it became repetitive and conventional.
However, two early North American practitioners of this art are noteworthy because of their sympathetic approach to the subject, the quality
of their books, and their effort not only to entertain, but also to instruct
the reader: Alexander Sliddel Mackenzie and Severn Teackle Wallis.

Mackenzie, a sailor and storyteller (whose first book was modestly
ascribed to A Young American) wrote two popular books, *A Year in Spain*
(1831) and *Spain Revisited* (1836). He travelled extensively throughout the

country, visiting places that were not accessible to the leisurely voyager and mixing easily with Spaniards from all walks of life. His prose reveals a curious intellect as well as an energetic and adventurous spirit. He was critical of political repression and religious bigotry but found much that was positive in Spanish everyday life, including learned societies that had survived from more enlightened times. The following is his description of a hydrographical institution that he visited in Madrid:

> There is another institution more remarkable than those just enumerated. It is called the Hidrográfica, and its object is to collect information relative to naval affairs. For this purpose the principal of the establishment is in constant correspondence with the officers of government in Spain and the colonies, and with men of science in every country, in order to receive the earliest information of newly discovered land or dangers in the ocean, or of corrections in the positions of such as are already known. These are forthwith inserted and made public in the charts, which are, from time to time, published by the Hidrográfica. Connected with the establishment is a press; a shop where all the books and charts published by it are sold at cost; and a well-selected library, in which one may find all books, in whatever language, of mathematics, astronomy, navigation, voyages, and travels; in short, every thing which in any way relates to the nautical art. Of two draftsmen employed in the Hidrográfica, I found one occupied in correcting a map of Cuba, the other in making a new chart of the coast of the United States. It was curious to see a Spaniard, in the heart of the Peninsula, laying down the soundings of Chesapeake Bay, which is scarcely visited once a year by the flag of his country. The execution of such charts as were finished was as good—nay, better, than that of any that are published in France or England.[19]

His youthful enthusiasm for the Spanish language was transformed into an outburst of hyperbolic praise.[20]

A Year in Spain went through several editions and retained its popularity with the reading public for over two decades. On account of its unflattering references to Fernando VII, the book was banned in Spain by royal order of July 26, 1832, and its author was forbidden from reentering the country. Mackenzie defied the interdiction and then published *Spain Revisited*—including the text of the royal order against him in the first volume—thereby providing empirical evidence that the severity of royal absolutism was occasionally tempered in practice by bureaucratic ineptitude.

During the reign of Fernando VII, official censorship discouraged the circulation of elementary information about the United States. Thus, the first encyclopedia written by a Spanish American that described the recently created North American republic, which was published in Madrid in 1786, was suppressed in its entirety.[21]

Wallis, a Baltimore lawyer and a leading member of the Maryland bar for several decades, visited Spain in 1847 and 1849. He was favorably impressed by the friendliness, dignity, and courtesy of the people, and by the improvements in national development that were becoming apparent after the end of the Carlist insurrection. Looking back upon his Spanish experience he concluded that

> in no country could I have enjoyed more fully the charm of novelty and freshness; from none could I have parted with kindlier or more pleasant recollections.
>
> The traveler who visits Spain, for pleasure or improvement, will fail egregiously, he may be sure, of both, unless he makes up his mind to forget the fables and the follies he has read and heard— the prejudices of his social, political and religious education. . . . Whatever may have been the case, heretofore, there is no room for doubt, that now, the face of things in Spain is changing, steadily and surely, for the better. This is not only obvious, from a comparison with what trustworthy travelers have written, but from what is daily going on before one's eyes. It may be, that the movement is a slow one, compared with what we see in other countries, and especially our own. It may be, that there are impediments not easy to surmount—delays, protracted and vexatious, demanding more than common energy and patience. But both of these are elements that enter largely into Spanish character; and when we think on all the past, and see what has been done in spite of it, instead of fearing for the future, we should see it full of hope and promise.[22]

The establishment of Hispanic Studies as an academic discipline in the United States in the first half of the nineteenth century came about as a result of the conjunction of favorable circumstances on both sides of the Atlantic. In the United States a group of intellectuals emerged—historians, philologists, teachers, and literati—whose work was inspired by a common interest in Spanish culture. In Spain, scholarly work on historical sources and archival collections that had begun during the reign of Carlos III, produced a wealth of documentary materials that became available in the 1820s. In addition, at the right time and place, there appeared competent intellectual entrepreneurs to perform the intermediation between scholars and archives in Spain and their counterparts in the United States. A description of this fortunate concurrence, and a brief reference to some of its principal protagonists provides the background for what became a successful instance of intellectual and institutional cooperation across academic disciplines as well as national boundaries.[23]

A decisive factor in the incorporation of Spanish into the university curriculum in the United States was a bequest of 1815, from Abiel Smith, a New England businessman and Harvard graduate from the class of 1764, to his alma mater for the purpose of teaching French and Spanish. This gift, which became effective at the time of the donor's death, endowed the famous Smith Professorship at Harvard University and became the building block for departments of Romance languages at Harvard and elsewhere. (Other centers of higher learning that incorporated Spanish language and literature into their courses of instruction were Bowdoin, Yale University, the University of Pennsylvania, and the University of Virginia.) The first three occupants of the Smith Professorship enhanced the prestige of that position by their scholarly distinction and their devotion to Spanish literature: George Ticknor, Henry Wadsworth Longfellow, and James Russell Lowell.[24] Ticknor's masterpiece, *History of Spanish Literature*, published simultaneously in New York and London in 1849, established his reputation as a historian and was acclaimed in Europe as well as North America.

The establishment of the Smith Professorship at Harvard was only a manifestation—albeit an important one—of a larger phenomenon. A literary and scientific effervescence was taking place in Massachusetts in the early decades of the nineteenth century as a result of the region's cultural and material prosperity. An advantageous combination of economic and intellectual factors produced an environment that favored the cultivation of the humanities and encouraged the study of history.[25] A robust demand for European source materials developed from the professional interests of a new generation of competent historians, and the literary tastes of an educated and affluent reading public.

The preparation of the supply side of the equation was associated most notably with the work of two Spanish historians, Juan Bautista Muñoz (1745–1799), a scholar and government official, and Martín Fernández de Navarrete (1765–1844), a naval officer and historian.[26] In turn, the process of intermediation between Spanish historians and scholars and institutions in the United States was set in motion by two Massachusetts-born diplomats who combined a strong literary inclination with the appreciation of Spanish culture: Alexander Hill Everett (1790–1847), minister plenipotentiary to Spain, and Obadiah Rich (1783–1850), consul in Madrid.[27]

Muñoz was commissioned by Carlos III in 1779 to write the history of the Spanish Indies based on original documents, a project that occupied him for the rest of his life. To accomplish his task, he was given privileged access to the various relevant departments and archives, Council of the Indies, Archives of Simancas, Indies House in Seville, and the Tribunal of Commerce in Cadiz. Muñoz was critical of the national archival organization. He advocated the creation of a centralized archival location for documents that were widely scattered and poorly kept. His research brought him into conflict with members of the Real Academia de Historia, over matters of archival jurisdiction and censorship. He was unable to complete his project. However, in 1793 the first volume of his *Historia del Nuevo Mundo* was published in Madrid by the Viuda de Ibarra Press. He left to posterity a remarkable assembly of extracts and copies of documents—the Muñoz Collection—that would benefit later generations of historians.

The archival research effort initiated by Muñoz was continued by Navarrete, who was commissioned in 1816 by Carlos IV to undertake a documentary history of Spanish discoveries in America. Navarrete accomplished the formidable task of assembling all the documents available in Spain related to Christopher Columbus and his voyages. These materials were printed in seven volumes between the years 1825 and 1844. The publication of the first two volumes set off a chain of events that opened a new chapter in the cultural relations between Spain and the United States.[28]

At the invitation of Alexander Everett, Washington Irving came from Bordeaux to Madrid for the purpose of translating Navarrete's work into English. Irving was attached to the United States Legation in Madrid and took lodgings in the family residence of Obadiah Rich. In addition, Rich's private library, which contained a superb collection of Spanish American manuscripts, was made available to him. What began as a mere translation, evolved into a book of his own, based upon Navarrete's work, a substitution to which Navarrete generously consented. Irving's book, *History of the Life and Voyages of Christopher Columbus* (1828), was well received by the reading public and by the critics. This literary enterprise marked a turning point in Irving's career, and was the beginning of his lasting and affectionate relationship with Spain.[29] Subsequent to

Irving's editorial success, major works in Spanish historiography appeared, written by a new generation of historians, that benefitted from the increasing liberalization of Spanish libraries and archives that took place during this period.[30] Foremost among them was William H. Prescott, whose bestseller *History of the Reign of Ferdinand and Isabella, the Catholic* (1838) was followed by *History of the Conquest of Mexico* (1843), *History of the Conquest of Peru* (1847) and *The Reign of Phillip II* (1855 and 1858). The trailblazing work of Muñoz, Navarrete, and Irving, facilitated by the initiatives of Everett and Rich, blossomed into a more systematic and direct relationship between scholars and institutions in both countries as interest in Hispanic culture became a permanent feature of academic and artistic life in the United States.

The impact of these scholarly efforts on the relations between the United States and Spain during the nineteenth century should be kept in a proper perspective. Notwithstanding its academic significance, the blossoming of hispanic studies in New England was limited to an intellectual and social elite. It could not be expected to overcome the deep-rooted cultural and religious differences that separated the two societies. Traditional misunderstandings continued to permeate political discourse, journalism, and the attitudes of the general public. Antagonism towards Spain in the United States, however, was more pronounced in the Southwest than in the North.[31] These prejudices surfaced—in Spain as well as in the United States—whenever bilateral tensions threatened to provoke a conflict.

Henry Adams described this conflictive relationship in the following terms:

> Between the Americans and the Spaniards no permanent friendship could exist. Their systems were at war, even when the nations were at peace. . . . Spain had immense influence over the United States; but it was the influence of the whale over its captors—the charm of a huge, helpless, and profitable victim. Throughout the period of Spain's slow decomposition, Americans took toward her the tone of high morality. They were ostensibly struggling for liberty of commerce; and they avowed more or less openly their wish to establish political independence and popular rights throughout both continents. To them Spain represented despotism, bigotry, and corruption; and they were apt to let this impression appear openly in their language and acts. They were persistent aggressors, while Spain, even when striking back, as she sometimes timidly did, invariably acted in self-defence. That the Spaniards should dread and hate the

Americans was natural; for the American character was one which no Spaniard could like, as the Spanish character had qualities which few Americans could understand. Each party accused the other of insincerity and falsehood; but the Spaniards also charged the Americans with rapacity and shamelessness. In their eyes, United States citizens proclaimed ideas of free-trade and self-government with no other object than to create confusion, in order that they might profit by it.[32]

After the ratification of the Adams-Onís Treaty, and the conclusion of the independence movements in continental Latin America, Spain's American empire was reduced to Cuba and Puerto Rico. Therefore, issues concerning those two islands acquired a prominent role in the overall relations between Spain and the United States. Differences in trade policies were a recurring source of friction between the two governments. Spain's preferential commercial practices with its colonies clashed with the free trade principles of the United States. In the second half of the century, the questions of slavery and the struggle for Cuban independence became increasingly important items in the bilateral agenda.[33]

Beyond the significance of any particular cause of disagreements concerning Cuba and Puerto Rico, what was ultimately at stake between the two nations was the balance of power in the Caribbean. The possession of Cuba and Puerto Rico conferred on Spain the status of a power in the Caribbean, a region where the economic and political influence of the United States was steadily growing. U.S. officials assigned a high priority to control of the Caribbean region, for commercial as well as strategic reasons. Spanish policy makers in turn, valued the Caribbean possessions not only as economic assets (Cuba "the pearl of the Antilles"), but even more significantly as symbols of international prestige. The preservation of an imperial role in the Americas became identified with great power status, and came to be regarded by Spanish political leaders as a question of national honor.[34]

Another factor contributing to Spanish intransigence on matters relating to Cuba and Puerto Rico was the conviction, shared by liberals and conservatives alike, that the reforms of 1812 had caused the loss of Spanish America. Hence the reluctance of successive Spanish governments to introduce reforms in the Antilles. The conflicting nature of the respective national objectives guaranteed that each government would tend to view the actions of the other with misgivings, and to regard them as potentially hostile. Diplomacy served to attenuate this rivalry but not to dispel it. By the end of the century, the emergence of the United States as a world power became incompatible with the existence of Spanish colonies in the Americas.

The attitude of the U.S. government toward Cuba evolved over the course of the century from favoring the continuation of Spanish rule, to annexation, and finally to independence with limited sovereignty within a North American sphere of influence. The initial policy with respect to Cuba and Puerto Rico was formulated by John Quincy Adams in a letter of instructions to Huge Nelson, U.S. minister to Spain:

> These islands, from their local position, are natural appendages to the North American continent; and one of them, Cuba, almost in sight of our shores, from a multitude of considerations has become an object of transcendent importance to the political and commercial interests of our Union. Its commanding position with reference to the Gulf of Mexico and the West India seas; . . . the nature of its productions and of its wants, furnishing the supplies and needing the returns of a commerce immensely profitable and mutually beneficial; give it an importance in the sum of our national interests, with which that of no other foreign territory can be compared, and little inferior to that which binds the different members of this Union together.
>
> Such indeed are, between the interests of that island and of this country, the geographical, commercial, moral and political relations, formed by nature, gathering in the process of time, and even now verging to maturity, that in looking forward to the probable course of events for the short period of half a century, it is scarcely possible to resist the conviction that the annexation of Cuba to our federal republic will be indispensable to the continuance and integrity of the Union itself. It is obvious however that for this event we are not yet prepared. . . . But there are laws of political as well as of physical gravitation; and if an apple severed by the tempest from its native tree cannot choose but fall to the ground, Cuba, forcibly disjoined from its own unnatural connection with Spain, and incapable of self-support, can gravitate only towards the North American Union, which by the same law of nature cannot cast her off from its bosom. . . .
>
> The transfer of Cuba to Great Britain would be an event unpropitious to the interests of this Union. . . . The question of both our right and our power to prevent it, if necessary, by force, already obtrudes itself upon our councils, and the administration is called upon, in the performance of its duties to the nation, at least to

use all the means within its competency to guard against and for-
fend it.[35]

According to this formulation, until the moment when the law of nature brought about the inevitable, the United States, while continuing to
press for trade liberalization, would support the political status quo in
Spain's Caribbean possessions. In addition to an explicit no-transfer policy, the United States would not give its support to local independence
movements for fear that political instability or racial strife could provoke
intervention by other European powers. Implicit in this formulation was
a departure from the policy towards independence in the rest of Latin
America, and an exception to the reasoning that led to the proclamation
of the Monroe Doctrine. Accordingly, a combined military operation
planned by Colombia and Mexico in 1825 to liberate Cuba from Spanish
rule was resolutely opposed by the United States.

From 1848 to 1861, the attitude of self-restrained expectation by the
United States gave way to a preference for the annexation of Cuba, by
purchase if possible, but without ruling out the option of acquiring it by
force. This greater assertiveness reflected the same popular sentiment in
favor of territorial expansion that had resulted in war with Mexico. With
the acquisition of California and Oregon—the ownership of which
having recently been acknowledged by Great Britain—the port of Havana had become a vital link in the maritime communications between
the eastern seaboard and the Pacific coast. Securing control of Havana
was regarded as necessary for the eventual protection of the West. The
change of policy was strongly supported by representatives of slave-
owning interests, who viewed the acquisition of Cuba, with its plantation
agriculture, as a means for protecting and preserving the institution of
slavery in the South. (For the same reason, the prospect of bringing Cuba
into the Union was resisted by the advocates of abolition.)

Official manifestations of interest in purchasing Cuba by U.S. diplomats were met by Spanish rejection, a position that was supported by
other European powers, in particular Great Britain. The British government, mindful of its own Caribbean possessions, favored a no-transfer
policy with regard to Cuba, as a safeguard against further expansion by
the United States into that region.

Several incidents highlighted the importance of Cuban concerns in the
relations between Spain and the United States during this period. One
of them was caused by Narciso López, a charismatic Venezuelan working for Cuban independence, who had been carrying out filibustering

raids on the island from the East Coast of the United States. In August 1851, he led a force of Cuban insurgents and North American sympathizers in an invasion attempt at Bahia Honda that was promptly frustrated by the Spanish army. López and a large group of his followers were summarily tried and executed. The severity of the repression signalled Spanish determination to forcefully resist any attempt to undermine colonial rule in Cuba. News of the executions, however, shocked public opinion in the United States; in New Orleans, the city where López had established his command, an outraged multitude attacked the Spanish consulate.

During the administration of Franklin Pierce (1853–1857), a relatively minor disagreement over the seizure in Havana in February 1854 of a U.S. merchant ship, the *Black Warrior*, by Spanish authorities, for port infractions, brought the nations close to an open conflict. The minister to Madrid, Pierre Soulé, a bellicose annexationist from Louisiana, going beyond his instructions, used the dispute as a pretext to provoke a confrontation between the two governments. This same official, along with the ministers to France and Great Britain, John Mason and James Buchanan, was responsible for an unprecedented diplomatic episode in October 1854, that became known as the Ostend Manifesto. At the suggestion of William Marcy, the secretary of state, the three diplomats drafted a set of policy recommendations with regard to Cuba, urging the purchase of the island from Spain, or its seizure in the absence of Spain's agreement to sell. Newspaper accounts of this initiative produced an unfavorable reaction in Europe and stiffened Spanish resistance to any negotiation with the United States concerning the status of Cuba. The episode became an embarrassment for the Pierce administration, domestically as well as internationally. Soulé was recalled from his post in Madrid. The Spanish government in turn offered to pay reparations for the losses incurred by the owners of the *Black Warrior*.

The prospect of acquiring Cuba became increasingly controversial in the United States as it became associated with the divisive issue of slavery. Northern opposition to the initiative was intensified by the perception that the Cuban venture was part of a Southern conspiracy to bring additional slave states into the Union. After the election of Abraham Lincoln as president, and the advent of the Civil War in April 1861, the incorporation of Cuba into the United States ceased to be a politically feasible option.

The Battle of Gettysburg (July 1863) was the beginning of the end for the Confederacy, and therefore, of that peculiar institution that had become an integral part of the social and economic fabric of the Old South. Once the eventual outcome of the Civil War ceased to be in doubt, the Spanish government had to come to terms with the growing awareness that the continuation of slavery in the Caribbean was no longer tenable. Opposition to slavery acquired an organized domestic constituency with the foundation of the Spanish Abolitionist Society (Sociedad Abolicionista Española) in Madrid on April 2, 1865, under the leadership of the Puerto Rican reformer Julio Vizcarrondo and the Cuban-born Spanish liberal Rafael Maria de Labra.[36] The issue of slavery also acquired greater foreign policy relevance once it became foreseeable that the United States would now contribute to increase the abolitionist pressure on Spain that Great Britain had been applying since the 1820s. On May 6, 1865, Antonio Maria Fabié, a conservative deputy, made the following statement in the Cortes:

> The war in the United States is finished, and being finished, slavery on the whole American continent can be taken as finished. Is it possible to keep Spanish provinces . . . while keeping this institution in the dominions? I don't think so, and therefore I say the question is urgent, that the Government must comply with great obligations. . . . I hope that the enlightenment necessary to solve this problem will be sought for in cooperation with the Cortes.[37]

In July 1865, Gabriel Tassara, the Spanish minister in Washington, fearing that the issue would provide a pretext for the United States to intervene in Cuba advised his government "to consider in one form or another the means for initiating the abolition of slavery."[38]

An armed uprising in Cuba in 1868 marked the beginning of a bitter and destructive struggle for independence that became known as the Ten Years' War (1868–1878). The leaders of the Cuban independence movement also embraced the abolitionist cause. The linkage of these two issues further stiffened the resistance of Spanish business interests, conservative politicians, and military officers to the introduction of any reforms in colonial administration. In addition, the severe political instability experienced by Spain during this period precluded the adoption of bold innovations in government policy. A revolution in 1868 brought about the dethronement of Isabel II. This action was followed by the brief reign of an Italian king, Amadeo I, the establishment of a republic, and, after the failure of the latter in 1874, the restoration of the monarchy.

The war in Cuba became a matter of concern for the United States on account of economic considerations and because of complications arising from geographical proximity. The Cuban revolutionaries looked to the United States for material assistance in funds and weapons and for political support in the form of recognition of belligerency status. They promoted sympathy for their cause in Congress and among the public at large through a vigorous propaganda campaign. The business community also took an interest in the conflict. The harshness with which the war was conducted, by both sides, was harmful to North American investments in the island and had a detrimental effect on trade between Cuba and the United States.

In June 1869, Hamilton Fish, the secretary of state during the administration of President Ulysses Grant, forwarded to Madrid a proposal that included granting independence to Cuba upon payment by the Cubans to Spain of a certain sum, whose amount would be guaranteed by the United States; the abolition of slavery in Cuba and Puerto Rico; and the declaration of an armistice through the mediation of the United States between the combatants. This formula was intended by Fish as an alternative to the recognition of belligerency status of the Cuban rebels. The latter was a policy that in his view would lead to war with Spain, and that he vehemently opposed. The Spanish government, at that time under the leadership of General Juan Prim, in effect rejected the proposal. It gave its approval, but with the condition that the rebels lay down their arms before the start of the negotiations, a condition that was unacceptable to the Cubans.

In November 1873, a maritime incident related to the Cuban insurrection brought Spain and the United States to the brink of war. The *Virginius*, a ship carrying supplies sent by the New York Cuban junta to the rebels, was intercepted by the Spanish patrol boat *Tornado*, declared a pirate ship, and taken into the port of Santiago de Cuba. After a summary court-martial ordered by General Juan Burriel, the Spanish governor of Santiago, most of the ship's crew, including several U.S. civilians, were condemned to death and executed. The reports of the massacre became headline news in the United States and led to manifestations of public outrage. Secretary Fish directed a formal protest to the Spanish government, and requested an apology, reparations, and the punishment of Burriel, in the absence of which by a predetermined date, diplomatic relations would be terminated. By means of a face-saving compromise, which Fish considered satisfactory, the Spanish government accepted responsibility for the incident and paid $80,000 in indemnities to the families of the civilians that had been executed.

The danger of war subsided, but the episode of the *Virginius* created long-lasting resentment against Spain in the United States. It also set in motion an effort to build up the U.S. Navy. At the height of the crisis, it had been decided to assemble a flotilla of warships at Key West, Florida, as a precaution in the event of war with Spain. What the navy was able to mobilize was a collection of old Civil War vessels that had not been out to sea in eight years. The sense of military inadequacy that was revealed on that occasion, provided the impetus for a program of modernization of the navy over the course of the next twenty years, the nature of which would fundamentally alter the balance of power in the Caribbean, to the detriment of Spain.

At the beginning of 1878, General Arsenio Martínez Campos, a popular and highly-regarded officer who commanded Spanish military operations in Cuba, was able to bring the Ten Years' War to an end mostly by diplomatic means. He negotiated with the rebels an agreement that was formalized in the Treaty of Zanjón, signed in February 1878. In exchange for the acceptance of Spanish allegiance and the cessation of hostilities, the insurgents were granted an amnesty and offered the implementation of colonial reforms.

The conclusion of a costly and unpopular war became a major achievement that brought prestige to the restored monarchy of Alfonso XII, and contributed to the political stability and economic progress enjoyed by Spain in the following twenty years. However, the government did not take advantage of these favorable circumstances to carry out the promised reform program in colonial administration. The root causes of the Cuban insurgency remained unchanged. As a result, the peace brought about by the Zanjón Treaty became a seventeen-year interlude in the Cuban war of independence. The resumption of the war in 1895 set in motion a chain of events that brought relations between Spain and the United States to a crisis, which the diplomats of both nations were unable to control.

NOTES

1. Miguel Artola, *La España de Fernando VII* (Madrid: Espasa-Calpe, 1968), 846.
2. Artola, op. cit., 846–847.
3. Recent Spanish historiography challenges the traditional, mostly negative interpretation of the nation's performance during the nineteenth century. See, for example, Gabriel Tortella Casares, *El Desarrollo de la España Contemporánea: Historia Económica de los Siglos XIX y XX* (Madrid: Alianza Editorial, 1995), and

Leandro Prados de la Escosura, *De Imperio a Nación: Crecimiento y Atraso Económico en España, 1780–1930* (Madrid: Alianza Editorial, 1988).

4. The source for the figures on population, education, and economic growth in this section is: Richard Current, Harry Williams, Frank Freidel, and Alan Brinkley, *American History: A Survey*, 6th ed., vol. 1, and 7th ed., vol. 2 (New York: Knopf, 1985, 1987).

5. "On the American Indians" (1530), published in Francisco De Vitoria, *Political Writings*, ed. Anthony Pagden and Jeremy Lawrence (Cambridge: Cambridge University Press, 1991), 250–251.

6. John W. Burgess, *Political Science and Comparative Constitutional Law*, vol. 1, *Sovereignty and Liberty* (Boston: Ginn and Company, 1902), 46–47.

7. John Fiske, "Manifest Destiny," *Harpers New Monthly Magazine* (March 1885): 578–590.

8. Josiah Strong, *Our Country: Its Possible Future and Its Present Crisis* (New York: The American Home Missionary Society, 1885), 160–161.

9. Burgess, op. cit., 45, 47, 48.

10. In 1741, for example, during the so-called War of Jenkin's Ear between Great Britain and Spain, Admiral Edward Vernon led an unsuccessful sea and land assault on Cartagena. Lawrence Washington, a half brother of George Washington, was a member of the North American colonial contingent that participated in the Caribbean expedition. He gave the name Mount Vernon to the family estate in Virginia, in honor of his commanding officer.

11. "Puritan New England, much more than the Anglican Middle Colonies, kept alive all those historic fears of Catholic Spain, the Inquisition, the Jesuits, and the Counter-Reformation, which had long before disturbed Elizabethan Old England. The strict Puritan lived by the theological argument. All in all, however a blend of European theology, Old World royalist rivalries, European trade interest in the Indies, historical myth, mass psychology, and the real nearness of Spain-in-America ought to be used to explain the whole attitude of British Americans towards Spanish Americans. The myths about Spain lived for a long time; there was little change in the belief. For those who believed it, the points were the same in the nineteenth century as they were in the sixteenth, when they were born. Such ideas, or rather, images never seem to grow or evolve. They depended upon a static nightmare of Spain, an abnormally enduring fear, timeless and stubborn." Harry Bernstein, *Making an Inter-American Mind* (Gainsville: University of Florida Press, 1961), 3.

12. Cotton Mather, *La Fe del Christiano: en Veyntequatro* [sic] *Articulos de la Institucion de Christo* [sic] *Embiada* [sic] *a los Españoles para que abran sus ojos, y para que se conviertan de las tinieblas a la luz, y de la potestad de Satanas a Dios*: para que reciban por *la fe que es en Jesuchristo,* [sic] *remission* [sic] *de peccados* [sic] *y suerte entre los santificados*. 1699. The original is in the library of the American Antiquarian Society. The New York Public Library has a film copy.

13. Until the beginning of the eighteenth century, the principal North American sources of information on Spanish America were from European sources. Some of them had received wide dissemination as part of a deliberate anti-Spanish propaganda campaign orchestrated by Great Britain, which produced the enduring legend of Spanish wrongdoing and obscurantism known as la le-

yenda negra. Foremost among these was Bartolomé de Las Casas's *The Destruc-tion of the Indies* (1552). Other popular publications were *The English American, or A New Survey of the West Indies* (London, 1648), written by Thomas Gage, a ren-egade Dominican friar and advisor to Oliver Cromwell, and the voluminous writings of Richard Hakluyt, a British geographer and promoter of Elizabethan overseas expansion. He wrote *Divers [sic] voyages touching the discoverie [sic] of America* (1582), and translated Antonio Galvano's *Discoveries of the World* (1601) and Hernando de Soto's account of the discovery of Florida (1609).

14. Following in the footsteps of the Logan Collection, other institutions as well as bibliophiles in Pennsylvania, Massachusetts, and New York enlarged and diversified their collections of Spanish and Spanish American materials. The for-mer include the American Philosophical Society in Philadelphia, the American Academy of Arts and Sciences and the Massachusetts Historical Society in Bos-ton, the Harvard College Library in Cambridge, the New York Society Library (founded in 1754), and the New York Historical Society (founded in 1804). Prom-inent among the private libraries were those of John Carter Brown, John Jacob Astor, and Hubert H. Bancroft. Some of the principal book collectors were Wash-ington Irving, Henry Stevens, Buckingham Smith, George Ticknor, and Obadiah Rich. Rich was the U.S. consul in Valencia and Madrid during the reign of Fer-nando VII, at a time when political unrest and the persecution of intellectuals brought about the dispersal of valuable archives and libraries. His acquisitions eventually enriched the collections of the Boston Athenaeum, the Boston Public Library, and the New York Public Library. See Bernstein, op. cit., 12–28, and Norman P. Tucker *Americans in Spain* (Boston: Atheneum, 1980), 2–9.

15. For a list of Spanish, Portuguese, and Latin American members of North American learned societies in the nineteenth century, see Bernstein, op. cit., ap-pendix, 178 ff.

16. For a description of this trade see Bernstein, op. cit., 33–67 passim. Also, Harry Bernstein, "The Latin American Book Trade before 1900," *Publisher's Weekly* 148, 22 (December 1, 1945): 2416–2419.

17. *Port Folio*, series III (July–December 1809): 282–283, cited in Bernstein, op. cit., 36–37.

18. Cited in Bernstein, op. cit., 31.

19. *Alexander Sliddel Mackenzie, A Year in Spain* (London: John Murray, 1831), 1:241–242.

20. "In its present state, the Spanish language is perhaps the most excellent of all. Like the Italian, full of vowels, it lends itself with ease to the uses of poetry, and furnished the most graceful garb to a happy idea. . . . As a spoken tongue the Spanish is unequalled; for whilst its graceful inflictions and sonorous ca-dences please the ear even of one who does not understand them, the mind is delighted and self-love flattered and gratified by a thousand happy proverbs and complimentary expressions, which have grown into use among a witty and cour-teous people. In the pulpit the Spanish is dignified and solemn, requiring but a little skill and feeling to kindle it into eloquence; at the head of an army it is prolonged, powerful, and commanding; in ordinary discourse it is expressive, sprightly, and amusing; from an enraged voice, its gutturals are deeply expres-sive of hatred and detestation; as a language of a lover, as the vehicle of passion,

the Spanish has an earnest eloquence, an irresistible force of feeling; in the mouth of a woman it is sweet, captivating, and fraught with persuasion." Mackenzie, op. cit., 2:366–367.

21. *Diccionario Geográfico-Histórico de las Indias Occidentales, O América* (1786–1789) by Antonio de Alcedo Madrid. The Boston Athenaeum has one of the few existing copies outside of Spain. For information about the author and his unpublished *Biblioteca Americana*, which was acquired by Obadiah Rich, see Tucker, op. cit., 8.

22. Severn Teackle Wallis, *Glimpses of Spain* (New York: Harper and Brothers, 1849), 362, 368.

23. This narrative focuses on the origins of Hispanic studies in the United States, and therefore, omits the significant professional and institutional developments that took place in this field at the end of the nineteenth and the beginning of the twentieth centuries. For a knowledgeable and comprehensive treatment of this subject see Stanley T. Williams, *The Spanish Background of American Literature* (New Haven: Yale University Press, 1968).

24. Both Ticknor and Longfellow were German trained. Ticknor chose to study at the University of Göttingen because of the reputation of its library and the influence of his reading of Madame de Stael's *De l'Allemagne*. French scholarship also played a considerable role in the early years of Hispanic studies in the United States. Two eminent Spanish teachers of this period were French: Father Peter Babad, an emigré priest who taught Spanish for twenty years at Saint Mary's College in Baltimore, and Francis Sales, who for thirty-five years did the actual day-to-day teaching at Harvard as instructor and assistant to the distinguished lecturers who occupied the Smith Professorship. Sales produced his own textbooks, among them an adaptation of Augustin Louis Josse's *A Grammar of the Spanish Language* (1822), his *Colmena española; o, piezas escogidas, de varios autores españoles, morales, instructivas y divertidas* (1825), and his *Selección de Obras Maestras Dramáticas por Calderón de la Barca, Lope de Vega y Moreto* (1828). Before coming to Harvard in 1817—at the start of the Smith Professorship—Sales had given private lessons in French and Spanish in Boston. One of his pupils from that time was George Ticknor.

25. "Here in New England the independent fortunes, like those of Prescott and Ticknor, made research in Europe possible. Here, too, were the most fertile libraries in America, and here was a book-buying public. In all these libraries this curious public found shelves of history; simultaneously in the bookstores this 'middle group' of historians now provided others. The reading of history was fashionable; there was, one historian laments, little else to read. History adorned the cultivated reader's library; it was so obviously 'polite and entertaining literature'. In Boston, in 1837, Prescott's *Ferdinand and Isabella* was a standard Christmas present. As we look back now from our own machine age in scholarship with its professionals and steel filing cabinets, this phase of the 'Renaissance of New England' resembles a gentleman-scholar's paradise. These rich and talented men collected manuscripts and hired agents abroad to explore the archives. They assembled priceless libraries, and they wrote history which, at least so they believed, was literature.

"Indeed these famous historians were really a literary coterie. Most of them

lived in Massachusetts, were associated with Harvard University, used the libraries of Boston, and were intimate friends, as in the case of Ticknor and Prescott. All were learned, gifted writers, working together in a medium partly
scientific, partly belletristic. They wrote biographical articles, they annotated
manuscripts, and they imported books. In particular, they were able to initiate
colossal projects demanding prolonged research, extensive travel, and uninter-
rupted periods of writing. Notably absent were the formal organizations, the
foundations, the professional connections between university and investigator.
Nor did these skillful amateurs, like some modern scholar-historians, compose
merely for each other. They wrote for this book-buying, history-reading, genteel
public which in turn accorded their productions an admiration unparalleled to-
day for works equivalent in solidity of scholarship." Williams, op. cit., 139–140.

26. Several other Spanish personalities served as friends and mentors to U.S.
scholars, or provided them with access to restricted family or ecclesiastical archives. They included Leandro Fernández de Moratín; Angel de Saavedra Ra-
mírez de Baquedano, duque de Rivas; and other members of the aristocracy.
Antonio de Uguina provided Washington Irving with the link to the Muñoz
Collection. Irving was also given access to the Royal Library of the Jesuit's College of San Isidro. José Antonio Conde, librarian of the Escorial and Arabic
scholar, was a friend and tutor of George Ticknor during Ticknor's visit to Madrid in 1818. Conde's library was purchased by Obadiah Rich.

27. For biographical sketches of Everett, Rich, Muñoz, and Navarrete, see
Tucker, op. cit., 2–13.

28. Martín Fernández de Navarrete, *Colección de los Viajes y Descubrimientos que
hicieron por mar los Españoles desde fines del Siglo XV* (Madrid: Imprenta Real, 1825).

29. Irving spent a total of seven years in Spain, of which four (1842–1846) were
in his capacity as U.S. minister plenipotentiary. In addition to the Columbus
biography, he wrote about Spanish themes in three other books: *A Chronicle of
the Conquest of Granada* (1831), *Voyages of the Companions of Columbus* (1831), and
The Alhambra (1832). Sponsored by Navarrete, Irving became a member of the
Real Academia de Historia, the third citizen of the United States to receive that
honor, after Benjamin Franklin and George Ticknor.

30. When Irving attempted to consult the Archives of the Indies in Seville, in
1828, he was informed by the keeper of the archives that a special permission
from the king was required for that purpose. After a delay of three months and
several communications between Everett and the first secretary of state, the royal
permission was granted. See Stanley Williams, *The Life of Washington Irving* (New
York: Oxford University Press, 1935), 1:337–338.

31. "There grew up in the Southwest a vindictive hatred of Spain which
showed itself as soon as the struggles for Mexican independence began. . . . When
in 1870 a Spanish Governor shot seventy passengers from the *Virginius* in Santiago without even the form of a trial, those men in the Southwest said, 'This is
the same old Spain!' When in 1897 Weyler committed worse atrocities, these
people said, 'It is the same old Spain'.

"We in the North could not conceive of this. To us, Spain was the Spain of
Isabella II, our true friend in the Rebellion; the Spain of Gayangos, of Navarrete,
of Irving, of Cervantes and Gil Blas; the Spain of Sancho Panza and of Don

Quixote. We did not hate Spain. But the people of the Southwest did. To them, Spain was the Spain of murder, of fraud, and of violated promise. And so the mills of the gods ground in their time. Those mills grind slowly, but they grind exceeding fine." Edward Everett Hale, *Memories of a Hundred Years* (New York: Macmillan, 1904), 1:84–85.

32. Henry Adams, *History of the United States of America during the Administration of Thomas Jefferson*, 2 vols. (New York: Albert and Charles Boni, 1930), 1:339–341.

33. For a comprehensive study of the question of slavery in Cuba, see Arthur F. Corwin, *Spain and the Abolition of Slavery in Cuba, 1817–1886* (Austin: University of Texas Press, 1967). On the evolution of North American attitudes towards Cuban independence, see Lester D. Langley, *The Cuban Policy of the United States: A Brief History* (New York: Wiley, 1968). For a description of Spain's foreign policy during this period, see Jerónimo Bécker, *Historia de las Relaciones Exteriores de España durante el Siglo XIX*, 3 vols. (Madrid: Establecimiento Tipográfico de J. Ratés, 1924).

34. Several assertions of Spanish power throughout the hemisphere contributed to heighten mistrust of Spain's intentions, in the United States as well as in Latin America. Among them were the participation with France and Great Britain in a military expedition against Mexico in 1862, the reincorporation of the Dominican Republic into the metropolis (1861–1865), and a war with Chile and Peru that resulted in the bombardment of Valparaiso and Callao by a Spanish fleet in 1866.

35. Adams to Nelson, April 28, 1823, *The Writings of John Quincy Adams*, ed. Worthington Chauncey Ford (New York: Macmillan, 1913), 7:372, 373, 379.

36. Spanish abolitionists were predominantly identified with the anticlerical, freethinking movement characteristic of nineteenth-century Spanish liberalism. They tended to favor either a republican form of government or a constitutional monarchy; they also advocated the establishment of freedom for dissident religious sects. Prominent members of this group were, among others, Emilio Castelar, Francisco Pi y Margall, Manuel Ruíz Zorrilla, and Nicolás Salmerón. Representative leaders of the Spanish church were conspicuously absent from the ranks of the abolitionist movement. Catholic authors typically identified with the conservative attitude towards slavery. Even when deploring it in principle, they opposed immediate abolition, arguing that it would destroy the civilizing influence of the master over the slave. See Corwin, op. cit., 164–171.

37. Diario, Congreso (1864–1865), III, No. 79 (6 de mayo de 1865), p. 1701, cited in Corwin, op. cit., 162–163.

38. Tassara to Ministry of Foreign Affairs, July 19, 1865, A. H. N. Ultramar, Leg. 3547 (1827–1869), cited in Corwin, op. cit., 161–162.

Chapter 4

An Empire Lost, an Empire Gained

Although in strict chronological sense, the war between Spain and the United States corresponds to the end of the nineteenth century, the consequences of that war are illustrative of the trajectories that both nations were to follow during the twentieth century. For Spain, the loss of its overseas possessions brought about a reorientation of its external relations. The result was a foreign policy primarily focused on Europe and northern Africa, as it had been in earlier centuries. For the United States, the "splendid little war" brought international recognition of its emergence as a world power, the acquisition of a colonial empire, and the commitment to defend territorial, economic, and strategic interests in Asia and the Caribbean.[1]

The war itself was brief and anticlimactic, given the overwhelming maritime superiority of the United States and the characteristics of Spain's far-flung colonial empire. The naval battles of Manila Bay and Santiago, May 1 and July 3, 1898, respectively, which resulted in the destruction of the Spanish Asiatic and Caribbean Fleets, effectively determined the outcome of the war and the fate of the colonies.

The hostilities between Spain and the United States were the culmination of the second war for Cuban independence. However, the terms of reference of this study do not allow for an adequate coverage of the Cuban war effort, a topic that is an essential part of Cuba's national history.[2] The linkage between the Cuban independence movement and the decision of the United States to go to war with Spain can be described as follows.

The insurrection that began in February 1895, had been preceded by years of organization among the Cuban emigré groups in the United States—cigar workers, teachers, and professionals—a process in which José Martí played a leading intellectual and political role. This external support network became a crucial complement to the military operations on the island that were under the direction of General Máximo Gómez y Báez, a veteran of the Ten Years' War. It provided the revolution with financial resources, weapons, supplies, and skilled manpower. It also enabled the insurgents to influence public opinion in the United States. The cigar workers mobilized the support of the labor unions to the cause of Cuban independence. The intellectuals in turn, contributed copy to newspapers that had not yet established their own sources of foreign news, thereby acquiring an effective vehicle for revolutionary propaganda.

A revolutionary junta that was established in New York promoted the cause of the provisional government of the Republic of Cuba. It issued communiqués, held rallies, raised funds, and organized filibustering activities in Cuban waters, much to the annoyance of Spanish officials.

The destructiveness of the tactics employed by both sides of the Cuban-Spanish struggle became a matter of growing concern for the U.S. government and a major source of friction in the relations between Washington and Madrid. The insurgents sabotaged railroads, destroyed the mills, and set fire to the sugar plantations of those owners that refused to support the revolution. Total sugar production dropped from 1,054,000 tons in 1894 to 225,221 tons in 1896.[3] As part of their military operations against the rebel forces, the Spanish authorities under the command of Governor-General Valeriano Weyler evacuated the rural populations from their homes and concentrated them in garrison towns, where deplorable conditions of food supply and sanitary facilities prevailed.

The Cuban conflict caught the attention of public opinion in the United States on account of geographical proximity, business interests, humanitarian considerations, and ample newspaper coverage. Total trade between the United States and Cuba dropped from $96 million in 1894 to $25 million in 1896. The disruption of economic activity caused by the actions of the insurgents and the subsequent reprisals by the army affected U.S. private investment in the island, which amounted to $46 million in 1896.[4] Claims for consular protection of people and property became entangled with Spanish complaints about the revolutionary activities of Cubans who had acquired U.S. citizenship. The harshness of Weyler's military rule, particularly the reconcentration policy, was denounced in U.S. newspapers as evidence of Spanish cruelty and misrule. Real and imaginary reports of the plight of the displaced persons—the reconcentrados—and of military atrocities made Weyler the focus of anti-Spanish propaganda in the popular newspapers, where he became known as "Butcher Weyler."

Popular support for the Cuban cause in the United States was reflected in demands for governmental action on behalf of the insurgents. State legislatures, universities, trade unions, chambers of commerce, and other civic organizations sent petitions to Congress, expressing sympathy for the Cuban independence struggle and requesting the recognition of belligerency rights to the Republic of Cuba. On April 6, 1896, after several months of debate in both houses, Congress approved a concurrent resolution in favor of the recognition of Cuban belligerency, recommending to President Grover Cleveland that the United States extend its good offices to Spain to ensure peace on the basis of Cuban independence. President Cleveland abstained from implementing a recommendation that would have led to war. Instead, he offered Spain the good offices of the United States to achieve peace on the basis of substantial political and economic reforms in Cuba, within the framework of Spanish sovereignty. In a note to Enrique Dupuy de Lôme, the Spanish minister to the United States, Richard Olney, the secretary of state, referred to the anxiety with which the president regarded the situation in Cuba. After reviewing the progress made by the insurgents, the devastation that was being inflicted on the island's economy, and the popular sentiment in favor of U.S. intervention as a means of putting an end to the conflict, he stated:

> that the United States cannot contemplate with complacency another ten years of Cuban insurrection, with all its injurious and distressing incidents, may certainly be taken for granted. The object of the present communication, however, is not to discuss intervention, nor to propose intervention, nor to pave the way for intervention. The purpose is exactly the reverse—to suggest whether a solution of present troubles cannot be found which will prevent all thought of intervention by rendering it unnecessary. What the United States desires to do, if the way can be pointed out, is to cooperate with Spain in the immediate pacification of the island on such a plan as, leaving Spain her rights of sovereignty, shall yet secure to the people of the island all such rights and powers of local self-government as they can reasonably ask. To that end, the

United States offers and will use her good offices at such time and
in such manner as may be deemed most advisable.[5]

The Spanish government, under the direction of Prime Minister Antonio Cánovas del Castillo declined President Cleveland's offer, and
suggested instead that the United States hinder the assistance being provided to the insurgents from its territory by a more vigorous enforcement
of its neutrality laws. The reply, signed by the minister of state, Carlos
O'Donnell, the duke of Tetuán, affirmed the government's policy regarding Cuba in the following terms:

> it is not possible to think any benefit can come to the island of Cuba
> except through the agency of Spain, acting under her own convic-
> tions, and actuated, as she has long been, by principles of liberty
> and justice. . . . In brief, there is no effectual way to pacify Cuba
> apart from the actual submission of the armed rebels to the mother
> country. . . . Until that happy state of things has been attained,
> Spain, in the just defense not only of her rights but also of her duty
> and honor, will continue the efforts for an early victory which she
> is now exerting regardless of the greatest sacrifices.[6]

These exchanges contained the outline of the fundamental differences
underlying the approach of the two governments to the same problem,
differences that were to prove irreconcilable: on the part of the United
States, increasing impatience and assertiveness with respect to developments in Cuba; on the part of Spain, resentment of foreign interference
and a haughty intransigence. By 1896, the leaders of the Cuban insurrection were committed to oppose peace terms offering anything less
than full independence from Spain. Presumably, they would have rejected the terms of the mediation proposed by President Cleveland. Nevertheless, their acceptance by Prime Minister Cánovas would have placed
the influence and the resources of the U.S. government on the side of a
Cuban solution that allowed for the maintenance of Spanish sovereignty.
By turning down the president's offer of good offices, the Spanish cabinet
opted for a course of action that would place that influence and those
resources on the side of Cuban independence.

During the last year of the administration's term of office, President
Cleveland continued to resist popular and congressional demands in favor of U.S. intervention in Cuba. His message to Congress on December
7, 1896, affirmed the government's objections to the recognition of Cuban

belligerency or of Cuban independence, and argued in favor of the pacification of Cuba on the basis of a genuine autonomy consistent with
Spanish sovereignty. Mindful of the interventionist mood in Congress
and in large sectors of public opinion, the president included in his message an explicit warning to Spain and a notification that time was run-
ning out:

> It should be added that it cannot be reasonably assumed that the
> hitherto expectant attitude of the United States will be definitely
> maintained. While we are anxious to accord all due respect to the
> sovereignty of Spain, we cannot view the impending conflict in all
> its features, and properly apprehend our inevitably close relations
> to it and its possible results, without considering that by the course
> of events we may be drawn into such an unusual and unprece-
> dented condition as will fix a limit to our patient waiting for Spain
> to end the contest, either alone and in her own way, or with our
> friendly cooperation.
>
> When the inability of Spain to deal successfully with the insur-
> rection has become manifest and it is demonstrated that her sov-
> ereignty is extinct in Cuba for all purposes of its rightful existence,
> and when a hopeless struggle for its re-establishment has degen-
> erated into a strife which means nothing more than the useless
> sacrifices of human life and the utter destruction of the very subject-
> matter of the conflict, a situation will be presented in which our
> obligations to the sovereignty of Spain will be superseded by higher
> obligations, which we can hardly hesitate to recognize and dis-
> charge.[7]

The year of 1897 brought changes in government in the United States
as well as in Spain. In March, William McKinley, a Republican, succeeded Cleveland as president, and in August, Cánovas, the prime minister and leader of the Conservative Party, was assassinated by an Italian
anarchist. Several weeks later, Queen Regent Maria Cristina called upon
Práxedes Mateo Sagasta, leader of the Liberal Party, to form a new government.

President McKinley hoped for a peaceful solution to the strife in Cuba,
but was less willing than his predecessor to contravene popular sentiment in favor of intervention. The platform of the Republican Party for
the 1896 elections offered support to the Cuban people in their struggle
for independence. His party also favored a more assertive role on the
part of the United States in international affairs, and called for a policy

of territorial expansion. John Sherman was appointed secretary of state, but the assistant secretary, William Day, who effectively ran the department, handled relations with Spain, which ranked as the most important problem in the nation's external affairs. General Stewart Woodford was chosen to head the Legation in Madrid, the most sensitive diplomatic post at the time, with instructions to report directly to President McKinley. Although the overall framework of the bilateral relationship was maintained, the new administration was willing to apply greater pressure on Spain to reach a prompt settlement in Cuba. President McKinley did not hesitate to formulate requests to the Spanish government in the imperative. The tone of the mutual exchanges, therefore, became less cordial. In June, President McKinley registered his objections to General Weyler's conduct of military operations in Cuba in unusually blunt language:

> Against these phases of the conflict, against this deliberate infliction of suffering on innocent non-combatants, against such resort to instrumentalities condemned by the voice of humane civilization, against the cruel employment of fire and famine to accomplish by uncertain indirection what the military arm seems powerless to directly accomplish, the President is constrained to protest, in the name of the American people and in the name of common humanity. . . . He is bound by the higher obligations of his representative office to protest against the uncivilized and inhuman conduct of the campaign in the island of Cuba. He conceives that he has a right to demand that a war, conducted almost within sight of our shores and grievously affecting American citizens and their interests throughout the length and breadth of the land, shall at least be conducted according to the military codes of civilization.[8]

In his message to Congress of December 6, President McKinley expressed his satisfaction with the first measures of the Sagasta government, which included the recall of General Weyler, a proclamation of clemency on the part of the new military commander, a relaxation of the reconcentration policy, and the offer of a scheme of autonomy for Cuba. He requested that Spain "be given a reasonable chance to realize her expectations and to prove the asserted efficacy of the new order of things to which she stands irrevocably committed." But the message also contained an implicit deadline for the reforms to bring about peace, and an explicit threat of unilateral action if in the judgment of the U.S. government those expectations had not been fulfilled within a certain period of time:

> The near future will demonstrate whether the indispensable con-
> dition of a righteous peace, just alike to the Cubans and to Spain
> as well as equitable to all our interests so intimately involved in
> the welfare of Cuba, is likely to be attained. If not, the exigency of
> further and other action by the United States will remain to be
> taken. When that time comes that action will be determined in the
> line of indisputable right and duty. It will be faced without mis-
> giving or hesitancy in the light of the obligation this Government
> owes to itself, to the people who have confided to it the protection
> of their interests and honor, and to humanity. . . .
>   If it shall hereafter appear to be a duty imposed by our obliga-
> tions to ourselves, to civilization and humanity to intervene with
> force, it shall be without fault on our part and only because the
> necessity for such action will be so clear as to command the support
> and approval of the civilized world.[9]

The virulent denunciations of Spanish policies that were repeatedly
made in Congress and in newspapers throughout the United States contributed to stimulate anti-American sentiments in Spanish public opinion. The form as well as the content of the communications from the U.S.
government, in its dealings with Madrid, was resented by Spanish officials:

> Whatever may be the political views of the men constituting the
> present Government of Spain, they can not, without protest, permit
> the severe condemnation passed upon those who preceded them in
> power. . . . nor can they consent to a foreign cabinet's making use of
> them as a basis for its arguments or as a foundation for its views in its
> diplomatic relations, as they are, on the contrary, domestic matters
> entirely foreign to the judgment or decision of other nations. . . . The
> Spanish Government assuredly did not admit that reasons of prox-
> imity or damages caused by war to neighboring countries might give
> such countries a right to limit to a longer or shorter period the dura-
> tion of a struggle disastrous to all, but much more so to the nation in
> whose midst it breaks out or is maintained . . . [10]

By the beginning of 1898, the tempo of events accelerated, but time
was no longer working in favor of peace. The autonomy scheme adopted
by the Sagasta government at the end of 1897 was rejected both by the

insurgents and by the Spanish landowning and business interests in Cuba. On January 12, 1898, riots erupted in Havana, during which Spanish army officers attacked the premises of proautonomy newspapers. The fate of the government's initiative to end the war on the basis of political reforms was thereby sealed. On January 24, the battleship U.S.S. *Maine* was dispatched to Havana, reportedly on a friendly visit, but in reality to protect U.S. citizens and their property in case of further unrest.

On February 9, the *New York Journal* published the text of a private letter written by Minister Dupuy de Lôme to José Canalejas, editor of the Madrid *Heraldo*, who was investigating the situation in Cuba. The letter, which had been stolen by a Cuban agent and delivered to the newspaper, contained disparaging remarks about President McKinley. This incident, which was given sensational publicity, resulted in Dupuy's resignation and a further deterioration in the bilateral relations. Shortly thereafter, the *Maine*, still stationed in Havana Harbor, was destroyed by an explosion with the loss of some 260 members of its crew.

Dupuy's letter and the destruction of the *Maine* exacerbated anti-Spanish sentiment in the United States. The bilateral negotiations on the Cuban question that took place during the following weeks became a frantic race against the bellicose sentiment of Congress, the newspapers, and the general public.[11] On March 9, Congress approved a bill appropriating $50 million for national defense. On March 28, the report of the navy's court of inquiry into the loss of the *Maine* was sent to Congress. The court concluded that the *Maine* had been destroyed by the explosion of a submarine mine. A separate investigation, conducted by the Spanish navy concluded that an internal explosion had caused the destruction of the ship. That report was disregarded by Congress and Spain was held to be responsible for the loss of the *Maine*.[12]

A final démarche, in the form of an ultimatum, was attempted by President McKinley towards the end of March, before sending a message to Congress on the crisis in Cuba, a step that, given the mood of Congress, would lead to war with Spain. Spain was asked to declare an armistice, revoke the reconcentration order, and acknowledge that she would grant independence to Cuba if the president came to the conclusion that it was necessary to do so.

The Spanish government accepted the first two conditions but not the third. On April 11 the president sent his message to Congress, adding to it the most recent information concerning Spain's declaration of an armistice in Cuba. On April 19, Congress approved a resolution demanding that Spain relinquish sovereignty over the island, authorizing the president to use the armed forces, and pledging that the United States would not assume sovereignty, jurisdiction, or control over Cuba. On April 25, Congress declared that a state of war existed with Spain as of April 21. Thus, the Cuban insurrection that started in 1895 served as a pretext for a war that neither of the two governments had foreseen or wanted. President McKinley, responding to various motivations—economic, psychological, and strategic—led his country into a war of aggression for the sake of Cuban independence, a cause in which he did not believe.[13] In order to preserve the dynasty and maintain political stability, Prime Minister Sagasta and his cabinet accepted war and certain defeat, for the sake of a colony that in practical terms had already been lost. Faced with the alternative of losing Cuba after a war with the United States, or capitulating to an ultimatum, they opted for the course that in their judgment was the least dishonorable for a proud nation.

On April 22, immediately after the adoption of the Joint Congressional Resolution, the Atlantic Fleet began to blockade Cuban ports, in accordance to plans developed by the recently created Naval War College for the eventuality of war with Spain. In the absence of significant Spanish naval power in Cuban waters, the blockade was established without encountering resistance. The Pacific Fleet under the command of Commodore George Dewey had been ordered on February 25, by Theodore Roosevelt, the acting secretary of the navy, to assemble in Hong Kong, to keep full of coal, and to be prepared to commence offensive operations in the Philippine Islands in the event of declaration of war with Spain. On April 24, it was ordered to proceed to the Philippines and destroy the Spanish Asiatic Squadron, a collection of obsolete, ill-equipped vessels that could not possibly have represented a threat to the West Coast of the United States. The commencement of offensive military operations in such a remote area suggested the existence of an additional purpose for the conflict, beyond the elimination of Spanish sovereignty over Cuba. Dewey's decisive victory in Manila Bay created a propitious conjuncture for the implementation of the "large policy" of territorial expansion advocated by Alfred Mahan, Theodore Roosevelt, Henry Cabot Lodge, and Whitelaw Reid, editor of the *New York Tribune*. An expeditionary force dispatched from San Francisco in late May to secure Manila, captured the island of Guam on June 20 on its way to the Philippines. At the request of President McKinley, ostensibly for its use as a naval base to conduct the war against Spain, the annexation of Hawaii was approved by Congress on July 6. The treaty requirement for approval of the annexation was sidestepped by means of a joint resolution requiring only a majority vote. The president signed the resolution the following day.

Spain's Atlantic Squadron, under the command of Admiral Pascual Cervera y Topete was ordered to leave the Cape Verde Islands for the Caribbean, in spite of reasoned recommendations to the contrary from the responsible naval officers and from Cervera himself.[14] The Spanish navy was totally unprepared for hostilities against a major maritime power. Several of its warships were still under construction or undergoing repairs in foreign shipyards. The crews had not had sufficient time to become familiarized with the recently installed equipment and technological innovations. As a result, some of the naval guns were fired for the first time in actual battle. The squadron was short of ammunition and of fuel. One of the principal ships, the *Cristobal Colon*, was without its main guns. After crossing the Atlantic, deprived of repair facilities and coaling stations, the squadron would have to confront an adversary whose modern ships were fully supplied, had three times as much firepower, and enjoyed the additional advantage of proximity to home ports. Cervera was able to sail the squadron into Santiago harbor on May 19, where it was soon detected and blockaded. In early July, following orders, he gallantly led his ships into battle against a vastly superior force and certain destruction. A protagonist of that uneven encounter describes the fateful moment in the following terms:

> The bugle gave the signal for battle to begin, an order repeated by all the batteries and followed by a murmur of approbation amongst all those poor sailors and marines anxious to fight because they did not know that those warlike sounds would thrust the nation at the feet of the victor by depriving her of the only force . . . that could carry weight in the peace treaty. . . . My bugle sounded the last echo of those that history tells sounded in the conquest of Granada; it was the signal that the history of four centuries of greatness was coming to an end and that Spain was passing into the ranks of a fourth-class nation. Poor Spain!, I said to my esteemed and noble Admiral and he assented meaningfully, as if to say that he had done everything possible to avoid it (the battle) and his heart was at ease.[15]

Confronted with the loss of the fleets in Asia and the Caribbean, the fall of Santiago, and the operations of U.S. troops in Puerto Rico and the Philippines as well as Cuba, Spain sued for peace. Although Spain had an army of two hundred thousand troops in Cuba, it was dispersed through the island, harassed and frustrated by the guerrilla tactics of the Cuban insurgents, decimated by the harsh tropical climate and by disease, and demoralized by inadequate supplies as well as by arrears of several months in the payment of wages.[16] Peace talks with U.S. officials were initiated in Washington by Jules Cambon, the French ambassador to the United States, who was acting on behalf of the Spanish government. On August 12 an armistice was signed. On October 1, commissioners from Spain and the United States met in Paris to negotiate a peace treaty. No representatives from either Cuba or the Philippines were allowed to take part in the Paris negotiations. The U.S. government did not wish to restrict its freedom of action with respect to these territories. Furthermore, it had systematically avoided taking any action that implied recognizing the Cuban or the Philippine insurgents as valid political interlocutors. Spanish officials in turn, had no interest in bringing their rebellious colonial adversaries into the proceedings.

Given the position of weakness from which the Spanish side was negotiating, the terms of the treaty were basically those demanded by the United States. The transfer of Puerto Rico and Guam to the United States had been agreed to by means of the armistice protocol in lieu of a financial indemnization on the part of Spain. The relinquishment of Spanish sovereignty in Cuba, which had been the reason invoked by the United States for the intervention, was a foregone conclusion. It was left to the delegates to the peace treaty negotiations in Paris to establish how the cession of Cuba would be accomplished, as well as the disposition of the Philippine Islands.

The Spanish commissioners proposed that sovereignty over Cuba be transferred permanently to the United States. The Spanish government considered that this formula offered better protection to Spanish interests in Cuba, than the prospect of an independent Cuban government. This proposal was rejected by the United States notwithstanding the desirability of such an outcome to the advocates of expansionism. Outright annexation of Cuba, in disregard of the self-denying clause of the Joint Congressional Resolution—the Teller Amendment—would have undermined the support that was required for approval of the treaty by the Senate. In addition, annexation would have brought along with it the Cuban debt, amounting to over $400 million plus interest. The control and administration of Cuba was ceded to the United States, as a preliminary step, once the pacification of the island had been achieved, towards its eventual transfer to a properly constituted Cuban government that would guarantee stability and the protection of life and property.

Reluctantly, Spain accepted responsibility for the Cuban debt, a large part of which had been incurred to finance military operations on the island.

The request for all of the Philippine Islands came as a surprise to the Spanish commissioners. In the case of the Philippines, the right of conquest by U.S. forces could not be invoked, because the surrender of Manila had taken place two days after the signing of the armistice in Washington. Furthermore, the congressional resolution that authorized the use of the armed forces by the president had made no mention of the Philippines. Nonetheless, the U.S. delegates insisted that Spain also give up the Philippines.

The decision to take the Philippines was President McKinley's, based on his own inclination and on his perception of the prevailing public sentiment in favor of expansionism.[17] In a celebrated, self-revelatory passage, he attributed his decision to advice from Divine Providence, justified on the grounds of humanity, civilization, Christian duty, and self-interest.[18]

As a form of compensation for these harsh terms, and in order to secure the successful outcome of the negotiations, the United States agreed to pay Spain the sum of $20 million three months after the ratification of the treaty.

The treaty was signed on December 10. On April 11, 1899, after exchange of ratifications of the peace treaty by the two governments, the war between Spain and the United States formally ended. The result of the war was consistent with the existing economic and military disparity between the two belligerents. Nevertheless, its brevity, and the decisiveness as well as the implications of the outcome came as a surprise to foreign observers and even to some of the participants. Although by the 1890s the United States had already acquired the material prerequisites of great power status, that fact had not yet been explicitly acknowledged. After the war and the annexations of 1898–1899, the United States became the seventh member of a select group of countries internationally recognized as great powers, along with Austro-Hungary, France, Germany, Great Britain, Italy, and Russia.[19]

The changes that had taken place in international relations as the nineteenth century came to a close worked to the detriment of Spain and to the advantage of the United States. The last two decades of the century witnessed an intensification of European colonial expansion in Africa and Asia, within the context of nationalistic rivalries between the major powers. As a result, dynastic inheritance or tradition were no longer, by themselves, sufficient requisites for the possession of colonies. In the pre-vailing competitive struggle for commercial and strategic advantage of the period, legal title of ownership had to be buttressed in practice by administrative, technological, and military resources that Spain did not possess. According to the cold logic of Realpolitik, Spain's colonial em-pire of the 1890s had become an anachronism that few outsiders were inclined to preserve, let alone help to defend. As the war over Cuba approached, none of the major European powers were prepared to risk jeopardizing their respective commercial and diplomatic relations with the United States for the sake of Spain's colonial possessions. Even while expressing their sympathy for the Spanish monarchy, the European pow-ers offered it no real support beyond a polite and ineffectual joint dé-marche before President McKinley on April 6, 1898, appealing to feelings of humanity and moderation in the resolution of the existing differences with Spain.

A comparable situation prevailed in Asia. After the successful outcome of the war with China in 1895, Japan was regarded as the emerging regional power. Therefore, the expansion of the United States to Hawaii and the Philippines was a matter of understandable concern to Japan, for commercial as well as strategic reasons. Nevertheless, the Japanese government maintained its opposition to the annexation of Hawaii within the limits of diplomacy and acquiesced to U.S. possession of the Philippines as conducive to preserving the peace in East Asia.[20]

The transfer of colonial possessions stipulated in the peace treaty rep-resented a triumph for the advocates of expansionism by the United States as the nation's Manifest Destiny and the fulfillment of the mission assigned by Providence to the Anglo-Saxon race. But the perception that a humanitarian intervention was being transformed into a war for em-pire gave rise to the organization of a small but influential opposition movement. On June 15, 1898, the American Anti-Imperialist League was founded at a meeting in Faneuil Hall, Boston. The league included among its members, former president Grover Cleveland, the industrialist Andrew Carnegie, Samuel Gompers, president of the American Federa-tion of Labor, the novelist and social critic Mark Twain, the black leaders Booker T. Washington and W. E. B. Du Bois, members of Congress, uni-versity professors, and clergymen. The league and its supporters op-posed the imposition of U.S. sovereignty over the Philippine Islands against the wishes of their inhabitants and worked for the defeat of the treaty in the Senate, by means of articles, speeches, protests, and peti-tions.

While the peace treaty was still under consideration in the Senate, Yale Professor William G. Sumner argued against colonial expansion in the following terms:

> Spain was the first, for a long time the greatest, of the modern imperialistic states. The United States, by its historical origin, its traditions and its principles, is the chief representative of the revolt and reaction against that kind of state. I intend to show that by the line of action now proposed to us, which we call expansion and imperialism, we are throwing away some of the most important elements of the American symbol, and are adopting some of the most important elements of the Spanish symbol. We have beaten Spain in a military conflict, but we are submitting to be conquered by her on the field of ideas and policies. . . . The most important thing which we shall inherit from the Spaniards will be the task of suppressing rebellions. If the United States takes out of the hands of Spain her mission, on the ground that Spain is not executing it well, and if this nation, in its turn, attempts to be school-mistress of others, it will shrivel up into the same vanity and self-conceit of which Spain now presents an example. To read our current litera- ture one would think that we were already well on the way to it. . . . The doctrine that we are to take away from other nations any possessions of theirs which we think that we could manage better than they are managing them, or that we are to take in hand any countries which we do not think capable of self-government, is one which will lead us very far. . . . The thirst for glory is an epidemic which robs a people of their judgement, seduces their vanity, cheats them of their interests, and corrupts their consciences.[21]

The peace treaty was approved by the Senate on February 6, 1899, by a margin of one vote more than the required two-thirds majority. Two days earlier, the war against the Philippine Republic, under the leader- ship of Emilio Aguinaldo, had begun. The characteristics of that war, and the methods used by U.S. military forces to suppress any local resistance to the occupation, contributed to weaken support for expan- sionism, as policy makers in Washington—and eventually the general public—discovered some of the less glamorous aspects of the business of empire and of shouldering the "white man's burden."

The aftermath of the war with Spain in Cuba as well as the Philippines resulted in a de facto alliance between the former adversaries against the local inhabitants. The surrender of Manila was arranged between United

States and Spanish military commanders in a manner that would keep Aguinaldo's forces out of the city. Likewise, at the surrender of Santiago, the Cuban army was not allowed to enter the city. Spanish and U.S. soldiers alike felt contempt towards people whom they considered uncivilized and racially inferior.[22]

The outcome of the war, by removing Cuba as a source of friction between the two countries, contributed to the establishment of amicable relations between Spain and the United States. During the next thirty-seven years, however, their bilateral diplomatic exchanges reflected the low priority that each government assigned to its relations with the other. But in contrast to what had taken place during the middle decades of the nineteenth century, the two countries did not turn away from each other in an atmosphere of animosity and mutual suspicion. Instead, after the climactic events of 1898, they followed divergent paths. The United States, from a position of economic and military strength, moved outwards as the unchallenged hegemonic power in the Caribbean and as an increasingly important protagonist in the Asia-Pacific region. Spain, shaken by the magnitude of the defeat and the loss of her empire, turned inward to cope with the threat of fragmentation caused by regionalism and by tensions between the military and civilians, between the church and civil society, and between social classes, in urban centers as well as rural areas. Adapting to a more modest role in international affairs, Spain assigned priority to the Mediterranean region and to northern Africa, while trying to implement a policy of ideological and cultural entente with Latin America, known as hispanismo.[23]

For Spain, 1898, the year of the Disaster, became a historical watershed and a political reference point during the first half of the twentieth century.[24] The military defeat followed by the loss of the empire undermined the legitimacy of the political system associated with the Restoration and the liberal monarchy. However, there was no immediate collapse similar to what had happened in France after the defeat of Sedan in 1870. The limitations of Spain's level of social and political modernization contributed to the survival of the weakened institutional framework for another twenty-five years.[25]

NOTES

1. The expression "splendid little war" was coined by John Hay, U.S. minister to Great Britain, in a letter to Theodore Roosevelt in July 1898. The second adjective appropriately describes the duration of hostilities between the United

States and Spain, which lasted 114 days. However, neither of the two adjectives properly describes the military occupation of the Philippines and the subsequent suppression of the Philippine struggle for independence led by Emilio Aguinaldo. That enterprise became a costly and brutal counterinsurgency war that lasted until 1902.

2. For a comprehensive and sympathetic treatment of this subject from a U.S. perspective, see Philip Foner, *The Spanish-Cuban-American War and the Birth of American Imperialism, 1895–1902* (New York: Monthly Review Press, 1972). For an authoritative Cuban treatment of the same subject, see Ramiro Guerra y Sanchez, et al., eds., *Historia de la Nación Cubana*, Tomo VI, 1952.

3. Ramiro Guerra y Sanchez, ed., *Historia de la Nación Cubana* (La Habana: Editorial Historia de la Nación Cubana, 1952), 1: xii. Guerra estimates that the war of independence resulted in the destruction of sixty-seven percent of the national wealth and the loss of twelve percent of Cuba's population, equivalent to 228,000 persons. Ibid, ix.

4. Lester D. Langley, *The Cuban Policy of the United States: A Brief History* (New York: Wiley, 1968), 84.

5. Olney to Dupuy de Lôme, Washington, April 4, 1896, *Spanish Diplomatic Correspondence and Documents, 1896–1900; Presented to the Cortes by the Minister of State*, translation (Washington, D.C.: Government Printing Office, 1905), 7.

6. Tetuán to Dupuy de Lôme, Madrid, May 22, 1896, *Spanish Diplomatic Correspondance*, op. cit., 10–13.

7. Annual Message to Congress by the President of the United States, Washington, December 7, 1896, op. cit., 18.

8. Sherman to Dupuy de Lôme, Washington, June 26, 1897, op. cit., 26. The Spanish government, in reply, rejected the charges of inhumanity against the army, denounced the scorched earth policy being implemented by the insurgents, and referred to the tactics employed by General William Tecumseh Sherman, brother of the secretary of state, in his march through Georgia and South Carolina during the Civil War. Tetuán to Dupuy de Lôme, San Sebastián, August 4, 1897, ibid., 28–35.

9. Annual Message to Congress by the President of the United States, December 6, 1897, op. cit., 50.

10. Gullón, Minister of State, to Woodford, U.S. Minister to Spain, Madrid, February 1, 1898, op. cit., 72–73.

11. For a description of the war fever that afflicted the country during this period see Ernest May, *Imperial Democracy: The Emergence of America as a Great Power* (New York: Harcourt, Brace and World, 1961), and Walter Millis, *The Martial Spirit* (Cambridge: Riverside Press, 1931).

12. A study conducted in 1976 by Rear Admiral Hyman G. Rickover, with the assistance of technical specialists and a physicist from the U.S. Navy, using the advancements in knowledge on the effect of explosions on hulls acquired during two world wars, concluded: "We have found no technical evidence in the records examined that an external explosion initiated the destruction of the *Maine*. The available evidence is consistent with an internal explosion alone. We therefore conclude that an internal source was the cause of the explosion. The most likely

source was heat from a fire in the coal bunker adjacent to the 6-inch reserve magazine. However, since there is no way of proving this, other internal causes cannot be eliminated as possibilities." Cited in George O'Toole, *The Spanish War: An American Epic—1898* (New York: Norton, 1984), 400.

13. For an interpretation that explores the link between economic conditions in the United States and the decision to go to war, see Walter La Feber, *The New Empire: An Interpretation of American Expansion, 1860–1898* (Ithaca, N.Y.: Cornell University Press, 1963). La Feber, in a later article titled *That "Splendid Little War" in Historical Perspective (The Texas Quarterly* 11, no. 4 [Winter 1968]: 98) claims that "It was a war to preserve the American system." An interpretation of the war as an imperialist venture can be found in Foner, op. cit.

14. Between February 16 and April 24, Cervera described to the minister of the navy the inadequacies of the Spanish fleet, and explained his objections to the proposed expedition to the Caribbean, which in his judgment would have disastrous consequences. These and other relevant communications were published by him after his court-martial for the destruction of the squadron under his command. See Pascual Cervera y Topete, *Guerra Hispano-Americana: Colección de Documentos Referentes a la Escuadra de Operaciones de las Antillas* (El Ferrol: El Correo Gallego, 1900), 30–84. This collection contains a remarkable document, dated June 3, 1898, when Cervera's squadron was blockaded in the harbor of Santiago, in which the minister of war asked the governor-general of Cuba for his opinion on the advisability of moving the squadron to the Philippines temporarily, to confront the enemy in Manila, after which it would "return to Cuba without loss of time and strongly reinforced." Miguel Correa to Ramón Blanco, ibid, 129. In a vigorous defense of Cervera and the navy, and an indictment of Spain's political leadership, the captain of the flagship *Infanta Maria Teresa* refers to the deplorable conditions encountered by the squadron in Santiago, and the fact that the foundry date on the cannons defending the entrance to the harbor was 1724. See Victor Concas y Palau, *La Escuadra del Almirante Cervera*, 2nd. ed. (Madrid: Librería de San Martin, 1899), 99–102.

15. Concas, op. cit., 142–143. The description of the battle, in which he was wounded, is in ibid., 143–165.

16. In a file describing the situation he found upon taking office, Prime Minister Sagasta kept reports on conditions in Cuba from Governor-General Blanco and from the journalist and statesman José Canalejas. Blanco described matters in the island as follows: "The administration is in the last degree of disorganization and confusion. The army is anemic and exhausted, crowding the hospitals, lacking the strength to fight or even to hold up its weapons." Cited in Alvaro Figueroa y Torres, Conde de Romanones, *Sagasta o el Político* (Madrid: Espasa-Calpe, 1930), 191–192. Canalejas described the army as numerous "but disorganized and destroyed by disease and by misery." Ibid., 193–194.

17. For an elucidation of the shift in public sentiment towards expansionism, which helped to transform the intervention for Cuban independence into a war of conquest, see Ernest May, *American Imperialism: A Speculative Essay* (Chicago: Imprint Publications, 1991).

18. More than a year after the fact, speaking to a delegation from the General Missionary Committee of the Methodist Episcopal Church, President McKinley

stated: "The truth is I didn't want the Philippines, and when they came to us as a gift from the gods, I did not know what to do with them . . . I walked the floor of the White House night after night until midnight; and I am not ashamed to tell you, gentlemen, that I went down on my knees and prayed [to] Almighty God for light and guidance more than one night. And one night late it came to me this way—I don't know how it was, but it came: (1) That we could not give them back to Spain—that would be cowardly and dishonorable; (2) that we could not turn them over to France or Germany—our commercial rivals in the Orient— that would be bad business and discreditable; (3) that we could not leave them to themselves—they were unfit for self-government—and they would soon have anarchy and misrule over there worse than Spain's was; and (4) that there was nothing left for us to do but to take them all, and to educate the Filipinos, and uplift and civilize and Christianize them, and by God's grace do the very best we could by them, as our fellow men for whom Christ also died. And then I went to bed and went to sleep and slept soundly." Cited in Millis, op. cit., 383– 384.

19. "The war and the annexations of 1898–1899 seemed to me out of keeping with both previous tradition and subsequent practice, but I saw them as marking a transition from a past of comparative non-engagement in world politics to a future increasingly marked by such engagement. Previously, neither Americans nor others had made up their minds as to how the United States compared with other nations. After 1898–1899, though there continued to be much controversy about specifics, the United States was seen, from within and from without, as a world power in many respects comparable to Great Britain or Russia or Imperial Germany." May, op. cit., xxx. For a further elaboration of this theme, see also May, *Imperial Democracy*, 263–270.

20. Akira Iriye, *Pacific Estrangement: Japanese and American Expansion, 1897– 1911* (Cambridge: Harvard University Press, 1972), 53–57.

21. William G. Sumner, "The Conquest of the United States by Spain (a lecture before the Phi Beta Kappa Society of Yale University, January 16, 1899), 1, 9, 14, 15.

22. For a description of the aftermath of the war with Spain in the Philippines see Leon Wolff, *Little Brown Brother: How the United States Purchased and Pacified the Philippine Islands at the Century's Turn* (Garden City, N.Y.: Doubleday, 1961). For a sense of the growing animosity between North Americans and Cubans as the war came to an end, see Louis Pérez, *Cuba between Empires, 1878–1902* (Pittsburgh: University of Pittsburgh Press, 1983), 211–227.

After the end of the war, a letter from a Spanish soldier addressed to Soldiers of the American Army, that was widely circulated among U.S. troops, and in the newspapers, stated "We have been vanquished by you . . . but our surrender and the bloody battles preceding it have left in our souls no place for resentment against the men who fought us nobly and valiantly. . . . You have complied exactly with all the laws and usages of war as recognized by the armies of the most civilized nations of the world; . . . We wish you all happiness and health in this land, which will no longer belong to our dear Spain, but will be yours . . . but the descendants of the Congos and Guineas mingled with the blood of unscrupulous Spaniards and of traitors and adventurers—these people are not able to exercise or enjoy their liberty. . . . [signed] Pedro López de Castillo, Soldier of

Infantry. Santiago de Cuba, August 21, 1898. Cited in Gregory Mason, *Remember the* Maine (New York: Henry Holt, 1939), 279–280.

23. For an authoritative study of the contradictions and limitations of hispanismo during the early decades of the twentieth century see Frederick B. Pike, *Hispanismo, 1898–1936: Spanish Conservatives and Liberals and Their Relations with Spanish America* (Notre Dame: University of Notre Dame Press, 1971).

24. For an insightful study of the far-reaching consequences of the debacle of 1898 see Sebastian Balfour, *The End of the Spanish Empire, 1898–1923* (Oxford: Clarendon Press, 1997).

25. "The Restoration state survived for twenty-five years principally because Spain remained a largely unmodernized society for most of that time. The residual strength of the regime lay in the fact that the potential base for political change was largely confined to the cities amongst a relatively small number of middle and working classes, while huge areas of Spain remained in the thrall of traditional social relations dominated by the Church, the landlord and the cacique. No pluralist, modernizing alternative emerged either because political culture in Spain became increasingly drawn towards the opposite poles of revolution and reaction." Balfour, op. cit., 228–229.

Chapter 5

Dictatorship and Ostracism

As the United States and Spain adjusted to the major changes brought about by the war of 1898, the priority that each government assigned to its relations with the other was sharply reduced. For that reason, in terms of the bilateral relationship, the first decades of the twentieth century were relatively uneventful. After the ratification of the peace treaty and the normalization of diplomatic relations, both governments found that it was in their mutual interest to deal with potentially controversial matters in an amicable way.

Thus, the issue of two islands in the southwestern corner of the Philippine archipelago, Cagayan and Sibutú, which had been omitted from the exact border description demanded by the United States during the Paris peace conference, and therefore, remained legally Spanish, was resolved by negotiation. The United States acquired jurisdiction over the islands in January 1901, upon payment of $100,000 to Spain. In 1902 the two governments signed a limited commercial agreement. In August 1906, a more comprehensive agreement was signed, lowering tariffs on most traded commodities. (U.S. imports from Spain included wines, cork, olives, furniture, and luxury items. Spanish imports from the United States included cotton, coal, machinery, barrels, and manufactured consumer goods.) A further mutual reduction of duties took place in 1910.

From the outbreak of World War I until the beginning of 1917, the interests of the two governments coincided, as neutral nations. Both governments tried to protect their citizens and their trade from the actions of the belligerents. Likewise, both governments favored a negotiated conclusion of the war. That coincidence of interests ceased to exist in the spring of 1917 when the United States entered the war as an ally of France and Great Britain, while Spain, which had remained aloof from European conflicts since 1814, maintained its neutrality until the end of the war.

During the 1920s, both governments again found a convergence of views on the issue of world disarmament. Spain advocated world disarmament from within the League of Nations. The United States, as a nonmember nation, pursued the same objective outside the league, by means of ad hoc international conferences. A major foreign policy initiative by Spain during this period, one that required a substantial military effort, was the attempt to reestablish a colonial empire in Morocco. This costly and unpopular enterprise touched on Spain's relations with Great Britain as a Mediterranean power and with France as a neighboring colonial power in North Africa. It was of negligible concern to the interests of the United States in the region.

In Spain, the debacle of 1898 and the loss of the empire gave rise to an anguished reassessment of the national identity and to an overly pessimistic evaluation of the recent past. The predictable military defeat by a stronger, technologically more advanced, and better equipped adversary, was transformed by journalists, intellectuals, and politicians into a judgment on the Spanish character and interpreted as a symptom of national "degeneration." The year of the Disaster, 1898, became a watershed in Spanish modern history and a point of reference in the political discourse of the following decades.[1]

A variety of proposals from across the political spectrum were put forward for the "regeneration" of Spain. Some stressed the need to "Europeanize" Spain by means of educational and scientific reforms. Some argued, instead, in favor of a return to the Catholic, hierarchical, authoritarian, preindustrial, Castille-centered values of Spain's sixteenth century. Others, in turn, advocated schemes of river management and irrigation. Joaquín Costa, a prominent exponent of regenerationism called for an "Iron Surgeon" that would apply drastic remedies to the nation's body politic. Some of these concepts were incorporated into a nationalist ideology, which since the end of the nineteenth century was shifting to the political right.[2] This development, added to the military's feelings of humiliation and resentment after the defeat of 1898, contributed to set the stage for the two dictatorships experienced by Spain in the twentieth century. However, the turmoil that characterized Spanish politics during the early decades of this century was by no means caused by economic stagnation. The political system of the Restoration proved incapable of incorporating the new constituencies—labor unions, industrial bourgeoisie, and urban middle class—that accompanied a process of economic and social modernization.[3]

The military coup of September 1923 that led to the dictatorship of General Miguel Primo de Rivera y Orbaneja, Segundo Marqués de Estella, (1923–1930) did not disrupt normal diplomatic relations between the United States and Spain. This coup was one among several instances of the emergence of authoritarian regimes in Europe during the turbulent years following the end of World War I (Hungary in 1920; Italy, 1922; Bulgaria and Turkey, 1923; and Portugal and Poland, 1926). Furthermore, business leaders and conservative politicians in the United States, alarmed by the establishment of a Communist regime in Russia, looked favorably upon right-wing authoritarianism as a protection against the spread of bolshevik revolution.[4]

In the United States, the foreign as well as the domestic policies of the Warren Harding, Calvin Coolidge, and Herbert Hoover administrations reflected the conservative outlook of the business community and the Republican Party. Diplomatic exchanges between the United States and Spain during the years 1923 to 1925 dealt with negotiations to renew the 1906 Commercial Agreement and routine matters such as the effect of Prohibition on the wine trade and the embargo placed by the Department of Agriculture on the importation of Spanish grapes and oranges on account of the Mediterranean fruit fly.[5]

U.S. business interests benefitted from some of the decisions of Primo de Rivera's regime. In 1925 the International Telephone and Telegraph Company (ITT) was granted exclusive rights to operate the telephone system in Spain. Some aspects of the regime's economic dirigisme, however, had the opposite effect. In June 1927 the government nationalized the petroleum industry, a decision that was detrimental to the interests of Standard Oil of New Jersey, Vacuum Oil Company, and Atlantic Refining Company. The affected companies were not satisfied with the payments received as compensation for their properties. The State Department provided diplomatic support to the affected companies during the course of these developments. However, the disagreement about the settlement did not disrupt relations between the two governments.

The conservative inclination of U.S. foreign policy during this period was reflected in the manner in which the State Department reacted to the proclamation of the Republic on April 14, 1931, upon the departure of Alfonso XIII. Irwin Laughlin, the U.S. ambassador to Spain, deplored the departure of the king, described the new situation in bleak terms, and advised the State Department against recognition of the Republic.[6] Henry Stimson, the secretary of state, authorized Laughlin to extend recognition of the Provisional Government, but only after ascertaining that Great Britain had previously done so, and without using the term "Spanish Republic," in order not to "give the appearance of prejudging events."[7]

During the 1920s and 1930s, nongovernmental relations between the two countries were stimulated by a growing number of U.S. tourists travelling to Spain and by renewed cultural exchanges. During this period, Georgiana King, a professor of Comparative Literature and History of Art at Bryn Mawr, published two travel books of enduring literary merit, *The Way of Saint James* (1920), and *Heart of Spain* (1926). John Dos Passos and Ernest Hemingway reflected the impact of Spanish culture and society in their writings. In addition to his works on Spain, *The Sun Also Rises* (1926), *Death in the Afternoon* (1932), and *For Whom the Bell Tolls* (1940), Hemingway dealt with Spanish themes and current affairs in his newspaper articles.

The early decades of the twentieth century were accompanied by a renewal of interest in Hispanic Studies in the United States. In 1904, the philanthropist and scholar Archer Milton Huntington founded the Hispanic Society of America in New York. This research institution, focused on Spanish culture, was endowed with an outstanding art museum and a valuable collection of rare books and manuscripts. In 1916, Federico de Onís came to Columbia University, where he became head of the Department of Spanish Literature. In 1920, the Casa Hispánica, Spanish House, was established at Columbia University. It became a center of Spanish cultural and intellectual activity in New York. Charles Chapman and Roger Bigelow Merriman continued the tradition of their nineteenth-century academic predecessors with their scholarly work on Spanish history. In sharp contrast to the negative stereotypes of Spain that were so common in U.S. publications during the nineteenth century, the early twentieth century witnessed the emergence of a romantic mystification of Hispanic values and social customs. The disillusionment that followed World War I, and the discomfort felt by intellectuals with life in industrialized capitalist countries, led some authors to discover admirable qualities in a premodern society that had not been spoiled by the pursuit of material wealth. Hemingway, who became acquainted with Spain in the 1920s, fell in love with the country. He was fascinated by bullfighting, by ritual, and by Spanish attitudes toward nature, life, and death. "Spain is the very best country of all. It's unspoiled and unbelievably tough and wonderful."[8]

Waldo Frank gave the following idealized description of Spanish manhood:

> He has the virtues of his state. His personal development brings him a personal integrity, a true personal pride unknown in Europe. He has natural dignity. Whatever his rank, he is a *caballero*: a true microcosm of the Spanish nation. There is no artifice in him. He is clean, self-controlled and independent. In his veins lives the impulse of heroism; in his mind is the knowledge and the acceptance of heroism's price. Cowardice, compromise, hypocrisy are traits more common in more social races.[9]

These flattering observations were more useful as a reflection of the predispositions of the respective authors than as a guide to the conditions of the Spanish people prevailing at the time.

The international implications of the Spanish civil war and World War II interrupted the quiet hiatus in governmental relations that followed the ratification of the peace treaty in 1899. In the midst of an international crisis, under particularly unfavorable circumstances, the two nations renewed and reassessed their governmental bilateral relations.

The military uprising of July 17, 1936, that marked the beginning of the Spanish civil war, confronted officials in the United States with the need to formulate a policy with respect to the conflict. Although the revolt against the Republic began as a domestic affair, the struggle that ensued soon acquired an international dimension on account of the foreign assistance that both sides actively sought. The Spanish government turned to the Western democracies and the Soviet Union for support in its efforts to suppress a military rebellion. The rebels requested aid from the Fascist regimes in Germany and Italy. The significant air support provided by Adolf Hitler and Benito Mussolini to the insurgent leader, General Francisco Franco, was a decisive factor in the early stages of the war, by facilitating the transport of the Army of Africa under Franco's command, from Morocco to southern Spain. President Franklin Roosevelt and Secretary of State Cordell Hull adopted a policy of nonintervention with regard to the war in Spain, within a framework of close cooperation with the governments of France and Great Britain.

These basic policy guidelines, which were established during the initial stages of the conflict, remained unaltered for the duration of the civil war (July 1936–April 1939). The initial response by the U.S. government to the events in Spain has been described by a diplomatic historian as guided not so much be a clearly defined set of intentions as by "inertia joined with hope."[10] Overwhelming public sentiment against U.S. involvement in European conflicts and the proximity of a presidential election in November 1936, were factors that argued against any initiative that would have implied active support for either side in the Spanish war.[11]

During the first months of the war a "moral" embargo was announced on the sale or transportation of weapons and military supplies to Spain. The administration appealed to voluntary compliance with the embargo on the part of U.S. firms and individuals, in the absence of neutrality legislation specifically applicable to cases of civil war. In December 1936, the moral embargo was challenged by a request for licenses to export aircraft materials to Republican Spain, a request that the State Department could not legally refuse. On January 6, 1937, President Roosevelt sent a message to Congress requesting emergency legislation to cover the contingencies raised by the civil strife in Spain. Congress complied with the president's request promptly and almost unanimously (by majorities of 81–0 in the Senate and 406–1 in the House). The Spanish Embargo Act, signed into law on January 8, extended the provisions of the American Neutrality Act of 1935 to the situation prevailing in Spain. In May, Congress approved the Neutrality Act of May 1937, which remained in force throughout the year. The neutrality legislation of this period, curtailing the president's discretionary power in the conduct of foreign affairs, reflected the isolationist sentiment prevailing in Congress and in public opinion.

The hearings of the Nye Committee on the profits of arms manufacturers and bankers during World War I, served to strengthen the cause of those who advocated a policy of U.S. aloofness from European conflicts. Although the arms embargo applied to both belligerents, in practice it was detrimental to the Republic and helpful to Franco, who throughout the war received the overt support of Germany and Italy in the form of weapons, equipment, airplane pilots, and troops. Notwithstanding protests from the diplomatic representatives of the Spanish Republic and the pressure for repeal of neutrality by supporters of the Republic in the United States, the policy of nonintervention remained in force for the duration of the war.[12]

By the beginning of 1939, after the collapse of Catalonia in January, the military situation of the Spanish Republic had become untenable. France and Great Britain recognized the Franco government on February 27. On March 28 Madrid fell to the insurgents. On March 31, the Republic's ambassador to Washington, Fernando de los Rios, visited Secretary of State Cordell Hull, to say good-bye and to inform him that his embassy was being closed. On April 1st, Franco, who was still in Burgos, the Nationalist capital, announced the end of the civil war following the unconditional surrender of the Republican armies. On April 3, an exchange of cables between Secretary Hull and Count Francisco Jordana, the Nationalist foreign minister, confirmed the recognition of the Franco government by the U.S. government.

The defeat of the Republic, which coincided with a rapidly deteriorating international situation in Europe, was perceived as a victory for Fascist Italy and Nazi Germany and as a setback for the Western democracies. Against the background of an approaching European war, relations between the United States and Spain became for both governments a relatively secondary part of the overall international context.

In the light of the behavior of Germany, Italy, and Japan, the wisdom of the neutrality laws was brought into question in the United States. In an address to Congress on January 4, 1939, President Roosevelt stated:

> There are many methods short of war, but stronger and more effective than mere words, of bringing home to aggressor governments the aggregate sentiments of our own people.... At the very least, we can and should avoid any action, or any lack of action, which will encourage, assist or build up an aggressor. We have learned that when we deliberately try to legislate neutrality, our neutrality laws may operate unevenly and unfairly—may actually give aid to an aggressor and deny it to the victim. The instinct of self-preservation should warn us that we ought not to let that happen any more.[13]

Sumner Welles, who was appointed undersecretary of state in May 1937, was even more explicit in his retrospective assessment of U.S. policy towards the conflict in Spain:

Of all our blind isolationist policies, the most disastrous was our attitude on the Spanish civil war. . . . It has been our traditional policy to permit the legitimate and recognized government of a foreign country, confronted by a revolt within its own borders, to obtain from this country such military supplies as it may require. . . . The crucial point was whether in a crisis such as this, where our own interests were involved, the traditional policy of the United States should be reversed—to the great benefit of the Nazi and Fascist governments. . . . In the long history of the foreign policy of the Roosevelt Administration, there has been, I think, no more cardinal error than the policy adopted during the civil war in Spain.[14]

The attitude of the Roosevelt administration towards the new Spanish government was shaped by the lack of democratic legitimacy of the Franco regime, and by its close association with the fascist states. Franco joined the anti-Comintern Pact on March 27, 1939. On March 31 a friendship treaty between Spain and Nazi Germany was signed. Although Spain declared its neutrality at the beginning of World War II, the foreign policy of the regime was favorable to Germany. When Hitler launched Operation Barbarossa, the invasion of the Soviet Union, Franco proclaimed a two-war policy: Spain would remain neutral in the war between Germany and the European democracies but would take the side of Germany in the war against the Soviet Union. On June 28, 1941, shortly after the attack on the Soviet Union began, the Blue Division was created. Some eighteen thousand Spanish volunteers, commanded by a Spanish general, fought alongside the German army on the eastern front between 1941 and 1944. The United States also declared its neutrality at the beginning of World War II, but it was a neutrality unambiguously favorable to Great Britain and France.

Relations between the United States and Spain between 1939 and 1945 were characterized by the fundamental differences between the two governments: one was a liberal democracy, committed to the survival of democratic values, the other was a right-wing pro-Axis military dictatorship. During this period, despite their feelings of mutual mistrust and animosity, the two governments conditioned their dealings with each other to the exigencies of the war and to what each one considered to be convenient, according to the changing circumstances. The priority of the Roosevelt administration was the defeat of the Axis powers. Franco's priority was the survival of the regime. U.S. policy towards Spain during World War II followed a similar pattern to the one that had prevailed from 1936 to 1939, during the civil war. Spain was regarded by U.S. policy makers (along with Portugal and the western Mediterranean) as a region of primary interest to Britain, commercially, strategically, and diplomatically. Therefore, the United States was willing to coordinate its policy towards Spain with that of Britain, tacitly accepting British leadership on Iberian matters, particularly in wartime.

Between 1939 and 1941, for example, the United States concurred with Britain's Iberian policy objective, which was to provide sufficient economic incentives to Franco (credits and supplies of critical commodities such as petroleum, rubber, and wheat) to keep Spain from joining the Axis. As long as Spain remained neutral, Britain was ready to enforce the Continental Blockade selectively, allowing Spanish ships—subject to inspection by the Royal Navy and provided with special permissions called Navicerts—to sail from the Western Hemisphere to Spanish ports. The United States helped enforce this policy, even before entering the war.

From 1942 to 1945, Britain and the United States cooperated closely in a deliberate and carefully managed operation, designed to provide Franco with the minimum amount of petroleum necessary to keep the economy functioning: a yearly amount no larger than sixty percent of the five-year average 1931–1936. This and other elements of the British economic warfare policy with respect to Spain (i.e., preemptive buying of strategic materials and black-listing of firms doing business with the Axis) were adopted in toto by the U.S. government upon entering the war.[15]

British officials, concerned with the safety of Gibraltar and the Mediterranean sea lanes, were willing to overlook Spanish partiality to the Axis and to refrain from punishing Franco for his Fascist rhetoric and his deliberately insulting behavior. Because of its economic backwardness and military weakness, Spain was of little intrinsic importance as an eventual belligerent. (Lack of fuel and food stocks restricted full-scale military operations to a maximum duration of one month.) However, its geographic location would be a significant asset to the Axis powers, should Spain become an adversary. To avoid this contingency, British officials were willing to pay a reasonable economic price, to suffer Spanish official truculence with toleration and condescension, and to recommend similar patience to Washington.

During the first years of the war, when it appeared that Germany would be victorious, and Spanish partiality towards the Axis was most pronounced, relations between the United States and Spain were strained.

The U.S. ambassador to Spain, Alexander Weddell, and Franco's foreign minister, Ramón Serrano Suñer, shared a mutual dislike of one another and for practical purposes were not on speaking terms. On September 13, 1941, Secretary of State Hull expressed to Juan Francisco de Cárdenas, the Spanish ambassador, his indignation over Madrid's treatment of Ambassador Weddell in the following terms:

> While it is most disagreeable even to recall our experiences in dealing with the Spanish Government, I must state that in all the relations of this Government with the most backward and ignorant Governments in the world, it has not experienced such a lack of ordinary courtesy or consideration customarily prevailing between friendly nations as it has at the hands of the Spanish Government. Your Government's course has been one of aggravated discourtesy and contempt in the very face of our offers to be of aid.
>
> We could not think of embarrassing, not to say humiliating, ourselves by further approaches of this nature, bearing in mind the coarse and extremely offensive methods and conduct of Serrano Suñer in particular and in some instances of General Franco. When I think about the details of the conduct of the Spanish Government toward this Government, what has happened is really inconceivable.[16]

In addition to the strong language of the secretary of state, the displeasure of the U.S. government was manifested in a more tangible form: unexplained delays began to take place in the severely restricted level of petroleum shipments, thereby bringing about a serious fuel shortage in Spain. Winston Churchill appealed to Roosevelt for moderation, in terms that reveal a realistic perception of British (and Allied) interests: "Please will you kindly consider giving a few rationed carrots to the Dons to stave off trouble at Gibraltar? Every day we have the use of the harbour is a gain, especially in view of some other ideas we have discussed" (Operation Torch, the invasion of North Africa).[17]

After the successful Allied landings in North Africa in November 1942, and the German defeat at Stalingrad in February 1943, which marked the beginning of the Russian counteroffensive, the capacity of Franco to benefit from Allied fears that Spain would join the Axis was sharply reduced.[18] Spain, which had shifted away from neutrality to nonbelligerency on June 12, 1940, at the time of the defeat of France, shifted back to neutrality in October 1943. By early 1944, in preparation for Operation Overlord, the invasion of Normandy, the United States and Britain cut off oil supplies to Spain completely. Franco's leverage vis-à-vis the Allied powers by then was nonexistent. Spain was required to disband the Blue Division, to restrict shipments of tungsten to Germany, to close the German consulate in Tangiers, and to curtail German espionage.

After the invasion of Normandy, Spain ceased to be a matter of military concern to the Allied governments. Relations between the Allied powers and the Franco regime after the defeat of Germany became a political question to be addressed within the context of the general postwar settlement. As the war in Europe entered its final phase in early 1945, the Spanish government found itself in an unfriendly external environment, confronted by a hostile public opinion in the Western democracies, and encumbered by the memories of its association with the Axis during the early years of the war.

INTERNATIONAL OSTRACISM OF SPAIN, 1945–1947

At the governmental level, the leaders of the victorious Allied powers had grievances to settle with General Franco for his wartime cooperation with Hitler and Mussolini, despite Spain's formal nonbelligerency and neutrality. The Soviet government held Franco accountable for the disgraceful behavior of the Spanish Blue Division incorporated into the German army on the eastern front.[19]

The British Foreign Office and the U.S. State Department resented Spanish partiality to the Axis, covert assistance provided to the German war effort, and the hostile behavior of Spanish officials towards the Allied governments when it seemed that Germany would be victorious. In the early months of 1945, as the Allied forces advanced towards Berlin, the guidelines of Anglo-American postwar policy towards Spain were explicitly formulated. In January, Churchill rebuffed an offer by Franco to establish an Anglo-Hispanic anti-Soviet alliance and rejected Franco's request for Spanish participation in the peace settlements.[20]

In March, President Roosevelt explained U.S. policy towards the Franco regime in a letter to Norman Armour, the newly-appointed ambassador to Madrid.

Having been helped to power by Fascist Italy and Nazi Germany, and having patterned itself along totalitarian lines the present regime in Spain is naturally the subject of distrust by a great many American citizens who find it difficult to see the justification for this country to continue to maintain relations with such a regime.

Most certainly we do not forget Spain's official position with and assistance to our Axis enemies at a time when the fortunes of war were less favorable to us, nor can we disregard the activities, aims, organizations, and public utterances of the Falange, both past and present. These memories cannot be wiped out by actions more favorable to us now that we are about to achieve our goal of complete victory over those enemies of ours with whom the present Spanish regime identified itself in the past spiritually and by its public expressions and acts.

The fact that our Government maintains formal diplomatic relations with the present Spanish regime should not be interpreted by anyone to imply approval of that regime and its sole party, the Falange, which has been openly hostile to the United States and which has tried to spread its fascist party ideas in the Western Hemisphere. Our victory over Germany will carry with it the extermination of Nazi and similar ideologies.

. . . The form of government in Spain and the policies pursued by that Government are quite properly the concern of the Spanish people. I should be lacking in candor, however, if I did not tell you that I can see no place in the community of nations for governments founded on fascist principles.[21]

Ambassador Armour communicated the contents of this letter to the Spanish foreign minister and to General Franco at the beginning of his mission in Madrid.[22]

Differences in attitude regarding the Spanish question between the Allied powers became evident in the discussions of the Big Three during the Potsdam Conference in the summer of 1945. Stalin took the strongest position against the Franco regime, describing it as a "cancer in Europe" and recommending that all relations be broken off with Franco's government; he considered that this effort to overthrow it by international pressure "was no internal affair, because the Franco regime had been imposed on the Spanish people by Hitler and Mussolini." Churchill disagreed. While affirming his government's "strong distaste for General Franco and his government" Churchill pointed out that "there was more to Spanish policy than drawing rude cartoons of Franco." He was "against interfering in the affairs of a country which had not molested the Allies and believed it was a dangerous principle to break off relations because of Spain's internal conduct." He warned against promoting another civil war in Spain and argued that the United Nations Charter prohibited interference in a nation's domestic affairs. He also pointed to the valuable trade relations that Britain maintained with Spain, stating that unless he were convinced "that breaking relations would bring about the desired result, he did not want this old and well-established trade with Spain stopped." Harry S. Truman supported Churchill's position, implicitly recognizing the differences between a statesman's personal dislikes and the requirements for international peace and stability. "I made it clear that I had no love for Franco and also that I had no desire to have any part in starting another civil war in Spain. There had been enough wars in Europe. I said that I would be happy to recognize another government in Spain but that I thought Spain itself must settle that question."[23]

The compromise that emerged from this discussion was a joint condemnation of the Franco regime and the agreement to exclude it from membership in the United Nations (UN) Organization. The section on Conclusion of Peace Treaties and Admission to the United Nations Organization of the Potsdam Communiqué, issued on August 2, 1945, stated:

> The Three Governments feel bound however, to make it clear that they for their part would not favor any application for membership [in the UN] put forward by the present Spanish Government, which, having been founded with the support of the Axis Powers, does not, in view of its origins, its nature, its record and its close association with the aggressor States, possess the qualifications necessary to justify such membership.[24]

In March 1946, the governments of Britain, France, and the United States took the unprecedented action of issuing a joint statement expressing their hope that "leading patriotic and liberal-minded Spaniards may soon find means to bring about a peaceful withdrawal of Franco, the abolition of the Falange, and the establishment of an interim or caretaker government under which the Spanish people may have an opportunity freely to determine the type of government they wish to have and to choose their leaders." It was hoped that these goals were to be achieved without again subjecting the Spanish people "to the horrors and bitterness of civil strife."[25]

The manner in which this praiseworthy political transformation was to be achieved under the circumstances then prevailing in Spain, however, was left unexplained. This statement, along with fifteen secret documents describing Franco's wartime cooperation with the Axis, and his friendship with Hitler and Mussolini, was released to the press by the State Department. The proscription of the Franco regime from the international community was formalized in 1946 by the adoption of two resolutions by the UN General Assembly: Resolution 32 of February 9 reaffirmed Spain's ineligibility for UN membership, and Resolution 39 of December 12 excluded the Franco government from membership in any international agencies related to the UN, and further, recommended that all Member States immediately recall their accredited ambassadors and ministers plenipotentiary from Madrid.[26] Compliance with this recommendation was almost universal, with the exception of Argentina, Portugal, and the Vatican. Since December 1, 1945, when Armour had departed from Madrid, the United States did not have an ambassador in Spain. U.S. diplomatic representation in Madrid was maintained at the level of chargé d'affaires until February 1951.

By the end of 1946, U.S. policy towards Spain, patterned closely on that of Britain, included the following elements: dislike for the regime, moderated by an attitude of nonintervention; a preference for nonviolent evolution towards democracy; and low priority to Spain itself, except as part of the larger context of overall objectives in Europe and the western Mediterranean.

The dislike of the regime, however, although clearly and vigorously expressed by the U.S. government, did not take the form of direct retribution, but rather the form of denial of the benefits of American friendship. In the words of President Roosevelt:

> There are many things which we could and normally would be glad to do in economic and other fields to demonstrate that friendship. The initiation of such measures is out of the question at this time, however, when American sentiment is so profoundly opposed to the present regime in power in Spain.[27]

U.S. displeasure with Franco in the immediate postwar period took the form of denying his regime respectability and admission to the UN and economic assistance. More drastic punitive measures, such as the French proposal of March 25, 1946, to impose a gasoline embargo and cut off all trade relations with Spain, were in conflict with the British and American policy objective of avoiding a renewal of civil strife in Spain.[28]

The Anglo-American hope "that any successor regime in Spain will be based on democratic principles, moderate in tendency, stable, and not indebted for its existence to any outside influences" did not coincide with the preferences of the Soviet Union.[29] According to George Kennan, the U.S. chargé d'affaires in Moscow, Soviet leaders believed that the conditions prevailing in Spain were similar to those of Tsarist Russia and therefore, conducive to social revolution. Furthermore, the Russians appreciated Spain's strategic value as well as its political usefulness as a base from which influence could eventually be exercised in France, Italy, Morocco, and Latin America. He considered Russian purposes to be "probably incompatible with all stability in Iberian Peninsula for coming years. As far as Spain is concerned Russians have learned nothing and forgotten nothing since [the] civil war. Their only program is to return to that struggle unabashed by chaos which might ensue."[30] Commenting on Kennan's message, William Butterworth, the U.S. chargé d'affaires in Madrid, underlined the differences between Soviet purposes in Spain and Anglo-American interests. He pointed out that the possibility of an abrupt political change helped to strengthen Franco's position, given the generalized "fear of violence and bloodshed." He urged patience to the State Department regarding the pace of political evolution that could be expected, given the bitterness of the civil war. He urged that a distinction be made between the indictment of the regime for its character and practices and condemnation of the Nationalists for their victory in the civil war. "While the first line of attack assists and impels to action moderate forces working for peaceful change, the second course drives them back into their '39 roles as mere allies of the victorious Franco."[31]

These communications to Washington suggested the possibility that under the prevailing circumstances, the two policy objectives, getting rid of Franco while at the same time avoiding civil strife in Spain, could be mutually exclusive, should Franco not be willing to give up power peacefully. It was precisely this contradiction, upon which Franco seized, that allowed the regime to survive. His reaction to external pressure was to stir up nationalist feelings, presenting the international condemnation as a conspiracy against Spain, promoted by Freemasons, communists, and Spanish traitors. Unity, discipline, and endurance were demanded of the supporters of the regime. Press censorship and harsh repression stifled any public dissent. A mass rally organized by supporters of the regime, was held in Madrid on December 9, 1946, to denounce the UN. International expressions of disapproval, by themselves, were not enough to displace the "Caudillo of Spain by the Grace of God."

The State Department still believed that Franco could be persuaded to step down. On April 7, 1947, Dean Acheson, the acting secretary of state, instructed the embassy in London to explore with the Foreign Office a joint initiative, on the basis that "Franco and any regime perpetuating the principles of his control must go." Both governments would then undertake to communicate their conviction to the army chiefs, to the opposition leaders, and to Franco himself. "Our resolve that we can no longer deal with him and our conviction that his proposed plan for succession is unsatisfactory should be made clear and an opportunity afforded him to depart in safety."[32] The British chargé d'affaires in Madrid objected to this course of action, which contradicted the publicly proclaimed policy of nonintervention in Spanish internal affairs. The Foreign Office doubted the success of such an initiative, and suggested "that the matter should, therefore, now probably be dropped."[33]

Despite persisting hostility to the Franco regime, by 1947 U.S. policy makers were confronting more pressing demands upon their attention. On March 12, 1947, President Truman asked Congress for urgent assistance to Greece and Turkey in a major foreign policy initiative, which became known as the Truman Doctrine. And on June 5 of the same year, the secretary of state, in a speech at Harvard University, called for an economic recovery program for Europe, a proposal that became the basis of the Marshall Plan.

RELUCTANT POLICY CHANGE 1948–1950

As U.S.–Soviet relations deteriorated, the State Department came under growing pressure to modify its policy toward Spain. The pressure originated from its own officials, from the military establishment, and from Congress, as a result of newly perceived threats to international stability and of a shift in public opinion towards a strongly anticommunist posture. This latter development became particularly helpful to Franco, as he sought to overcome U.S. hostility to his regime.

In October 1947, Kennan, from the recently created Policy Planning Staff of the State Department, transmitted to the secretary and the undersecretary, an evaluation of U.S. policy towards Spain, describing it as unsatisfactory "not only from the political point of view but from the viewpoint of our military planners." While granting that it would be desirable to replace Franco peacefully by a fully representative regime, the staff found no evidence of an effective opposition to Franco that could bring about an orderly change in government. In their view, the policy of diplomatic exclusion and economic isolation of Spain was harmful to the national interest, as well as counterproductive. Its net result had been to strengthen the Franco regime, to hinder Spain's economic recovery, and to obstruct Spain's friendly cooperation in the event of international conflict. The staff recommended that the department should begin working toward normalization of political and economic relations with Spain "irrespective of wartime ideological considerations or the character of the regime in power." As concrete steps in that direction, the staff was in favor of eliminating the existing controls to private trade and financial transactions, and of supporting the reversal of UN Resolution 39 of 1946 that excluded Spain from UN–affiliated agencies and called for the withdrawal of ambassadors from Madrid.[34]

The Policy Planning Staff document was approved by Secretary of State George Marshall on October 24. The U.S. embassy in Madrid was notified of the policy change in guarded terms. Normalization was to be gradual and could not be complete in the absence of "substantial political and economic changes within Spain."[35] The departure of Franco was no longer a policy objective, but this would not be made public in the absence of an evolutionary process towards democracy. The United States would continue to abide by UN Resolution 39. Export restrictions to Spain would be lifted and there would be no objection to private credits for Spanish importers. No government credits were contemplated yet. Participation of Spain in the European Recovery Program (ERP, also known as the Marshall Plan) would depend on the highly unlikely approval of the sixteen European countries concerned. The new policy hoped to obtain a gradual and orderly liberalization of the regime rather than to force Franco out. "What we need before we give him any sympathy or material assistance is convincing evidence of his intention to undertake orderly democratization."[36]

The policy change was adopted by the department, with serious political reservations about the convenience of putting relations with the Franco regime on a normal basis. The economic component of the new policy was quite limited. In the absence of public financial flows, significant private credits were not to be expected given the fragility of the Spanish economy. The diplomatic component was relatively modest. The U.S. government modified its attitude from one of open hostility to one of grudging toleration of Franco. But Franco obtained toleration without changing the authoritarian nature of the regime, and without disbanding the Falange or ending the repression. Even if only slightly, the mountain had moved in his direction.

The directives from Washington received a lukewarm response from the U.S. embassy in Madrid. Paul Culbertson, the chargé d'affaires, regarded the new policy as a step in the right direction, but felt that it did not go far enough. He was skeptical with regard to the effectiveness of the measures envisioned—given their modest scope—as an inducement to bring about meaningful change in the Spanish regime.

> On Franco's side, he has been cursed and condemned by all the world. No loophole has been left for him in any of the announced policies of the United States or other powers. With nothing but opposition to confront him, Franco has had two alternatives: one, to commit suicide or, two, to pull in and tighten the dictatorial reins. . . . Our policies, for whatever reason adopted, have failed and continue to fail to obtain material political and economic liberalization for the Spanish people. We say, quite rightly, that it is for the Spanish people to determine what they want. At the same time our policies tend to exclude those people who, for whatever the reason may be, support Franco and who are not prepared to plunge into the unknown. . . . On the question of economic policy . . . the easing up of present economic and financial restrictions . . . will in my estimation have practically no effect (a) on the economic situation in Spain or (b) in bringing about evolution politically or governmentally. For that reason I suggested . . . the implementation of our policy by present willingness to consider direct governmental assistance. I appreciate that such action may be out of the realm of the practical from the standpoint of problems in Washington, but I suggest it as the practical one for Spain if we want to keep the Spanish economy from going to pot.[37]

On February 2, 1948, Culbertson met with Foreign Minister Alberto Martín Artajo and Director General of Foreign Policy José Sebastián de Erice to notify them of the new policy. He also conveyed to them the need for concrete steps toward economic and political liberalization as a precondition for the complete normalization of relations between the two countries.[38]

After consulting with Franco and with the Cabinet, Artajo gave Culbertson a reply to the principal points raised in the previous meeting. He expressed the hopes of the Spanish government that the new attitude on the part of the United States would result in the granting of private and official credit. With respect to the latter, the government considered that direct dealings with Washington would be preferable to participation in the Marshall Plan. State control of the economy was attributed to the force of circumstances and described as temporary. The appropriateness of attempting to judge the internal affairs of another country was questioned. According to Artajo, the Spanish government desired collaboration and rapprochement with the United States but felt that the relationship should not be disturbed through mingling the two countries' common interests and ability to serve the world "with differences of ideology or political thinking which are exclusive to each people."[39]

Secretary Marshall was disappointed by this response, which in his view would not be conducive to changing existing U.S. policy of refusing government credits, facilitating Spain's participation in European cooperative arrangements, or modifying the position of the UN toward Spain.[40]

On March 26, 1948, Secretary of Defense James Forrestal called Assistant Secretary of State for Political Affairs Norman Armour to inquire about the possibility of changing existing policy toward Spain. He offered to send someone over to provide the background of the reason for his call.[41] Three days later, an air force major general and the U.S. air attaché in Madrid explained to State Department officials that the Joint Chiefs would like to secure base rights given the necessity "of having three airfields in Spain constructed and equipped to handle the heaviest U.S. bombers." The director of Western European Affairs informed them that securing base rights or furnishing military aircraft to Spain was politically inadvisable but raised no objection to a "privately financed program involving airport equipment and the largest civil aircraft, such as the DC-6."[42] On the same day, Culbertson recommended additional steps toward normalization of relations, including support for the participation of Spain in the ERP.

> It is my understanding that in general American military authorities consider continental Spanish territory to be of major importance to strategic military operations in the Mediterranean and to the keeping of operational lines open to the Middle and Near East. Certainly our military authorities have not at all times seen eye to eye with the State Department with regard to American policy toward Franco Spain. . . . If we are interested in Spain for purely military reasons and we can foresee the need to use Spain and Spanish territory, it should be borne in mind that Spanish transport and her military establishments are presently so antiquated that considerable time would be required to build them up to a point of real value and usefulness. . . . A busted economy in Spain certainly is not going to make European economic recovery easier and certainly is not going to be a help to political stability . . . the march of world

events is not slow and military considerations could, the way things look from here, overtake objections to ideologies of the Franco brand, and as a result we would be confronted with the problem of further modification of policy toward Spain. If there be likelihood of this situation arising, I recommend that further moves be made now . . . your statements and those of Congress have laid the foundation for Spain's inclusion in ERP on purely economic grounds. . . . If it is not too late I would like to see us informally and orally indicate to the ERP countries that we think that Spain should be included in the Program on economic grounds. It is the only way I can see which affords a partial bypass of the political question.[43]

The House of Representatives expressed a similar opinion on March 30 when it approved a resolution, introduced by Representative Alvin E. O'Konski of Wisconsin, to make Spain eligible to participate in the ERP as an amendment to the Foreign Assistance Act of 1948. President Truman expressed his opposition to the inclusion of this amendment to the bill. The amendment was excluded from the final version of the bill, which became Public Law 472, 80th Congress. On April 2, the State Department notified the embassy in Madrid that the inclusion of Spain under existing conditions would be contrary to the purposes of the ERP, such as the strengthening principles of individual liberty and free institutions.

View of this Government has been and continues to be that initiative on Span [sic] inclusion lies with original CEEC countries. They have made it crystal clear that it is politically impossible for them to cooperate with Spain along lines ERP under present conditions there. Immediate and violent reaction in West European countries and here against proposed inclusion Spain underlines views of this Government which you expressed to FonMin February 2 and since.[44]

During the first week of April, Secretary Marshall, who was in Bogota to attend the Ninth International Conference of American States, replied to an aide-mémoire from the British ambassador in Colombia, Gilbert MacKeneth, conveying the concern of Foreign Minister Ernest Bevin at the proposal for the inclusion of Spain in the ERP. Marshall expressed his understanding of Bevin's concern and assured him that the U.S. government policy on the matter remained unaltered.[45]

In a policy statement on Spain of July 26, 1948, the State Department incorporated military considerations but still subordinated them to the prevailing situation in Europe that was described as "primarily political, not military," and as such to be dealt with in political terms. The primary objective was "the reintegration of Spain, politically, economically and militarily into the free western European community of nations through the progressive normalization of Spanish relations with those countries and with the U.S." The military aspects were defined as

> the strategic value of Spain's geographic location and the impor-tance of preventing Spain from coming under the control of a Com-munist or Communist-dominated government. In this connection, our military authorities believe it is important, as we do, to assist Spain in the rehabilitation of its economy. . . . While a recent loan from Argentina and the new commercial agreements with France and the UK will undoubtedly partially relieve Spain's economic problems . . . capital equipment and long term loans are still re-quired in the rehabilitation of Spain's economy. These are matters in which assistance is required primarily from the US. . . .
> . . . the most desirable course of action for the present is to avoid international pressure on Spain and to continue our efforts to em-phasize the need for political liberalization, disabusing Spanish minds of the conviction that US public opinion will eventually force us to accept Franco on his own terms.
> Politically and militarily our two principal Allies in Europe are Great Britain and France. Their strategic interest in Spain is greater than ours . . . both governments consider public acceptance of Spain into the international community politically impossible at this time. . . . In the implementation of our policy toward Spain, therefore, we must have due regard for the political effect our actions in Spain have on the problems which confront US policy in the rest of Eu-rope.[46]

The decision to subordinate U.S. policy toward Spain to relations with the Western European democracies was formulated even more explicitly by John Hickerson, the director of the Office of European Affairs, in a message to Lincoln MacVeagh, the U.S. ambassador to Portugal.

> Essentially, we want to see Spain reintegrated into the Western Eu-ropean community, economically and militarily, as quickly as prac-ticable. However, England and France are more important to us than is Spain and Spain is more important to them than to us. Spain

is still a highly controversial subject in domestic politics in England, France, the Low Countries and Scandinavia.[47]

In 1948, the disagreements between the Western powers and the Soviet Union settled into the pattern of systematic antagonism and mistrust that characterized the "cold war," a term that became part of international usage during that year. In January, the communists acquired complete control in Hungary. In February, a communist coup took place in Czechoslovakia. In March, several Western European nations signed the Brussels Pact, providing for mutual defense against Soviet aggression. President Truman's Special Message to Congress on the Threat to the Freedom of Europe (March 17, 1948) committed the United States to cooperate with the free nations of Europe, not only in their economic rehabilitation but also in their search for protection against internal and external aggression. In June, the Soviet Union closed the border between its occupation zone in Germany and the Western-occupied zones. By denying the Western powers access by road or by rail to their sectors in Berlin, the Soviets effectively blockaded West Berlin, making it necessary for the United States, Great Britain, and France to supply it by means of a massive airlift. By mid-1948 all of Eastern Europe (except for Yugoslavia, which had left the Soviet-bloc in April) was sealed off from the West.

The danger of an East-West confrontation offered Franco hope that his anti-Communist credentials would help mitigate democratic hostility to his regime and open the door for its eventual acceptance by the Western community of nations. Furthermore, in addition to the perceptible symptoms of international tension, the Spanish government was receiving encouraging signals that indicated the existence of discrepancies in the United States with respect to the policy formulated by the State Department. On July 31, 1947, for example, a report from the General Staff of the Navy to the Ministry of Foreign Affairs described the visit of Captain Burnice Rutt, the U.S. naval attaché, to the naval commander of Málaga. Rutt, who had returned from a meeting on military strategy in London, claimed to be in Málaga on vacation. As a pretext for his visit he said he wished to present his greetings to the navy on the feast of her patron, Nuestra Señora del Carmen. He requested information about the local beaches and the conditions for an eventual disembarkation—his specialty—in case the United States should have to provide assistance to Spain. He believed that war with Russia was inevitable and that in such an eventuality Spain would have to be an ally of the United States. He expressed his hope that U.S. policy toward Spain would change in the near future but described his comments as private, to a friend, and not in an official capacity.[48]

Admittedly, this episode was a relatively early instance of disclosure of military dissatisfaction with the State Department's policy toward Spain. However, from 1948 onward, statements from members of Congress, prominent U.S. business and civic leaders, as well as military officers encouraged Franco to hope that Spain's geographical location and his anti-Communist reputation would suffice to bring about normalization of relations between his regime and the Western democracies.

On September 30, 1948, Senator Chan Gurney of South Dakota, chairman of the Armed Services Committee of the U.S. Senate, who went to Madrid accompanied by several military officers, was received by Franco. After the conference with Franco, Gurney held a meeting with the press during which he recommended the reestablishment of diplomatic relations with Spain by the United States and the other great powers.[49]

There were tangible reasons, other than giving satisfaction to wounded pride, for Franco to seek the friendship of the Western democracies. The immediate postwar years were a period of severe hardship for the Spanish people. The problems caused by the civil war and misguided economic policies were compounded by five years of consecutive drought that devastated agriculture and sharply reduced the supply of hydroelectric power, thereby crippling industrial production. The late 1940s in Spain came to be remembered as "the hunger years." The country was in dire need of foreign exchange to purchase foodstuffs, fuel, fertilizer, and raw materials as well as capital goods and transportation equipment.

In order to overcome these shortages, an effort was made to reach an understanding with the United States. In November 1948, shortly after the reelection of President Truman, Franco made a public bid for better relations with the United States, and requested a loan for $200 million for the rehabilitation of the Spanish economy. In an interview with Cyrus L. Sulzberger of the *New York Times*, he described the elements of what he hoped would be fuller and more cordial relations between Spain and the United States: better understanding in the United States of Spain's problems; a preference for direct economic assistance from the United States over participation in the ERP; and the willingness of Spain to participate in a Western alliance against the Soviet Union.

I, and the Spanish people desire greatly to improve relations between our country and the United States. . . . In a certain way, we feel ourselves to be American. In these days the seas tend to unite nations more than the land; there is no intervening nation between. . . .The United States has not quite understood the problems we have faced and those we have to face. . . . For Spain, an agreement with the United States and a loan would be excellent. Spain would recover more rapidly and thereby would more swiftly be in a position to aid in the over-all recovery of Europe. . . . Spain does not really desire to join the European Recovery Program for the reason that the other nations that participate in it do not appear to want us. . . . The United States is a curious nation. It provides the money, but lets the recipient nations state the conditions. Spain prefers to deal directly with the United States and thus avoid political confusion . . . there is a danger of war if Russia feels that no important resistance will be offered. Certainly an organization must be created to avoid such a potential danger. Spain would be willing to take part in such an alliance of the Occident.[50]

Franco's exploratory sounding was followed up a few days later by a request for bilateral economic assistance from the United States formulated to Culbertson, the chargé d'affaires, along with the offer of military bases on Spanish territory.

last evening I had one of my occasional longish, all-subject talks at the Foreign Office with José Sebastián de Erice, Director General of Foreign Policy, in which he asked, as he had done before, for suggestions in the field of economic liberalization in Spain. Spain, he said, wants and needs help but she wants it on a basis of a bilateral arrangement with the United States and not under Marshall Plan aid. If Spain could receive such aid as to give solidity to her economic structure, liberalizing action could and would be taken and Spain would be prepared to meet such reasonable conditions as we might be prepared to suggest. Furthermore, and I have never encouraged or left the door open to suggestions of a military character, Erice said that, could some understanding be reached between the two countries, we could, if we so desired, have bases in the Canary and Balearic Islands and facilities on the Spanish mainland. I did not follow up this last suggestion.[51]

An attempt to consult a record of this conversation in the Spanish diplomatic archives proved fruitless, because the documents related to negotiations with the United States for the establishment of military bases remain classified.[52] However, on the basis of circumstantial evidence, a strong case can be made for the inference that Erice's treatment of a highly delicate issue—because of its domestic as well as international implications—was the bona fide offer of a bilateral military alliance, and one that could only have been made with Franco's express authorization and in accordance to his direct instructions. The meeting with Culbertson took place five days after Franco was interviewed by Sulzberger. Erice's proposal coincided precisely with the guidelines formulated by Franco, and only made explicit and specific some of the matters that Franco had implied or raised in general terms. As an official in a hierarchical, extremely centralized regime, Erice was dealing with two matters that belonged to Franco's sole and exclusive domain: military affairs and relations with the major powers. An unauthorized initiative of this nature, therefore, would have been inconceivable. Likewise, the Ministry of Foreign Affairs could not, on its own initiative, make commitments to modify the regime's economic policy. The careful choice of message bearer revealed great caution, a characteristic feature of Franco's governing style. Erice's official rank within the government was sufficiently high for the offer to be taken seriously, but not high enough to run the risk of a diplomatic impasse in case it were rejected.

Contrary to Franco's expectation, the time was not yet ripe for an agreement of this kind. Erice's offer produced no immediate result. However, the exchange between Erice and Culbertson is noteworthy for several reasons. It officially placed the possibility of military cooperation on the bilateral agenda. The elements of the bargain eventually agreed to in 1953 were basically the same as those suggested by Erice in November 1948. The timing and the form of the proposal also indicate that the initiative to establish military bases in the Iberian Peninsula came in fact from the Spanish side.

In February 1949, the U.S. embassy in Madrid reported on the precarious economic conditions prevailing in Spain and warned of the possibility of an economic breakdown affecting political stability.[53] In April, the State Department dropped its objection to the filing of applications for Export-Import Bank loans by Spanish agencies and enterprises, a step that had been recommended by Culbertson.[54]

During the same month, Dean Acheson, the recently appointed secretary of state, notified Germán Baraibar, Madrid's chargé d'affaires in Washington, that Spain would be excluded from the North Atlantic Treaty for political reasons.[55] On May 4, at a press conference, Acheson expressed doubts about Spain's creditworthiness, a statement that provoked a vehement protest from the Spanish Ministry of Foreign Affairs.[56]

A week later he referred to the Franco regime as one "which was patterned on the regimes in Italy and Germany, and was and is a Fascist
government and a dictatorship."[57] Later that month, citing anti-Franco
sentiment in Western Europe, the State Department objected to the provision of direct military assistance to Spain under the Military Assistance
Program.

> The most important consideration in omitting any provision for
> military assistance to Spain is the political effect which such aid
> would have in Western Europe. Official and public opinion in var-
> ious Western European countries is slowly becoming more favor-
> able toward readmission of Spain into the international community.
> Many non-Communist elements in Western Europe, whose support
> we desire in providing for the security of Western Europe and the
> North Atlantic area, have, however, a strong repugnance for
> Franco. . . . These elements oppose Spanish participation in the de-
> fense arrangements for these areas and would object to U.S. mili-
> tary assistance to Spain. . . . As long as Spain is not a participant in
> the defense arrangements of Western Europe, any move to provide
> military assistance to Spain outside the scope of these arrangements
> would be immediately interpreted in Western Europe as undercut-
> ting the basic principle of those programs. Furthermore, military
> assistance to Spain would be readily construed as a design on the
> part of the United States Government to establish the real line of
> defense on the Pyrenees. . . . The fear in Western Europe, particu-
> larly in France, that this may be the intention of the United States
> is real and any encouragement of it could have very serious con-
> sequences. . . . While the military authorities in many of those coun-
> tries [of Western Europe and the North Atlantic area] desire the
> earliest possible integration of Spain into the defense arrangements
> of Western Europe, most of the Governments consider public ac-
> ceptance of Spain politically impossible at this time. . . . It is con-
> sequently the Department's feeling that a move at this time to
> provide direct military assistance to Spain outside the MAP [Mili-
> tary Assistance Program] for Western Europe would jeopardize
> rather than promote our basic policies in Western Europe.[58]

The secretary of state and the chargé d'affaires in Madrid held different views as to the best means of implementing U.S. policy toward Spain.
While Acheson favored taking a hard line toward Franco, insisting on
political liberalization as a precondition for economic assistance, Cul-

bertson pointed to the shortcomings of that policy and recommended that the sequence be reversed.

> I am not a supporter of the idea that we should base policy on the concept of molding the rest of the world in our own democratic image . . . people the world over are not the same and won't mold the same. Certainly not the Spanish. Stable democracy in Spain is a possibility only in the indefinite future. . . . Franco is not to blame for all the things that are wrong here in Spain. . . . From the standpoint of religion the Spanish church and people are bigoted and backward. Franco may be a dictator but he would never get by with any crusade on behalf of Protestants. . . . The peasant, the laborer, the clerk and on up the line are more concerned today with the actual problem of living than they are with the establishment of political liberties such as we know them. . . . The refusal of material aid to Spain punishes the Spanish people, not Franco and his cohorts or the rich. There are lots of very hungry folk in Spain today, and there are going to be more before the end of the year.[59]

Culbertson's arguments notwithstanding, the State Department refused to make any further modifications in the policy toward Spain.[60]

Although the State Department remained firm in its arms-length policy toward Franco, the requirements of military containment of the Soviet Union, and the development of contingency planning in the event of war, added another dimension, as well as new actors to the bilateral relationship. Among the latter, Admiral Richard Connolly, commander of the U.S. naval forces in the eastern Atlantic and the Mediterranean, and Admiral Forrest Sherman, appointed chief of naval operations in 1949 after a two-year command of the Sixth Fleet in the Mediterranean, became influential advocates of a change in policy toward Spain. On September 3, 1949, with President Truman's authorization, Admiral Connolly took units of the fleet to Spain for a courtesy call, the first time warships from the United States had entered a Spanish port since 1936. This was one of several instances in which President Truman, at the request of the military, allowed strategic considerations to supersede his strong dislike for the Franco regime. The U.S. Navy was interested in gaining friendly access to Spanish ports for the protection of the eastern Atlantic and western Mediterranean sea lanes. High-ranking naval officers became early advocates of giving a more amicable orientation to U.S. policy toward Spain.

During his port call at El Ferrol, Admiral Connolly, accompanied by four admirals, two generals, and the U.S. naval attaché in Madrid, visited Franco at his summer residence.[61] Shortly thereafter, units of the Sixth Fleet paid a call at Barcelona. New channels of communication with Washington were opening up for Franco. These interlocutors were less concerned with Spain's political system than the State Department officials. They were also more receptive to Franco's admonitions about the communist menace in Europe.

During 1949, several events, unrelated to Spain, contributed to intensify anticommunist feelings in the United States. In Asia, the defeat of the Nationalist army by Mao Tse-tung's forces brought about the flight of Chiang Kai-shek to Taiwan, and the proclamation of the People's Republic of China. The State Department issued a white paper in August explaining this outcome as a consequence of the shortcomings of the Nationalist regime. Acheson came under acrimonious attack from right-wing critics who blamed communists and fellow travelers in the U.S. government for having obstructed aid to the Nationalists. As a result, the Roosevelt and Truman administrations were accused of having "lost China." In October, President Truman announced that the Soviets had tested an atomic device, an event that created alarm in the United States and in Western Europe. By the end of 1949, the secretary of state had become politically vulnerable. His critics in Congress and in the media took advantage of unfavorable developments abroad to question the sincerity of his anticommunist posture. The State Department, therefore, was placed on the defensive before public opinion. Under these circumstances, dissenting groups and individuals found that the issue of U.S. relations with Spain served as a convenient pretext to challenge the administration's foreign policy.

By early 1950, the State Department was ready for a further modification in the policy toward Spain. In a letter to Senator Tom Connally, chairman of the Senate Committee on Foreign Relations, Acheson admitted that the withdrawal of ambassadors from Madrid had been a mistake and recognized the inconsistency of maintaining that situation while accrediting ambassadors in countries of Eastern Europe whose regimes the United States did not condone. He signalled support for a revision of the 1946 UN Resolution 39. He acknowledged that there was no evidence of an alternative to the existing government in Spain. He also stated that controversy had magnified the Spanish question "to a position among our present day foreign policy problems which is disproportionate to its intrinsic importance."[62]

In May 1950, General Omar Bradley, the chairman of the Joint Chiefs of Staff, forwarded a memorandum on Spain to Louis Johnson, the secretary of defense. The Joint Chiefs expressed their views on the existing policies of the State Department, which in effect excluded Spain from participation in the North Atlantic Treaty and precluded bilateral military cooperation outside the treaty because of its adverse political consequences on relations with the Western allies. The Joint Chiefs considered that relations with Spain were unsatisfactory, and that insufficient weight had been given "to the more important security and strategic interests of the United States in Spain." In their view, Spain could become the last foothold on the Continent in case of a major war in Europe. It was therefore "of paramount importance that the United States and its allies take proper steps to assure that Spain will be an ally in event of war." In order for the Department of Defense to make the necessary military arrangements, the Joint Chiefs recommended that the State Department take prompt action to ensure Spain's military cooperation either bilaterally or within the NAT framework.[63]

The argumentation of the Joint Chiefs was supported by the rationale of a top secret document approved by the National Security Council on April 14, 1950, NSC 68, which established the guidelines for U.S. foreign policy until the end of the cold war.

> Should a major war occur in 1950 the Soviet Union and its satellites are considered by the Joint Chiefs of Staff to be in a sufficiently advanced state of preparation immediately to undertake and carry out the following campaigns. To overrun Western Europe, with the possible exception of the Iberian and Scandinavian Peninsulas; to drive toward the oil-bearing areas of the Near and Middle East; and to consolidate Communist gains in the Far East; . . . It should also be possible for the Soviet Union to prevent any allied "Normandy" type amphibious operations intended to force a reentry into the continent of Europe.[64]

The reasoning of the Joint Chiefs, and of the State Department's Policy Planning Staff, prepared the groundwork for the adoption of a different policy toward Spain. Before proceeding with the description of that process, the first part of chapter 6 studies the initiatives taken by the Spanish government to improve its political, economic, and military relations with the United States.

NOTES

1. The manifesto issued from Barcelona by General Miguel Primo de Rivera y Orbaneja justifying his military coup, dated September 12, 1923, refers to "the spectacle of misfortunes and corruption which began in the year 1898 and which threaten Spain with an early end that will be both tragic and dishonorable." Cited in Dillwyn F. Ratcliff, *Prelude to Franco: Political Aspects of the Dictatorship of General Miguel Primo de Rivera* (New York: Las Americas, 1957), 89. Alfredo Kindelán, one of the generals who rose against the Republic and became air force chief on the Nationalist side, stated: "Although formally dissimilar, all the Army's political actions in this century have had an identical origin and substance. Their cause was none other than the psychological shock produced by the loss of the remnants of the colonial empire. Everything that happened, at least until 1936, was a consequence of the year 1898." Alfredo Kindelán, *Ejército y Política* (Madrid: Ediciones Ares, 1946), 176.

Francisco Franco's autobiographical movie script, *Raza*, begins with the destruction of Spain's Atlantic Squadron on July 3, 1898, tacitly establishing a link between Pascual Cervera's heroic sacrifice and Franco's victory in the Spanish civil war. In Francoist mythology, the "national rebirth" that began with the military revolt against the Republic, was a vindication of the humiliation of 1898.

2. See José Alvarez Junco, "The Nation-Building Process in Nineteenth-Century Spain," in *Nationalism and the Nation in the Iberian Peninsula*, ed. Clare Mar-Molinero and Angel Smith (Oxford: Berg, 1996). In the same publication see also Francisco J. Romero Salvadó, "The Failure of the Liberal Project of the Spanish Nation-State, 1909–1923," and Michael Richards, "Constructing the Nationalist State: Self-Sufficiency and Regeneration in the Early Franco Years."

3. See Juan Pablo Fusi Aizpúrua and Jordi Palafox Gamir, *España 1808–1996: El Desafió de la Modernidad* (Madrid: Espasa-Calpe, 1997).

4. For a study of the reaction in the United States to the Fascist regime in Italy, see John P. Diggins, *Mussolini and Fascism: The View from America* (Princeton: Princeton University Press, 1972).

5. Primo de Rivera assigned such importance to this matter that he took the unusual step of publishing an article in the December 18, 1925, issue of the *New York Times* appealing directly to public opinion in the United States, pointing to Spain's unfavorable bilateral balance of trade, asking for fair commercial treatment, and stating that Spanish agricultural products were not affected by the Mediterranean fruit fly. Text of the article, signed by Primo de Rivera, premier and former dictator of Spain, is in U.S. Department of State, *Foreign Relations of the United States* (Washington, D.C.: Government Printing Office, 1925), 2:718–720 (hereafter cited as *FRUS*).

6. "There are elements of the gravest nature in the resulting conditions. Communistic falsities have captivated the seventeenth century–minded Spanish people. All at once they see a promised land which does not exist. Ultimately they will be disillusioned. Then they will grasp at anything within their reach. Should the weak restraints of this newborn regime collapse, they will easily be captured by the widespread Bolshevistic influences.

"I do not believe immediate recognition of this regime is advisable." Laughlin to Henry Stimpson, the Secretary of State, Madrid, April 16, 1931, *FRUS*, 2:985–986.

7. Stimson to Laughlin, Washington, April 21, 1931, *FRUS*, 2:994.

8. Cited in Stephen Cooper, *The Politics of Ernest Hemingway* (Ann Arbor, Mich.: UMI Research Press, 1987), 85.

9. Waldo Frank, *Virgin Spain: Scenes from the Spiritual Drama of a Great People* (New York: Boni and Liveright, 1926), 243.

10. "It was hoped that the Spanish strife would not bring all Europe to war, that it would soon end, that the intervening nations would find it necessary to drop their schemes, and that Spain would not have a government controlled from Moscow, Berlin, or Rome. That the realization of its largest hopes was placed in the care of the British and French foreign offices was not particularly troubling to the State Department, as long as the Anglo-French approach did not kill those hopes." Richard P. Traina, *American Diplomacy and the Spanish Civil War* (Bloomington: Indiana University Press, 1968), 73.

11. Cordell Hull justified the policy adopted in terms of U.S. domestic considerations, and the overall international situation rather than on the basis of the bilateral relationship with Spain. He cited four factors that influenced the decision in favor of nonintervention: (1) the fact that Britain and France, the countries most directly concerned with developments in Spain, took the lead in establishing the Non-Intervention Committee; (2) the purpose of this committee was to prevent the spread of the conflict to the whole Continent, an objective that the United States also favored; (3) the peace and security of the United States; and (4) the desire to prevent the prolongation of the conflict. "Our policy had nothing to do with our views on the right or wrong in the Spanish Civil War. We were not judging between the two sides. . . . Both the Legislative and the Executive branches of the government joined, in singular harmony, in believing that to keep aloof from the Spanish conflict was to the best interest of the United States." In Cordell Hull, *The Memoirs of Cordell Hull* (New York: Macmillan, 1948), 1:481–492.

12. Growing sympathy for the Republic among public opinion and in Congress resulted in an attempt to repeal the arms embargo for Spain. In May 1938, Senator Gerald Nye presented a resolution to that effect. The initiative failed due to lack of support from the State Department and fear of alienating Catholic voters on the part of the Democratic leadership in Congress. The embargo, and the disruptions brought about by the civil war, restricted to a bare minimum the diplomatic exchanges between the United States and the Spanish Republic. Official relations with Franco's Nationalist rebels were nonexistent. See James W. Cortada, *Two Nations over Time: Spain and the United States, 1776–1977* (Westport, Conn.: Greenwood Press, 1978), 86–204, and Traina, op. cit. For an overview of the domestic political debate generated by the Spanish civil war in the United States, see Allen Guttmann, *The Wound in the Heart: America and the Spanish Civil War* (New York: The Free Press of Glencoe, 1962), and Allen Guttmann, ed., *American Neutrality and the Spanish Civil War* (Boston: D.C. Heath, 1963).

13. Hull, op. cit., 1:612–613.

14. Sumner Welles, *The Time for Decision* (New York: Harper and Brothers, 1944), 57–61.

15. For the lively, firsthand account of Britain's economic warfare policy in Spain and Portugal by one of its architects see David Eccles, *By Safe Hand: Letters of Sybil and David Eccles, 1939–1942* (London: Bodley Head, 1983). A brief but illustrative description of the U.S. economic weapon in Spain and of its skillful wartime use is given in Carlton Hayes, *Wartime Mission in Spain 1942–1945* (New York: Macmillan, 1946) 79–86. For a detailed description of U.S. economic warfare policy towards Spain, from the perspective of the State Department, see Herbert Feis, *The Spanish Story: Franco and the Nations at War* (New York: Knopf, 1948).

16. Hull, op. cit., 2:1187.

17. Churchill and Roosevelt, Vol. I, p. 313. Cited in Paul Preston, *Franco: A Biography* (London: HarperCollins, 1993), 451.

18. At the time of the Allied landings in North Africa, President Roosevelt wrote to Franco guaranteeing that Spanish sovereignty would be unimpaired by the impending military offensive. General Eisenhower was anxious to guarantee that the Spanish army in Morocco would not interfere with Allied operations.

19. "There is no doubt that participation of Spain in German attack on Russia and above all nefarious behavior of Spanish Blue Division aroused enormous resentment here and gave final hardening to Soviet hatred of Franco regime. Russians will not forget that Blue Division was largely responsible for wrecking and plundering of Catharine the Great's Palace at Tsarskoye Selo, perhaps the finest of Russian historical monuments, and that Spaniards quartered their horses in the ruins." George Kennan to Secretary of State, Moscow, February 3, 1946, *FRUS* 5:1034.

20. "It is out of the question for His Majesty's Government to support Spanish aspirations to participate in the future peace settlements. Neither do I think it likely that Spain will be invited to join the future world organization." Churchill to Franco, January 1945, cited in Samuel Hoare, *Complacent Dictator* (New York: Knopf, 1947), 310.

21. President Roosevelt to Ambassador Armour, March 10, 1945, *FRUS*, 5:667.

22. "I said (to Franco) that . . . my presence must not be interpreted as meaning that my Government was satisfied with the existing situation or approved the structure of the present regime in Spain." Armour to Secretary of State, Madrid, March 24, 1945, *FRUS*, 5:670.

23. Harry S. Truman, *Memoirs* (Garden City, N.Y.: Doubleday, 1955–1956), 1: 357–358.

24. Communiqué of the Potsdam Conference issued by President Truman, Chairman Stalin, and Prime Ministers Churchill and Atlee. Babelsberg, August 2, 1945, *FRUS*, 2:1510.

25. U.S. Department of State, *The Spanish Government and the Axis. Documents*, March 4, 1946 (Washington, D.C.: Government Printing Office).

26. U.S. Department of State, *A Decade of American Foreign Policy: Basic Documents 1941–1949* (Washington, D.C.: Government Printing Office, 1985), 605–606.

27. Roosevelt to Armour, March 10, 1945, *FRUS*, 5:668.

28. Text of the French proposal to Britain and the United States for a joint initiative on Spain in Caffrey to Secretary of State, Paris, March 25, 1946, *FRUS*, 5:1061.

29. State Department to British embassy, Washington, April 6, 1945, *FRUS*, 5: 672.

30. Kennan to Secretary of State, Moscow, February 3, 1946, *FRUS*, 5:1033–1036.

31. Butterworth to Secretary of State, Madrid, February 15, 1946, *FRUS*, 5: 1038–1042.

32. Acheson to Douglas, Washington, April 7, 1947, *FRUS*, 3:1066–1068.

33. Douglas to Acheson, London, April 19, 1947, *FRUS*, 3:1069–1073.

34. Kennan to Secretary of State, October 24, 1947, *FRUS*, 3:1091–1095.

35. Acting Secretary of State Lovett to Embassy in Spain, Washington, December 18, 1947, *FRUS*, 2:1096.

36. Theodore Achilles to Paul Culbertson, Washington, January 5, 1948, *FRUS*, 3:1017–1020.

37. Culbertson to the Secretary of State, no. 4402, Top Secret, Madrid, December 30, 1947, *FRUS*, 3:1100–1101.

38. Culbertson to the Secretary of State, no. 77, Top Secret, Madrid, February 6, 1948, *FRUS*, 3:1020–1025.

39. Culbertson to the Secretary of State, no. 167, Secret, Madrid, March 9, 1948, *FRUS*, 3:1026, 1027.

40. The Secretary of State to the Embassy in Spain, no. 171, Secret, Washington, March 23, 1948, *FRUS*, 3:1028.

41. Memorandum of Telephone Conversation, Washington, March 26, 1948, *FRUS*, 3:1030.

42. Memorandum of Conversation, Washington, March 29, 1948, *FRUS*, 3: 1034–1035.

43. Culbertson to the Secretary of State, Madrid, March 29, 1948, no. 182, Secret, *FRUS*, 3:1031–1034.

44. Telegram from the Acting Secretary of State to the Embassy in Spain, no. 201, Secret, Washington, April 2, 1948, *FRUS*, 3:1035:

45. The Acting Secretary of State to the Embassy in Spain, telegram transmitting Secretary Marshall's message to Foreign Minister Bevin, no. 207, Secret, Washington, April 6, 1948, *FRUS*, 3:1036.

46. Policy Statement by the Department of State on Spain. Washington, July 26, 1948, *FRUS*, 3:1041–1045.

47. Hickerson to MacVeagh, Washington, September 22, 1948, *FRUS*, 3:1007.

48. Ministry of the Navy, Naval General Staff, Second Section, to the Undersecretary of Foreign Affairs, Madrid, July 31, 1947, Ministerio de Asuntos Exteriores (hereafter cited as MAE), Legajo R2418 Expediente 33 (hereafter cited as L, E).

49. Marshall, who was attending the UN General Assembly in Paris, downplayed the significance of Gurney's declarations during a meeting at the Quai d'Orsay with Robert Schuman and Ernest Bevin, the foreign ministers of France and Great Britain, respectively. "I explained that the recent statement by Senator Gurney, which I had not yet read, was not inspired by the Government, but was

purely his own reaction, and that the military officers who accompanied him to Madrid were the liaison officers from the Army, Navy and Air to the Congress, and evidently had accompanied Gurney since he was the Chairman of the Armed Forces Committee of the Senate. They were not representing serious military considerations so far as I knew." Memorandum of Conversation, by the Secretary of State, Secret, Paris, October 4, 1948, *FRUS*, 3:1053.

50. *New York Times*, 12 November 1948, pp. 1, 17.

51. The Chargé d'Affaires in Spain to the Secretary of State, no. 661, Secret, Madrid, November 17, 1948, *FRUS*, 3:1063.

52. The question of foreign military bases on Spanish soil is linked with the historical memory of the French invasions of the nineteenth century and the long-standing friction with Great Britain over Gibraltar. Although the military bases built by the United States during the 1950s have lost their strategic raison d'être, and are no longer a major consideration in the overall bilateral relationship, the issue of the bases remains politically sensitive. Official Spanish documentation on the negotiations remains classified.

53. "If present drought continues (rainfall September to January inclusive 40 percent below thirty year average) causing poor crops and increasingly severe electricity restrictions (Barcelona factories now have public power six hours weekly), if private enterprises continue unable meet bank obligations, if Argentina does not supply wheat or should curtail present credits and Spain's grain crop should be failure, I do not see how Spain's economic and social structure can hold together indefinitely. . . . Economic and political breakdown or disintegration in Spain bound have severe repercussions on our aims economic political rehabilitation Europe. Such eventuality not in our interest nor that France and UK. I feel risk should be weighed carefully against present political objections." Culbertson to the Secretary of State, Madrid, February 17, 1949, no. 77, Secret, *FRUS*, 4:729–730.

54. The Secretary of State to the Embassy in Spain, no. 199, Secret, Washington, April 13, 1949, *FRUS*, 4:735.

55. The Secretary of State to Certain Diplomatic Missions, Confidential, For Chief of Mission, Washington, April 14, 1949, *FRUS*, 4:739.

56. *FRUS* (1949), 4:745. Reference to the note verbale no. 410 of May 19, 1949, of the Ministry of Foreign Affairs is in *FRUS*, 4:746.

57. "U.S. Spanish Policy. Remarks by Secretary Acheson" (released to the press May 11), *Department of State Bulletin*, May 22, 1949. U.S. Department of State (Washington, D.C.: Government Printing Office), 660.

58. "Why Spain is not included in MAP" (paper prepared by the Foreign Assistance Correlation Committee), Secret, MAP D-G/Gb, Washington, May 25, 1949, *FRUS*, 4:748–749.

59. Culbertson to the Secretary of State, no. 330, Confidential, Madrid, June 22, 1949, *FRUS*, 4:750–753.

60. "We obviously cannot engage in effusive government to government friendship nor, in the absence of favorable developments in Spain, can we (1) promote its participation in such programs as the ERP, MAP or NAT; (2) extend government to government financial assistance or an outright program of aid on a project basis; (3) take a strong lead in seeking to alter the UN position on Spain.

If the Spanish Government would show convincing concrete evidence of good intentions we could work progressively toward all three. However, we see little prospect of its being willing to do so in the near future." The Secretary of State to the Embassy in Spain A-287, Top Secret, Washington, October 31, 1949, *FRUS*, 4:762.

61. Elaborate measures were taken by the Spanish authorities to expedite procedures for the visit of the U.S. warships to El Ferrol September 3 to 8, 1949, and to welcome the officers and the crews. Hospitality included a bullfight and the arrangement of a visit to Santiago de Compostella for approximately five hundred Catholic sailors. Admiral Connolly's interview with Franco at Pazo de Meira on September 5 was very friendly. They discussed mostly naval matters, technical developments in naval armament, and the organization of the eastern Atlantic and Mediterranean command, with headquarters in London but the bases of the fleet in the United States. Connolly expressed his agreement with Franco's statement that a state of war existed and that the United States was trying to take effective steps to confront the possibility of an aggression. MAE, L R4230 E 15, Gabinete Diplomático.

62. Acheson to Connally, Washington, January 18, 1950, *FRUS*, 3:1549–1555.

63. Memorandum by the Chairman of the Joint Chiefs of Staff to the Secretary of Defense, Secret, Washington, May 3, 1950, *FRUS*, 3:1560–1562.

64. NSC 68: United States Objectives and Programs for National Security (April 14, 1950), cited in Ernest May, ed., *American Cold War Strategy: Interpreting NSC 68* (Boston: St. Martin's Press, 1993), 38. The document, drafted by Paul Nitze, who had replaced George Kennan as director of the Policy Planning Staff, argued for a major increase in military spending, against the objections of President Truman and Secretary Johnson who hoped to reduce the defense budget. As a result of the outbreak of the Korean War and the decision to implement NSC 68 taken by President Truman in September 1950, defense spending tripled. The subsequent militarization of the cold war shifted the balance of power over foreign policy from the State Department to the Pentagon. See ibid., 1–17.

Chapter 6

Reconciliation and Quasi Alliance

THE SPANISH DIPLOMATIC INITIATIVE

By 1948, government officials in Madrid had become aware that Spain would be the only Western European country barred from receiving assistance under the Marshall Plan. This outcome was the result of the prevailing anti-Franco sentiment in Europe, particularly in those countries that had been occupied by Nazi Germany. A significant number of European intellectuals and political leaders who had actively supported the Republic during the Spanish civil war—some as combatants in the International Brigades—remained adamantly opposed to Franco and his regime. The social-democratic orientation of many of the postwar governments of Western Europe gave organized labor, whose cooperation was critical for the task of reconstruction, a decisive influence in the shaping of public policies, domestic as well as foreign. Franco's suppression of unions and criminalization of strikes were anathema to labor leaders on both sides of the Atlantic. Therefore, the close intergovernmental cooperation required of the beneficiaries of the ERP became an insurmountable obstacle to the inclusion of Spain in the program, on political as well as on practical grounds. Similar considerations precluded Spain's membership in the Council of Europe and the Organization for European Economic Cooperation (OEEC). Opposition from European governments, other than that of Portugal, excluded Spain from the multilateral defense agreements of the North Atlantic Treaty, NAT, and therefore, from the possibility of obtaining NAT-related military assistance from the United States. European objections to Franco were also invoked by the State Department as the basis for its recommendation to block bilateral military support to Spain under the terms of the Military Assistance Program.

The change that had taken place in U.S. policy, from favoring the overthrow of the Franco regime to acknowledging it as a fait accompli, while welcomed by officials in Madrid, had been, until 1948, of little practical benefit. Spain remained excluded from the international community and from the U.S. government to government assistance, economic as well as military. Yet, even taking into account those external constraints, the regime was beginning to feel more secure, having survived the most perilous period of international hostility in 1946 and 1947. A 1947 law of succession, ratified by referendum, confirmed Franco's position as head of state, and effectively eliminated the possibility of a monarchist alternative to his personal rule. A catastrophic shortfall in the supply of foodstuffs during that year had been averted by means of large shipments of wheat and beef provided by Argentina on credit. In February 1948, France reopened the frontier with Spain—which had been closed since March 1946—allowing the resumption of trade and travel across the Pyrenees. Despite the unfavorable external environment, short-term political continuity had ceased to be the government's priority concern. The regime's foreign policy shifted to the initiative with a sustained effort to break out of the isolation imposed upon it by the international community. A diplomatic counteroffensive was launched to overcome the objections of the State Department, and to reach a bilateral agreement with the United States for military cooperation and economic assistance.

Part of this initiative was the formation in Washington of an informal group of friendly members of Congress, government officials, and influential persons that came to be known as the Spanish Lobby. Strictly speaking the lobby consisted of Charles Patrick Clark, a private lawyer with ample legislative experience as a former staff member of several congressional committees, who was retained by the Spanish embassy, as well as the Washington law firm of Commings, Stanley, Truitt and Cross, which acted as general counsel to the embassy. But in its extended version, the lobby brought together a diverse group of regional, economic, and political interests around the common objective of changing U.S. policy toward Spain. This larger group included members of key congressional committees (such as Foreign Relations, Appropriations, and

Armed Services), Catholic spokesmen, leading conservatives and anti-communists, military officers, representatives of southern cotton states, and political opponents of President Truman and Acheson.

The Spanish diplomatic effort in Washington was coordinated by José Felix de Lequerica, a right-wing politician from Bilbao who had served the regime as ambassador to Vichy France and as foreign minister. Lequerica was a member of the Basque bourgeoisie and a former conservative deputy in the Cortes under the Constitutional Monarchy, who had been a financial supporter of José Antonio Primo de Rivera, tercer marqués de Estella, the son of the late dictator and founder of the Falange. He studied in the London School of Economics and was fluent in English as well as French. He was evidently well regarded by Franco who appointed him to head Spain's most important foreign mission. Lequerica was sent to Washington in the spring of 1948 with the title of inspector of embassies and the rank of ambassador at large, since formally, Spain's diplomatic representation was entrusted to Germán Baraibar as chargé d'affaires. He occupied the embassy residence and took up the functions of an ambassador, under the pretense of performing a lengthy inspection. In January 1951, when diplomatic relations were reestablished at ambassadorial level, he was accredited as Spain's ambassador to the United States.

Lequerica's mission was two-fold: to restore diplomatic relations with Washington at the ambassadorial level, and to obtain economic and military cooperation from the United States outside the multilateral framework imposed by the Marshall Plan and the European defense agreements. The first objective, centered in New York, required repeal of the 1946 UN Resolution 39 on withdrawal of ambassadors from Madrid. The second objective, centered in Washington, implied a labor of persuasion in both the executive and legislative branches of government. Lequerica coordinated the work of the Spanish Lobby on both fronts. He also provided the link between the lobbying activities in New York and Washington and the principal policy makers in Madrid.

Lequerica's confidential correspondence with Alberto Martín Artajo, the foreign minister, reveals the priority that the Spanish government assigned to improving its relations with the United States. It also shows that in his pursuit of that objective, Lequerica had recourse to methods of persuasion other than dialectics and that he did not hesitate to recommend procedures that sidestepped the boundaries of conventional diplomatic propriety. The communications between the Spanish embassy in Washington and the Ministry of Foreign Affairs during this period testify to Lequerica's high standing within the hierarchy of the regime, a status that entitled him to send his titular superior recommendations and observations that normally flow in the other direction. Thus, in a letter to the minister about the composition of the Spanish commission that would travel to Paris to observe the 1948 meeting of the UN General Assembly, he wrote: "You know my thinking on the importance of this summer for military, ecclesiastic and propaganda matters. For those Spaniards competent in international affairs, this should be a period of maximum activity rather than a time for withdrawal to the pleasantness of Cantabria, regardless of what the thermometers may say . . ."[1] Lequerica regularly advised Artajo on the visits of influential persons to Spain who, in his opinion, merited special attention by officials in Madrid. In a letter informing the minister that Thomas H. Beck, chairman of the Board of *Colliers*, a weekly magazine, was travelling to Madrid, he added: "His Irish-Catholic wife, who is much younger than he, will be accompanying him. They are very interested in Madrid's society. For that reason, . . . I would be pleased if—as you have previously done with such success—you would kindly mobilize the ladies that govern our delightful social life. They would be performing, as so many times in the past, a patriotic task."[2]

Referring to Hector David Castro, El Salvador's ambassador to the United States, who planned to visit Spain after attending the meeting of the UN General Assembly in Paris, he stated: "As you know, the Ambassador of El Salvador is a most distinguished jurist. His twenty years of residence in Washington give him great authority with people in the State Department. For that reason, our Commission [to the UN meeting in Paris] should regard him, not only as a very useful person for its Spanish American activities, but especially, as a link to the North-American delegation."[3]

A frequent theme in Lequerica's correspondence is the request for ample discretionary funds for the purpose of expediting matters of interest to Spain, in New York as well as Washington. When explaining to the minister the need to provide material incentives in order to obtain results, Lequerica utilized euphemisms such as "means of action," "methods of persuasion," and "economic complement." The following text provides an illustration of his modus operandi.

1) Constantine Brown, our principal defender in the independent press, has never received from us the slightest gift, other than social invitations. Now we propose to: a) Appoint Mrs. Churchill, some-

body very close to him, for whom he has requested the job, as "Social Secretary" to the Embassy. This position, which is very useful, exists everywhere. But as with so many other things, we lacked it. b) Give him an important wedding gift. Something of gold or silver besides the customary remembrance. He is marrying . . . Mrs. Churchill. Until yesterday we had not associated one thing with the other, although it was not very difficult to surmise. . . . She is very well connected with the circles in the press that can be most useful to us.

2) This leads me to remind you that no movement on our part can be made without its corresponding economic complement. Oh, if we only had now—or had had in the past—a well stocked war chest![4]

Two letters related to his efforts to influence the vote in the UN General Assembly on repeal of the 1946 UN Resolution 39, are even more explicit. Referring to the vote of abstention by the U.S. delegation, whereby a two-thirds majority for repeal was not obtained, he commented:

Two thirds, almost within our reach if we had deployed in time— with more experience—certain means of persuasion. [The phrase "means of persuasion" appears underlined in red pencil and followed by an exclamation mark, apparently added by the minister.] . . . Conclusion. With reference to the means described in my handwritten letter: that in one degree or another they are to be employed in this delicate campaign. We have already begun to provide advances in number 5. [Presumably a code for an unnamed person.] . . . Taking a long-term view, I consider contact with the United Nations and its principal men of great interest for Spain. . . . We have become a first class country and we should behave accordingly. Distinguished travellers cannot abstain from rewarding generously those that take care of them at hotels and depart at dawn. Particularly if they intend to return the following season or someday, even to reside permanently.[5]

In a typewritten letter describing the influence of the U.S. delegation to the UN ("The Great Elector") as tremendous and decisive, he added:

Urgency of an Appropriation What is the sense of arguing? At the critical hour when an Assembly, whose form of functioning is proverbially known, is deciding the capital problem of re-establishing our diplomatic contact with the United States and a large part of the world, we have not received anything yet. To cover small invitations, flowers etc., we have to charge them to our account at the Ritz. Nobody would believe this. The memory of Gibraltar "defended" by seventy men when the British arrived comes again to mind, confronted by such a situation, unfortunately repeated throughout history due to some flaw in our character.

Attached to the letter was a handwritten note with the following message:

Urgently requires six that will be delivered tomorrow Monday 9, without further delay because it is necessary to push a lot of people. To that is added, also by request, a wedding gift of not excessive value. In God's name, keep a deadly silence about this. It suffices that you and His Excellency be informed. If any Prat [Pedro de Prat y Soutzo, Marqués de Prat de Nantouillet, policy director, America] should find out, it would not delay in being relayed here via Paul [Culbertson] with irreparable harm and closing the door on a promising future in the governmental department which is most hostile to us. The economic amount is not large, particularly if we move quickly. Much less than what we thought before we knew about the positive attitude of the [State] Department: It will not exceed twenty and may even be less.[6]

Neither the total amounts that were distributed nor the names of the recipients can be precisely determined from the available documentation, for obvious reasons. The sums transferred to the Spanish embassy in Washington for Lequerica's labor of persuasion came under the heading "Fondos Reservados" (secret funds), which did not require detailed accounting reports. As for the beneficiaries, they were rarely mentioned when communicating in writing with the foreign minister, and in such cases they were designated cryptically by means of a number. Lequerica feared that his communications were being intercepted by the U.S. Secret Service,[7] and was convinced that within the Ministry of Foreign Affairs in Madrid there existed an antiregime conspiracy of high-ranking Spanish diplomats who were working in tandem with leftist State Department officials to undermine his mission in Washington. The anticommunist paranoia in the United States that became associated with the McCarthy era was grist for his mill because it helped to buttress his own conspiracy theories.

When you read the unbelievable tale of the reds in the State Department you will get a better understanding of the scandal Culbertson-Dunham [chargé d'affaires in Madrid and chief of the Spanish Bureau in the State Department, respectively] with all their high Spanish collaborators, C, [Juan Francisco Cárdenas, former ambassador to the United States], dear Pericos [Marqués de Prat de Nantouillet] etc. etc. And the Senate here moves faster than Don Paco Rodriguez [presumably, director of intelligence] and his magnificent services.[8]

What can be surmised from the correspondence is that the intended beneficiaries of Lequerica's propaganda efforts were persons of influence in the media, Congress, and the State Department. The following document indicates that the magnitude of the resources mobilized to support Spain's diplomatic offensive was such as to require governmental decisions at the highest level.

Ambassador Lequerica has telephoned to say he needs urgently an extraordinary consignment of 100,000 dollars to bring to fruition those matters that are pending. The Minister of Industry, with whom I also spoke by telephone, tells me that I can dispose of it [the foreign exchange] on the condition that the Ministry of Foreign Affairs deposits in the Instituto de Moneda [the foreign currency bureau] the counterpart funds, equivalent to about one million two hundred thousand pesetas. Since the current budget does not include such a sum for this Ministry, it will be necessary to approve in the next Cabinet meeting, if Your Excellency thinks it is justified, a Decree-Law granting that sum as a supplement to the small credit assigned to this Ministry, in the same manner as was done last March for a similar amount.[9]

Lequerica's methods of persuasion were also applied to his Washington activities.

In my last handwritten letter I announced to you that it would be necessary to continue our propaganda campaign using the only known means, which I believe we have been doing with plentiful results. Specifically, I was thinking about our friends number 50. The details can be discussed, as well as the sums to be distributed. But to "stop" now would be to waste all that has been accomplished. I continue to have full confidence in the results obtained by this system. . . . Soon we will achieve our short term goals: full

diplomatic relations, loans of some kind, military contacts parallel
to the Atlantic Pact or even inclusion in the same. In the future it
will also be indispensable to maintain this activity, which for the
sake of comfort we will call propaganda.[10]

As a reinforcement to Lequerica's argument, this typewritten letter included as an addendum, a handwritten note from Baraibar, the chargé
d'affaires, to the minister, expressing "his identification with the Ambassador in his plans of action in this Embassy, which are so necessary
to Congressional and financial circles." Lequerica's eclectic approach to
international relations was not unanimously shared by the Spanish diplomatic establishment. In a letter to Artajo requesting funds to expedite
loans to Spain and a military agreement with the United States, he acknowledged, that apropos of his methods, the "party of Morality (!) of
our friend Merry and other exemplary men of the same style, thundered
and ex-communicated." [Merry del Val was a prominent Spanish family
with ties to the Vatican. Two brothers were in the Spanish diplomatic
service, and an uncle was a cardinal and papal secretary of state.][11]

Artajo himself had some qualms about the result-oriented methods of
his worldly ambassador, who had also briefly served as his predecessor
as foreign minister. "You, my dear Minister, without going to the extreme of those scandalized ones, have a propensity towards certain shy-
ness in this matter, and that is as it should be. But to your credit, and
that is a major achievement of your stewardship, from the beginning,
and with these minor, purely formal hesitations, you gave full support
to all aspects of our activity here. That is something of which we all
deserve to be proud."[12]

Franco was apparently not troubled by similar scruples. In contrast to
Artajo, who came to the ministry from the leadership of Accion Católica,
an association of devout Catholic laymen, Franco had acquired a disillusioned view of human nature from his dealings with tribal leaders in
Morocco. According to Don Juan de Borbón, pretender to the throne of
Spain (the father of King Juan Carlos), reporting on a recent meeting
with the Caudillo, "Franco is a complete cynic about men. I recall that
in our conference on the yacht, he remarked that anybody could be
bought."[13] Furthermore, Franco—like the previous military dictator,
Primo de Rivera—had a low opinion of political parties and of parlia-
ments. In all likelihood, Lequerica's methods, justified in terms of ex-
pediency, reason of state, and the higher interests of Spain, were not in

sharp contradiction with his views on how things worked in liberal democracies.

Two of Lequerica's closest and most prominent congressional allies were Senator Owen Brewster (Republican, Maine) and Senator Patrick McCarran (Democrat, Nevada). The following démarche on behalf of the latter illustrates the intimate relationship between the ecclesiastical and the political that prevailed during the national-Catholic phase of the Franco regime.[14] On July 22, 1949, Lequerica wrote the chief of the Diplomatic Cabinet of the Ministry of Foreign Affairs, informing him that McCarran had two daughters who were nuns, and that one of them, Sister Margarita, was particularly interested in obtaining a relic of Saint John of the Cross. The senator had requested Lequerica's help in the matter. He urged his colleague to make every effort to bring much happiness to a pious family and to earn its gratitude by complying with the senator's request. This communication produced a flurry of diplomatic-ecclesiastic activity involving the foreign minister, the bishop of Madrid-Alcalá and patriarch of the West Indies, the chief of the Diplomatic Cabinet, and the Spanish consul in Rome. On August 2, the consul in Spain wrote the chief of the Diplomatic Cabinet sending the relic that he hoped would be useful "to the interests of our Fatherland, given the purpose for which you request it." On August 9, eighteen days after being requested, the relic was on its way from San Sebastián, the Foreign Ministry's summer headquarters, to Washington.[15] The Spanish consul in Rome did not explain how he obtained the relic in that city, given the fact that the saint's remains were in Segovia. Neither did he describe the relic or refer to proof of its authenticity, but perhaps those were matters best left unmentioned. However, what is remarkable about this charming episode is that in this instance, a foreign service with a well-earned reputation for slowness, applied such speed and diligence to an enterprise close to McCarran's heart, despite the fact that several of the principal protagonists were away from Madrid for the summer recess.

Active participation in Washington's social life was part of Lequerica's overt effort to promote the cause of the Spanish Lobby, which a contemporary observer described as "a jumble of cotton, silver, cork, generals, society pages and cocktails."[16] In a letter to the foreign minister complaining about a reduction in his entertainment allowance, he stated that "in this month of May, 150 persons have dined at the Embassy."[17] In keeping with a practice that he had recommended to Artajo, he mobilized an influential group of ladies in support of his diplomatic objectives, including Mrs. Owen Brewster, the spouse of the senator from Maine, and Washington's society page columnists.[18]

Spain's foreign policy during this period was hampered by the intellectual limitations inherent in any dictatorship and by the peculiar world-view that had been developed by the regime's apologists to justify its perpetuation and to counter external criticism of its origins and its nature. In the words of a contemporary observer of Spain's governmental elite,

> Spain is run today by men of second-rate ability, men whose vision is obscured by Spain's glorious past. These men, in their thoughts and concepts, are as isolated from world thought as they are walled in physically by mountains and seas. Men of liberal thought and ability do not want to associate themselves with the Régime. Men of ability and training in statesmanship, journalism, law—the things that make for government—are rapidly disappearing in Spain. Ten years of dictatorship, plus three years of civil war, have laid a heavy toll on the development of men in the field of government and leadership.[19]

Three books from inside the regime serve to illustrate the intellectual underpinnings of governmental thinking, mythology, and propaganda. One was a sycophantic biographical sketch of Franco, proclaiming him not just as the savior of Spain but as the protector of Western civilization. The other was a self-serving eulogy of Franco's foreign policy during World War II. The third, a collection of articles written by Franco himself and published in 1951, interpreted all of modern history, from the Enlightenment to the twentieth century, as a conspiracy by Freemasons, liberals, and communists against Spain.[20] The articles, published under the pseudonym Jakim Boor, appeared in *Arriba*, the Falangist newspaper, from 1946 to 1951.

This intellectual nonsense could remain unchallenged domestically, thanks to a tightly controlled structure of political repression, press censorship, and the educational and cultural hegemony of an intolerant and reactionary church. But it was of little dialectical usefulness in a democratic setting where freedom of the press and unfettered political discourse prevailed. From time to time, Lequerica tactfully reminded his superiors in Madrid that the United States was a pluralistic society, and that within that context the regime's ideology did not travel well. To the foreign minister's suggestion that he have some of Franco's journalistic excursions translated into English and published in the United States, he replied: "The articles of 'Boor' are of exceptional interest and, in my judgement, have a most accurate point of view. In addition to those you sent me I have just come across a very good one in a recent issue of *Arriba*. My only fear about the translation is that in certain countries, even among those persons which require it most, there is little appreciation of those profound, authentic truths capable of untangling many plots. I suppose that you understand me correctly. Anyway, in agreement with Merry, we will make some soundings to see how far we can go. I will keep you informed."[21]

With a cautiously worded cover letter, he forwarded to Madrid a warning from a friend of the regime, about the harmful impression caused in the United States by a *New York Times* report on the persecution of Freemasons in Spain, of March 27, 1950, written by Sam Pope Brewer, the Madrid correspondent of that newspaper.[22] The following shows how he tried to explain to the foreign minister the need to adapt the activities of the Spanish Lobby to the complexities of religious pluralism. "If by friends you mean only Catholics, our good McCarran stands out among the most active and combative ones. But it would be a grave error to limit our friendships here only to Catholics. Thank God, there are enormous social and political sectors here separated from the only true Church, but nonetheless fervent defenders of Spain, that advocate assistance to her and promote her dignified union with the policy of the United States."[23]

At the same time, the characteristics of the regime provided Lequerica the advantage of enjoying a friendly press coverage in Spain. The foreign minister informed him that the director of *Arriba* was willing to publish as editorials the articles written by Lequerica "on American issues and on our affairs in the United States. If you prefer, you can send them directly to me and I will arrange to have them published."[24]

The State Department had misgivings about Lequerica's activities as de facto ambassador, under the pretense of carrying out his lengthy inspection. The U.S. embassy in Madrid was asked to inquire of the Foreign Ministry the purpose for which Lequerica had requested an assistant. The department also expressed curiosity about the expected duration of his mission in Washington.[25]

This inquiry was followed up several months later by an aide-mémoire, delivered personally to the foreign minister by Culbertson, chargé d'affaires ad interim, and a personal note on the same subject from Culbertson to Prat. "During the eighteen or more months, however,

of Ambassador Lequerica's stay in Washington his activities and his occupancy of the Embassy's residence have conveyed the impression that
he considers his duties primarily those of an accredited Ambassador
rather than those of an inspector making a temporary visit."[26] The foreign minister wrote Lequerica the same day, and asked him to prepare
a reply. "I have just received a visit from Culbertson, who handed me a
memorandum of which I enclose a copy. What seems to me the most
noble and loyal course of action toward you is to ask you to send me a
draft of the reply to be given, in the terms that you consider opportune."[27]

The text of the ministry's reply to the U.S. embassy in Madrid is noteworthy because it was drafted by Lequerica, who feared that his visa
was about to be revoked.

> The function of the Ambassador-Inspector, is by its nature, of in-
> definite duration. The prolongation of his mission should be no
> cause for concern, as long as he maintains his activities, as Mr.
> Lequerica does, within the limits of correct behavior required of all
> diplomatic representatives . . . nobody should take exception to the
> fact that the Spanish Government is interested in maintaining, in a
> nation of the worldwide importance of the United States, an ex-
> perienced observer and adviser such as Mr. Lequerica, besides the
> present Chargé d'Affaires.
>
> To conclude, the Spanish Government does not share the under-
> standing of the United States Embassy in Madrid about the con-
> venience of limiting the permanence in Washington of Mr.
> Lequerica, whose transparent and most correct activities have given
> no cause for complaint.[28]

On November 4, 1950, the UN General Assembly approved a resolution lifting the ban on ambassadors, with decisive help from the Latin
American bloc of delegates and with the favorable vote of the United
States. Simultaneously with this development, the gradual process of
Spain's incorporation into the technical agencies of the world organization began: Food and Agriculture Organization (FAO) in 1950; the International Postal Union, the World Health Organization and the
International Civil Aviation Organization in 1951; and the United Nations Educational, Scientific, and Cultural Organization (UNESCO) in
1952. On December 27, 1950, President Truman announced the nomi-
nation of Stanton Griffis as ambassador to Spain. Lequerica in turn, re-
alized the goal about which he used to joke, of remaining in Washington

until the ambassador at large becomes the ambassador at last. In his diplomatic objective of improving relations between Spain and the United States, he was strongly supported by events and forces that neither he nor the Spanish Lobby could control or influence.

THE TRIUMPH OF STRATEGY OVER POLITICS

The debate between Washington policy makers over relations with Spain was not, as Lequerica and some of President Truman's most virulent critics alleged, a conflict between friends of the Franco regime and communist sympathizers infiltrated into the State Department. A discrepancy existed, albeit a more subtle one, between those who stressed political diplomatic considerations and those who approached the problem from a military strategic standpoint.

The first group placed primary emphasis on the negative international repercussions of a rapprochement with the Franco regime, while the second group considered that the strategic advantages to be gained from Spanish military cooperation outweighed the corresponding diplomatic costs. Although both groups were in agreement about the ultimate goal, they disagreed on the cost-benefit estimates of bringing Spain into the Western European defense arrangements as part of the overall strategy of containment of the Soviet Union.

President Truman, who hoped to fund the social programs of his Fair Deal with a reduction in defense expenditures, sympathized with the position of the first group. This attitude was reinforced by his strong dislike for Franco and for the religious intolerance prevailing in Spain.[29] Until the spring of 1950, U.S. relations toward Spain reflected the prevailing political diplomatic views of the first group, notwithstanding criticism from Congress and the efforts of the Spanish Lobby.

In the summer of 1950, an unforeseen event—the outbreak of the Korean War, which was unrelated to Spanish considerations—began to shift the policy balance in the direction of the strategic planners. The fear that Pyongyang's decision to invade South Korea was part of a worldwide scheme of Soviet aggression gave urgency to the appeals for bolstering the military preparedness of Western Europe as a matter of national security. The heightening of international tensions brought about by the Korean War also provided opportunities for Congress to play a more assertive role on matters of foreign policy. In August 1950, taking advantage of the administration's request to provide support for Marshall Josip Broz Tito under the Yugoslav Emergency Assistance Act, the pro-

Franco bloc in Congress succeeded in including a sum of $62.5 million to be loaned to Spain by the Export-Import Bank in the general appropriations bill, despite the explicit opposition of President Truman. The original request had been for $100 million, but was reduced to $62.5 million in a House-Senate conference compromise. McCarran, the sponsor of that initiative, provided the following account of the congressional decision-making process.

> Congress voted the loan after hearing Administration men plead that our action would alienate European allies and repel millions who might eventually become allies. A dozen spokesmen predicted the act would nauseate the world, convince foreign people we were endorsing dictatorships and make a sham of our talk of democracy. . . . They threw the book at Franco, and when the exhortation was over, both Houses promptly voted the loan. Why? The shirt-sleeve boys in the Pentagon wanted it. Army men of Cabinet level kept out of the argument, but one notch below were the professionals, the men who have already fought Russia on a hundred blueprints. They saw that the Iberian peninsula had great value to the West if it comes to war. But the military does not make decisions if political questions intrude. Political decisions belong to the State Department and White House, and the President had made it clear he wanted no relations with Spain. This left the technical men in a spot. They could not openly advocate a policy which frightened their superiors, let alone contradict the President, yet their blueprints did just that. Unofficially, the lower echelon made known its views. . . . When the word drifted through congressional corridors, Congress caught the cue.[30]

By the beginning of 1951, U.S. policy toward Spain was under active reassessment within the administration. In February 1951, the National Security Council established the following immediate objectives of U.S. policy toward Spain:

a. To develop urgently the military potentialities of Spain's strategic geographic position for the common defense of the NAT area. . . .

b. To concentrate planning on the use of Spain for the common defense, not for the defense of the Iberian Peninsula. U.S. officials should emphasize in all discussions that the primary role envisaged for Spain is in support of the common policy of defending, not liberating Western Europe.

   c. To approach the Spanish Government in order to acquire such
     facilities as bases for long-range bomber and fighter operations
     and behind-the-lines staging areas. We should similarly ap-
     proach the Spanish Government for bases for naval operations.

The ultimate objective was to obtain early Spanish participation in the
North Atlantic Treaty, for which the provision of military assistance to
Spain was contemplated.[31]

On March 1, 1951, Ambassador Griffis presented his credentials to
General Franco, who received him with a spectacular display of Iberian
pomp and protocol.[32] Along with President Truman's recommendation
to press for the religious rights of non-Catholics he had received instructions from Secretary Acheson on security matters.

> The policy of the United States toward Spain is now under active
> study, particularly in the military field. . . . We fully realize that the
> gravity of the international situation emphasizes the desirability of
> including Spain in the common defense effort as soon as possible be-
> cause of the contributions which Spain could make. . . . One of our
> first objectives is to promote the inclusion of Spain in the Western
> European community. Besides the obvious advantages that would
> accrue to Spain from normal relations with its neighbors, progress
> along these lines will clear the way for Spanish participation in the
> joint defense effort. . . . In discussing this and other matters with
> Spanish officials, you may indicate our disposition to work out mu-
> tual problems in a spirit of cooperation based upon the recognition
> of our common interests as members of the Western World.[33]

In April 1951 provisions were made to complement the military policy
guidelines established by the National Security Council document NSC
72/4 approved by President Truman on February 1 with willingness to
offer financial and technical assistance to Spain. The rationale offered for
that decision was the following:

> The economic condition of the Spanish people is such that further
> deterioration may require the Spanish Government to request grant
> assistance from the United States in order to prevent the danger of
> starvation and the threat of political disorder. Moreover, the mili-
> tary capacity of Spain to make a contribution to Western European
> defense would require the support of the Spanish people. It might
> be difficult to obtain this support if it appeared to the Spanish peo-
> ple that United States interest in Spain extended only to expendi-

tures in behalf of the Spanish military establishment and disregarded the welfare of the Spanish people themselves. To make any military assistance or future military base program worthwhile requires some immediate improvement in the transportation network to be used in connection with the construction and operation of such bases. . . . Any financial assistance to be extended should, of course, be considered primarily in relation to the accomplishment of our military objectives. In accordance with the NSC policy paper, the provision of financial assistance to Spain should be related to the ultimate United States policy objective of bringing Spain closer to participation in NATO. Aside from purely military and economic considerations we must keep in mind that a strong demand exists in Congress that Spain should be included in Western European defense against aggression. . . . In view of the Administration's decision that for defense purposes grant assistance for Yugoslavia will be requested of the Congress, supporters of Spain will unquestionably demand that aid for Spain be authorized for the same reasons. We would have the greatest trouble in replying to this argument since the strategic importance of both countries in the defense of Western Europe makes untenable any presentation which attempts to justify aid for Communist dictator Tito and at the same time excludes anti-Communist dictator Franco.[34]

The approval of the military as well as the economic components of an eventual bilateral agreement between the United States and Spain prepared the ground for the next step, which was establishing a framework for negotiations between the two governments. The sensitive mission of initiating preliminary talks with Spanish officials was assigned to Admiral Forrest Sherman, chief of naval operations.[35]

The news of Admiral Sherman's proposed trip to Madrid was received with misgivings by some of the Western European allies.

British Cabinet has decided US Government must be strongly urged abandon policy to associate Spain more closely with West. . . . If US Government by unilateral action attempts associate Franco-Spain with West it would give severe shock to Scandinavians, Belgians, Dutch, possibly Italians, besides British and French. Western morale would be gravely disturbed by implication Europe is to be defended at Pyrenees. On material side Western Europe would be disturbed at prospect US arms and equipment being diverted to Spain for [sic] more urgently deserving countries. British

convinced US cannot pay Franco off with economic aid, but will
have to pay in military equipment. . . . British Government feels
very strongly on this matter. This question primarily of European
concern and British Government feels entitled ask its views be considered. French Ambassador being similarly instructed.[36]

On July 10, 1951, the British and the French embassies in Washington
delivered similarly worded aide-mémoire to the State Department with
the recommendation from their respective governments that the proposed military talks between Admiral Sherman and General Franco be
postponed.[37] Secretary Acheson informed both ambassadors that the
talks in Madrid would go forward, but indicated that he wanted the
event to pass off as quietly as possible and that as far as the State Department was concerned, there would be no publicity or fanfare associated with it. He acknowledged the validity of the political objections
invoked by their representations but pointed out that "we also had additional political problems of serious proportions."[38]

On July 16, Admiral Sherman, accompanied by Ambassador Griffis,
was received by General Franco at El Pardo, his official residence in the
outskirts of Madrid. Prat, from the Ministry of Foreign Affairs, acted as
interpreter. Admiral Sherman explained that he had been authorized by
the president to travel to Madrid, as a representative of the Defense
Department and the U.S. Chiefs of Staff, to explore matters related to the
defense of Western Europe and the United States, given the strategic
importance of Spain for air communications to and from Europe, and
for sea and air communications through the Mediterranean. In that context, he expressed the desirability of obtaining air operating and transit
privileges in Spain, Spanish Morocco, and the Canaries, as well as the
use of anchorages in Spanish territorial waters in those three areas and
the Balearics. As part of the envisaged measures of military cooperation,
Sherman referred to surveys of installations, the exchange of military
information, technical advice on questions of logistics and military supply, and consultations on plans for the defense of Spain. He added that
the development of these measures in detail would require conversations
at the staff level in the near future.

Franco expressed his agreement in principle to the commencement of
a bilateral negotiation. He pointed out that a great deal of time had been
lost in starting to prepare Spain to participate in the common defense.
He stressed the need for military equipment for the army (specifically
tanks, antitank weapons, and antiaircraft artillery), as well as Spain's

need for economic assistance. He made explicit the understanding that the use of bases and harbors would be regarded at all times as the use of Spanish property and that in accordance with existing treaty obligations, Portugal would have to be informed of any eventual defense agreements. With these reservations and the request that any further meetings be held in Madrid, Franco agreed to the initiation of detailed bilateral conferences at the staff level.[39]

On July 18, during a press conference, Secretary Acheson made the following announcement:

> Military authorities are in general agreement that Spain is of strategic importance to the general defense of Western Europe. As a natural corollary to this generally accepted conclusion, tentative and exploratory conversations have been undertaken with the Spanish Government with the sole purpose of ascertaining what Spain might be willing and able to do which would contribute to the strengthening of the common defense against possible aggression.
>
> We have been talking with the British and French Governments for many months about the possible role of Spain in relation to the general defense of Western Europe. We have not been able to find a common position on this subject with these Governments for reasons of which we are aware and understand. However, for the strategic reasons outlined above, the United States has initiated these exploratory conversations.[40]

This announcement, softened with reassuring words about NATO as the keystone to the defense of Western Europe, was an explicit recognition that U.S. policy toward Spain had changed, against the vehement opposition of London and Paris, and with less than enthusiastic support from the president.

Following up on the Franco-Sherman agreement, two survey teams were dispatched to Spain in August: a Joint Military Survey Team and a Temporary Economic Study Group, created by the Economic Cooperation Administration (ECA). The military team was headed by Major General James Spry, U.S. Air Force, who reported to the Joint Chiefs of Staff. The economic team was headed by Professor Sidney Suffrin of Syracuse University, who reported to the ECA. Both teams completed their task by the end of 1951. The opening of formal negotiations was announced in March 1952, after the Departments of Defense and State, and the Mutual Security Agency had studied the respective reports. Negotiations lasted for nineteen months and were completed during the first year of President Dwight D. Eisenhower's administration.

On September 26, 1953, three bilateral agreements were signed in Madrid by Artajo, the foreign minister, and James C. Dunn, the U.S. ambassador: a Defense Agreement for the construction and use of military facilities in Spain by the United States; an Economic Aid Agreement covering economic assistance to Spain under the Mutual Security Act of 1951; and a Mutual Defense Assistance Agreement covering military end-item assistance. As part of the agreements, $226 million were to be provided to Spain during the 1954 fiscal year, under the terms of the Mutual Security Act.[41] A U.S. Operations Mission was set up in Spain to organize the economic and technical assistance. Likewise, a military assistance advisory group was established to coordinate the military assistance program with the Spanish authorities.

The Pact of Madrid, as the three agreements came to be called, was a diplomatic triumph for the Franco regime. It signalled the beginning of the end of Spain's international isolation. The right to construct and operate military bases gave the United States a strong interest in the political stability of Spain, which under the circumstances implied acquiescence in the continuation of the regime. The characteristics of the regime guaranteed that the relationship was one between unequal partners, a feature that irritated Spanish officials.[42] The way in which the agreements were announced by the two governments illustrates the fundamental asymmetry in the bilateral relationship, as well as the desire of both parties to keep the relationship strictly circumscribed within the narrow and clearly defined boundaries of the common security interest. Given the opposition that still remained—domestic as well as foreign— to doing business with Franco, the agreements were given a low-key, understated treatment by Washington. They did not constitute a mutual defense treaty or an alliance. The respective texts were drafted as executive agreements, which did not require Senate approval, and became effective immediately.

Franco, on the other hand, sent the agreements to the Cortes for ratification, describing them as "the most important achievement of our foreign policy." Stretching somewhat the extent of the commitments that had been made, he claimed that the agreements obtained "the interest of the most powerful nation on earth in our defense." Furthermore, this had been brought about "without prejudice to our peculiar ideologies." Artajo, addressing the Cortes on the same subject, attributed the previous misunderstandings with the United States to "the malicious anti-Spanish policy of the governments of England and France" and to "pro-Communist elements infiltrated in the Administration."[43]

Although initiated by a circumscribed common security interest, the Pact of Madrid brought Spain and the United States into closer economic and political relations than either of the two governments had anticipated. It established the framework for an enduring rapprochement that brought to an end the alternating cycles of estrangement and hostility that characterized the relations between the two countries during the previous one hundred and eighty years.

NOTES

1. Lequerica to Artajo, Personal y Reservado, Washington, July 3, 1948, no. 25, Ministerio de Asuntos Exteriores (hereafter cited as MAE) Legajo R4224 Expediente 1 (hereafter cited as L, E).

2. Lequerica to Artajo, Washington, April 28, 1949, no. 243, MAE, L R4224 E 1.

3. Lequerica to Artajo, Reservada, Washington, September 13, 1948, no. 52, MAE, L R4224 E 1.

4. Lequerica to Artajo, Enteramente Confidencial (handwritten letter, sent via a personal friend who had spent a few days with the Lequericas), Washington, May 29, 1949, no. 113, MAE, L R4224 E 1.

5. Lequerica to Artajo, Enteramente Secreta, Washington, August 26, 1950, no. 225, MAE, L R4224 E 1.

6. Lequerica to Artajo, Washington, October 7, 1950, no. 228, MAE, L R4224 E 1.

7. In one instance Lequerica refers to security problems in the embassy and his fears concerning the safety of the code utilized to encrypt communications with Madrid. He suggests the possibility of utilizing couriers, saying that for sensitive documents he will use "reliable travellers" but send "nothing of interest" by telegram. Lequerica to Artajo, Enteramente Secreta, Washington, July 24, 1950, no. 218, MAE, L R4224 E 1.

In a previous communication, he refers to the use of private addresses (mail drops) for his letters to Artajo. The letter in question is being sent to D. Miguel Garcia Holgado, a person of his "full confidence" who will deliver it to Artajo. Lequerica to Artajo, Washington, July 3, 1948, no. 25, MAE, L R4224 E 1.

8. Lequerica to Artajo, (handwritten note on Spanish embassy stationery), Personal, Washington, March 29, 1950, no. 55, MAE, L R4224 E 1.

9. Unsigned copy for files of note from Artajo to General Francisco Franco, Ministry of Foreign Affairs, San Sebastián, August 4, 1950, no. 61, MAE, L R4224 E 1.

10. Lequerica to Artajo, Enteramente Confidencial, Washington, June 10, 1949, no. 114, MAE, L R4224 E 1.

11. Lequerica to Artajo, Enteramente Secreta (handwritten letter), Washington, June 11, 1951, MAE, L R4224 E 2.

12. Lequerica to Artajo, Reservado, Washington, June 26, 1952, no. 290, MAE, L R4224 E 3.

13. Memorandum of Conversation, by Mr. Theodore Xanthaky, Special Assistant to the Ambassador in Portugal (Lincoln MacVeagh), Lisbon, July 27, 1949, U.S. Department of State, *Foreign Relations of the United States* (Washington, D.C.: Government Printing Office), 4:754 (hereafter cited as *FRUS*).

14. During the national-syndicalist phase (1939–1945), the Falange was in the ascendant. During the national-Catholic phase (1945–1957), the Catholic organization Accion Católica, of which Artajo was a leading representative, played a prominent role. After 1957 the regime entered a technocratic, developmentalist phase, during which members of a semisecret Catholic society, Opus Dei, occupied key government positions.

15. The following documents describe the saga of Sister Margarita's relic:

1. Lequerica to Antero de Ussía, Chief of the Diplomatic Cabinet, Ministry of Foreign Affairs, Washington, July 22, 1949, no. 406.

2. Artajo to the Most Reverend Leopoldo Eijo y Garay, Bishop of Madrid-Alcalá and Patriarch of the West Indies, San Sebastián, July 27, 1949.

3. The Bishop-Patriarch to Artajo, Vigo, August 1, 1949.

4. Mario Ponce de Leon, Spanish Consul in Rome, to Antero de Ussía, Rome, August 2, 1949.

5. Antero de Ussía to Ponce de Leon, San Sebastián, August 9, 1949.

6. Antero de Ussía to Lequerica, San Sebastián, August 9, 1949. All in MAE, L R4224 E 1.

16. William V. Shannon, "The Franco Lobby," *The Reporter*, 20 June 1950, p. 19.

17. Lequerica to Artajo (letter by courier), Washington, May 31, 1952, MAE, L R4224 E 4.

18. Mrs. W. R. Hearst Jr., Evie Peyton Gordon, columnist for the Scripps-Howard papers, and Mrs. Maxwell Peter Miller, the niece of Colonel Robert R. McCormick, who had appointed her as editor of the *Times-Herald*. According to Shannon, "The highlight of the winter social season for this group was the party given by the Brewsters at the Mayflower Hotel in honor of Lequerica." Shannon, op. cit., 23.

19. Culbertson to the Secretary of State, Secret, Madrid, June 20, 1950, no. 792, *FRUS*, 3:1564.

20. Luis de Galinsoga, *Centinela de Occidente* (*Semblanza Biográfica de Francisco Franco*) (Barcelona: Editorial AHR, 1956); José Doussinague, *España Tenía Razón (1939–1945)*, 2nd ed. (Madrid: Espasa-Calpe, 1950), and Francisco Franco Bahamonde [Jakim Boor, pseud.], *Masonería* (Madrid: Fundacion Nacional Francisco Franco, 1981).

21. Lequerica to Artajo, Washington, August 8, 1949, MAE, L R4224 E 1.

22. "I suppose that Brewer as usual, at the service of his boss and of Dunham [Spanish bureau chief, State Department], has failed to grasp that Spanish Freemasonry is an anti-national, anti-Christian entity of a purely political combative nature. But because it is a useful, well-intentioned suggestion, I enclose Klein's letter for your information. [Max H. Klein, longtime President of the American

Chamber of Commerce in Spain, was a friend and ally of the regime.] The letter from Klein to Merry del Val, New York, March 27, 1950, says that the issue of Freemasonry is very delicate and that Brewer's press campaign could undo the progress made so far in improving relations with the United States. It appears in the archives underlined in red pencil with a handwritten note by Artajo, "Copia a S.E." (Copy to Franco). Lequerica to Artajo, Washington, March 29, 1950, no. 190, MAE, L R4224 E 1.

23. Lequerica to Artajo, Reservado, Washington, June 26, 1952, no. 290, MAE, L 4224 E 3.

24. Artajo to Lequerica, San Sebastián, September 2, 1949, no. 467, MAE, L R4224 E 1.

25. Internal note to the minister of foreign affairs, Madrid, April 23, 1949. The assistant in question was Don Carlos de Rafael, private secretary to Lequerica, for whom a visa to travel to Washington had been requested. MAE, L R4224 E 1.

26. The aide-mémoire was dated Madrid, December 7, 1949. The note to Prat, addressed "Dear Perico" and signed "Paul," was dated February 7, 1950. MAE, L 4224 E 1.

27. Artajo to Lequerica, Personal y Reservado, Madrid, December 7, 1949, MAE, L R4224 E 1.

28. Memorandum from the Ministry of Foreign Affairs to the United States Embassy in Madrid, no. 3, Madrid, February 14, 1950, MAE, L R4224 E 1. Fearing that the State Department would request his departure from Washington, Lequerica asked for help from Max Truitt, legal counsel to the embassy and son-in-law of Vice President Alben Barkley, and from Senator McCarran who telephoned the undersecretary of state on his behalf. Lequerica to Artajo, Personal y Reservada, Washington, July 6, 1949, no. 119, MAE, L R4224 E 1.

29. "There was and remains a deep conflict between the viewpoint of the Spanish on religious toleration and that of the President. Mr. Truman, as everyone knows, is a deeply religious man, a Baptist, and a little bit of what people have called a hardshell Baptist. He showed great feeling in discussing the religious problems in Spain as he said to me, 'I do not know what your religion is, I do not even know if you have any, but I am a Baptist and I believe that in any country man should be permitted to worship his God in his own way. The situation in Spain is intolerable. Do you know that a Baptist who dies in Spain must even be buried in the middle of the night?' " Stanton Griffis, *Lying in State* (Garden City, N.Y.: Doubleday, 1952), 269.

30. Senator Patrick McCarran, "Why Shouldn't the Spanish Fight for Us?" *The Saturday Evening Post*, 28 April 1951, 25.

31. Statement of Policy by the National Security Council, NSC 72/4, Top Secret, Washington, February 1, 1951, *FRUS*, 4:789–790.

32. "Three magnificent red and gold eighteenth-century coaches, each drawn by six horses, appeared in front of 5 Ramon de la Cruz, accompanied by more than two hundred of the picturesque Moorish guards of the Franco household, dressed in their native costumes and carrying lances, and with their horses' hoofs embellished with gold and silver. Never, I think, had there been a more picturesque procession through the streets to the mighty Oriente Palace. The emotional

and sentimental Madrileños were keenly aware of the history-making event of a new United States ambassador to Spain after five years." Griffis, op. cit., 283–284.

33. The Secretary of State to the Ambassador-Designate to Spain, at Washington, Secret, Washington, February 6, 1951, *FRUS*, 4:791.

34. Memorandum by the International Security Affairs Committee (ISAC D-12a), Top Secret, Washington, April 13, 1951, *FRUS*, 840–843.

35. Admiral Sherman was a prominent advocate of improving U.S. relations with Spain. His son-in-law, Lieutenant Commander John Fitzpatrick, was assistant naval attaché in Madrid. "Of Sherman's colleagues on the Joint Chiefs of Staff, Chairman Bradley particularly remained cool to the Spanish idea. According to former Secretary of Defense Johnson, Bradley's position changed in response to Sherman's forceful argument. . . . How vigorously and often Admiral Sherman broached the subject of Spain with the President will never be fully known. But there is no doubt that Sherman working with Secretary of Defense Marshall provided the critical force to change the President's mind. Reluctantly, the President did change it." Theodore J. Lowi, "Bases in Spain" in *American Civil-Military Decision: A Book of Case Studies*, ed. Harold Stein (Birmingham: University of Alabama Press, 1963), 692.

The Defense Department announced Admiral Sherman's trip that included visits to Spain, France, Great Britain, and Italy, as part of a process of familiarization with military conditions in Europe in preparation for a September meeting of NATO defense ministers. A few days after his meeting with Franco in Madrid, which cleared the way for the beginning of the negotiations for military bases, he died in Naples.

36. The Ambassador in the United Kingdom (Gifford) to the Secretary of State, telegram, Top Secret, Priority, London, July 8, 1951, *FRUS*, 4:827–828.

37. *FRUS* (1951), 4:828.

38. "Sec called in Brit and Fr Ambs separately this afternoon with regard to their recent representations on Spain. . . . Sec went on to say that . . . he, in company with Sec Marshall, General Bradley and Admiral Sherman, had reviewed problem in detail with Pres. After carefully weighing all elements latter had decided that we must proceed and to this end high Defense official will leave for brief visit to Madrid in few days. . . . Our military authorities were convinced of desirability of going ahead and to draw back at this time would merely result in deflecting political criticism to our Brit and Fr allies. In such a situation results on our Foreign Aid program cld well be imagined." Secretary of State to the Embassy in Madrid, telegram, Top Secret, Eyes only Amb., Washington, July 12, 1951, *FRUS*, 828–829.

39. Memorandum of Conversation, by the Chief of Naval Operations, Top Secret, Madrid, July 16, 1951, FRUS, 4:832–834. See also Griffis, op. cit., 294–295.

40. *FRUS* (1951), 4:834–835. Referring to the meeting in Madrid, President Truman acknowledged that U.S. policy toward Spain had changed "to some extent." When asked if the Franco-Sherman talks were the result of a National Security Council decision he replied, "It is the result of the advice from the Department of Defense." Griffis, op. cit., 835.

41. The text of the agreements was published in U.S. Department of State,

Department of State Bulletin, October 5, 1953 (Washington, D.C.: Government Printing Office), 435–442.

42. "The United States is not proposing to Spain a marriage but a concubinage. . . . What is required for the agreement between our countries is a wedding, even if it is not very luxurious nor celebrated in one of New York's most elegant churches." Report of conversation with Frank Nash, Assistant Secretary of Defense for International Security Affairs, Lequerica to Artajo, Enteramente Secreto, telegram no. 80, Washington, August 21, 1952, MAE, L R4224 E 3.

43. The presentation of the agreements to the Cortes took place on November 30, 1953. The texts of the speeches by Franco and Artajo were published by MAE, *Los Convenios con los Estados Unidos de América* (Madrid: Oficina de Información Diplomática, 1953).

Epilogue

The implementation of the base agreements brought the two countries into much closer contact through technical training, travel, cultural, and scientific exchanges. It soon became evident to U.S. officials that for the military program to succeed it was necessary to strengthen the Spanish economy and modernize the country's infrastructure. According to an estimate by the Strategic Air Command in 1958 "a wing of B-47's consumes in an afternoon more fuel than the entire Spanish railroad tanker fleet can transport in a month."[1]

The U.S. Operations Mission established sections that dealt with industry, electric power, transportation, agriculture, mining and commerce, economic analysis, and planning. The Economic Aid Agreement committed the Spanish government to stabilize the currency, maintain a valid exchange rate, and exercise fiscal and monetary discipline. For the members of the Operations Mission, this implied establishing close working relations with Spanish economic officials on issues ranging from sectorial investment priorities to macroeconomic policy. Between 1955 and 1958 the annual level of economic assistance received by Spain fluctuated between thirty-eight percent and fifty-five percent of the total exports. The United States provided decisive technical and financial support to the 1959 Stabilization Program that signalled the end of the policy of economic autarky and brought about a decade and a half of accelerated growth that propelled Spain into the ranks of the industrialized countries.[2] The successful reinsertion into the international economy, and the massive human exchanges brought about by tourism and migration during the 1960s transformed Spain's economy and society in ways that were neither anticipated nor always welcomed by the regime. The process of economic liberalization also facilitated closer cultural contacts between the United States and Spain. The Spanish reading public became familiarized with North American literature through the works of John Dos Passos, William Faulkner, and Ernest Hemingway. The latter was regarded by officials of the regime as a friend of Spain, notwithstanding his sympathy for the Republic during the civil war. His Nobel Prize for literature was celebrated as an award to Spanish culture.

An unexpected and profoundly disturbing shock from abroad originated in the Ecumenical Council Vatican II, where the country that had been described as the Light of Trent, the Sword of Rome, and the Cradle of Loyola, discovered that it had become theologically obsolete. The Spanish hierarchy, whose leaders argued that the situation prevailing in Spain of doctrinal intolerance and state-enforced religious conformity was the Catholic ideal, learned that this state of affairs was a historical aberration. Worse still, in the last religious confrontation between the United States and Spain, this time within two different interpretations of Catholicism rather than across separate denominations, the defeat of the Spanish bishops and of Cardinal Alfredo Ottaviani, the head of the Holy Office, represented by the Declaration on Religious Liberty—which upheld separation of church and state and advocated religious tolerance, even for atheists—came at the hands of the U.S. bishops, aided by John Courtney Murray of the Society of Jesus, a professor of theology in Woodstock College, Maryland.[3] The church reforms initiated by John XXIII's policy of aggiornamento undermined the intermingling of religion and politics that Franco had used to legitimize his regime.[4]

The widening of the bilateral relationship beyond the strictly military sphere proved to be a double-edged sword. It gave Franco the means to remain in power for life but it also helped to ensure that the regime would not survive his death. In June 1959, several months before his unprecedented trip to Madrid, President Eisenhower received the following description of the evolution of the relationship between the United States and Spain from Acting Secretary of State Douglas Dillon:

> The United States acquired a more than passive interest in what was going on in Spain by signing the 1953 Defense Agreement. Since then, we have actively, although often indirectly, pursued

policies that committed us in Spain's internal affairs. Our use of Spanish bases as a part of our cold war deterrent to Soviet aggression has removed Spain from among the neutrals, shattered tradition, and placed it on our side. Our military assistance to Spain's armed forces has been aiding them to develop a capability for defense of Spanish territory, and of the jointly used military facilities located thereon. It has also taught them United States' concepts and use of NATO–type equipment. Our economic aid, which since 1951 has exceeded $1.1 billion in the form of grants, loans, and sales of surplus agricultural commodities in pesetas, has contributed to economic stability in Spain, promoted some economic growth in that country and more than compensated for the impact on Spain's economy of our base construction program. . . . We have, in this manner, and to a greater degree than most Spaniards are willing to realize or recognize, taken Spain out of the cocoon of isolationism in which it has been sheltered for generations. Our policies in Spain and for Spain have been the catalysts of its present evolution into the modern society of nations. . . . It is largely due to United States' support that Spain was admitted to the United Nations in December 1955. We encouraged Spain's joining the International Monetary Fund and the International Bank for Reconstruction and Development, and we look forward to the early admission of Spain as a full and equal member of the Organization for European Economic Cooperation, a step which we have steadfastly supported. We continue to back the admission of Spain to NATO . . . The purpose of all these efforts is to Europeanize Spain, and to establish and nurture as many bonds as possible between the Spanish people and the Western world. Breaking down Spain's isolation will, we hope, give an impetus to the development of more democratic attitudes among its people, the majority of whom still appear to have understanding and good will for us. . . . We believe that this Europeanization of Spain offers the best hope that the change, which seems inevitable sooner or later, will be evolutionary rather than revolutionary.[5]

The favorable evolution of the postwar relations between Spain and the United States, which have endured until the present time, have had some paradoxical features. In contrast to what happened in the rest of Western Europe where the Marshall Plan preceded NATO, with Spain the military connection prepared the way for economic cooperation. In the long run, the ideologically neutral stance adopted by the United States after 1951 proved more effective in bringing about political change than the previous efforts to liberalize the regime by direct diplomatic pressure. The bilateral relationship with the United States prepared the way for Spain's eventual integration with Europe. The promotion of the "Europeanization" of Spain coincided with the objectives of a distinguished group of Spanish reformers such as Benito Jerónimo Feijoo, Gaspar Melchor de Jovellanos, Francisco Giner de los Rios, and José Ortega y Gasset.

In the seventeenth century, the route from Milan to Brussels, linking the Crown's possessions in Italy and the Netherlands, was known as the Spanish Road. Because of the unusual circumstances created by "the peculiar ideologies" of the Franco regime, during the second half of the twentieth century, the Spanish Road, connecting Madrid and Brussels (NATO and the European Community), took a transatlantic detour by way of Washington.

NOTES

1. Arthur Whitaker, *Spain and the Defense of the West: Ally and Liability* (New York: Harper Brothers, 1961), 66.

2. See Rodrigo Botero, *Reflections on the Modernization of Spain* (San Francisco, Calif.: ICS Press, 1992). See also Manuel-Jesús González, *La Economía Política del Franquismo (1940–1970): Dirigismo, Mercado y Planificación* (Madrid: Editorial Tecnos, 1979).

3. On this controversy, see Donald Pelotte, *John Courtney Murray: Theologian in Conflict* (New York: Paulist Press, 1976), and Dominique Gonnet, *La Liberté Religieuse à Vatican II: La Contribution de John Courtney Murray S. J.* (Paris: Les Éditions du Cerf, 1994.

4. During an official visit to Madrid in 1969, Botero observed that Franco's office in El Pardo—which had once displayed pictures of Hitler and Mussolini—was decorated with photographs of President Eisenhower and Pius XII.

5. Memorandum from Acting Secretary of State Dillon to President Eisenhower, Washington, June 4, 1959, U.S. Department of State, *Foreign Relations of the United States* (Washington, D.C.: Government Printing Office, 1958–1960), 7: 726–729.

Bibliography

Adams, Brooks. *The Law of Civilization and Decay. An Essay on History*. London: Swan Sonnenschein, 1895.

Adams, Henry. *History of the United States of America During the Administration of Thomas Jefferson*. 2 vols. New York: Albert and Charles Boni, 1930.

Adams, John Quincy. *The Memoirs of John Quincy Adams, Comprising Portions of his Diary from 1795 to 1848*. Edited by Charles Frances Adams. Philadelphia: J. B. Lippincott, 1874–1877.

———. *The Writings of John Quincy Adams*. 7 vols. Edited by Worthington Chauncey Ford. New York: Macmillan, 1913.

Artola, Miguel. *La España de Fernando VII*. Madrid: Espasa-Calpe, 1968.

———. *Los Afrancesados*. Madrid: Ediciones Turner, 1976.

Bailey, Thomas. *A Diplomatic History of the American People*. New York: Appleton-Century-Crofts, 1958.

Balfour, Sebastian. *The End of the Spanish Empire, 1898–1923*. Oxford: Clarendon Press, 1997.

Bancroft, George. *History of the Formation of the Constitution of the United States of America*. 2 vols. New York: D. Appleton, 1882.

Bécker, Jerónimo. *Historia de las Relaciones Exteriores de España durante el Siqlo XIX*. 3 vols. Madrid: Establecimiento Tipográfico de J. Ratés, 1924.

Bemis, Samuel Flagg. *Jay's Treaty: A Study in Commerce and Diplomacy*. New York: Macmillan, 1924.

———. *The Diplomacy of the American Revolution*. New York: D. Appleton-Century, 1935.

———. *Pinckney's Treaty: America's Advantage from Europe's Distress, 1783–1800*. New Haven: Yale University Press, 1960.

Bernstein, Harry. *Origins of Inter-American Interest, 1700–1812*. Philadelphia: University of Pennsylvania Press, 1945.

———. *Making an Inter-American Mind*. Gainville: University of Florida Press, 1961.

Botero, Rodrigo. *Reflections on the Modernization of Spain*. San Francisco, Calif.: ICS Press, 1992.

Brooks, Philip Coolidge. *Diplomacy and the Borderlands: The Adams-Onís Treaty of 1819*. Berkeley: University of California Press, 1939.

Burgess, John. *Political Science and Comparative Constitutional Law*. Boston: Ginn and Company, 1902.

Carr, Raymond. *Spain 1808–1975*. Oxford: Clarendon Press, 1982.

Cervera y Topete, Pascual. *Guerra Hispano-Americana: Colección de Documentos Referentes a la Escuadra de Operaciones de las Antillas*. 2nd ed. El Ferrol: El Correo Gallego, 1900.

Concas y Palau, Victor. *La Escuadra del Almirante Cervera*. 2nd. ed. Madrid: Librería de San Martin, 1899.

Cooper, Stephen. *The Politics of Ernest Hemingway*. Ann Arbor, Mich.: UMI Research Press, 1987.

Cortada, James. *Two Nations over Time: Spain and the United States, 1776–1977*. Westport, Conn.: Greenwood Press, 1978.

Corwin, Arthur. *Spain and the Abolition of Slavery in Cuba, 1817–1886*. Austin: University of Texas Press, 1967.

Current, Richard, Harry Williams, Frank Freidel, and Alan Brinkley. *American History: A Survey*. 6th ed., vol. 1. New York: Knopf, 1983.

———. *American History: A Survey*. 7th ed., vol. 2. New York: Knopf, 1987.

Deakin, James. *The Lobbyists*. Washington, D.C.: Public Affairs Press, 1966.

De Vitoria, Francisco. *Political Writings*. Edited by Anthony Pagden and Jeremy Lawrence. Cambridge: Cambridge University Press, 1991.

Diggins, John. *Mussolini and Fascism: The View from America*. Princeton: Princeton University Press, 1972.

Doniol, Henri. *Histoire de la participation de la France à l'établissement des États Unis d'Amérique. Correspondence diplomatique et documents. Complément du tome V*. 5 vols. Paris: Imprimerie Nationale, 1899.

Doussinague, José. *España Tenía Razón (1939–1945)*. 2nd ed. Madrid: Espasa-Calpe, 1950.

Eccles, David. *By Safe Hand: Letters of Sybil and David Eccles, 1939–1942*. London: Bodley Head, 1983.

Ellis, Havelock. *The Soul of Spain*. Boston: Houghton Mifflin, 1908.

Elson, Henry William. *History of the United States of America*. New York: Macmillan, 1914.

Feis, Herbert. *The Spanish Story: Franco and the Nations at War*. New York: Knopf, 1948.

Fiske, John. *The Critical Period of American History, 1783–1789*. Boston: Houghton Mifflin, 1888.

Foner, Philip. *The Spanish-Cuban-American War and the Birth of American Imperialism, 1895–1902*. New York: Monthly Review Press, 1972.

Franco Bahamonde, Francisco [Jakim Boor, pseud.]. *Masonería*. Madrid: Fundacion Nacional Francisco Franco, 1981.

Frank, Waldo. *Virgin Spain: Scenes from the Spiritual Drama of a Great People*. New York: Boni and Liveright, 1926.

Fugier, André. *Napoléon et L'Espagne, 1799–1808.* 2 vols. Bibliothèque d'histoire contemporaine. Paris: Librairie Félix Alcan, 1930.

Fusi Aizpúrua, Juan Pablo. *Franco: A Biography.* London: Unwin Hyman, 1987.

Fusi Aizpúrua, Juan Pablo, and Jordi Palafox Gamir. *España 1808–1996: El Desafío de la Modernidad.* Madrid: Espasa-Calpe, 1997.

Galinsoga, Luis de. *Centinela de Occidente (Semblanza Biográfica de Francisco Franco).* Barcelona: Editorial AHR, 1956.

Gilbert, Felix. *To the Farewell Address: Ideas of Early American Foreign Policy.* Princeton: Princeton University Press, 1961.

Godoy, Manuel. *Memorias del Príncipe de la Paz.* 2 vols. Madrid: Ediciones Atlas, 1956.

Gonnet, Dominique. *La Liberté Religieuse à Vatican II: La Contribution de John Courtney Murray, S. J.* Paris: Les Éditions du Cerf, 1994.

González, Manuel-Jesús. *La Economía Política del Franquismo (1940–1970): Dirigismo, Mercado y Planificación.* Madrid: Editorial Tecnos, 1979.

Griffis, Stanton. *Lying in State.* Garden City, N.Y.: Doubleday, 1952.

Guerra y Sánchez, Ramiro, ed. *Historia de la Nación Cubana.* 10 vols. La Habana: Editorial Historia de la Nación Cubana, 1952.

Guttmann, Allen. *The Wound in the Heart: America and the Spanish Civil War.* New York: The Free Press of Glencoe, 1962.

———, ed. *American Neutrality and the Spanish Civil War.* Boston: D.C. Heath, 1963.

Hale, Edward Everett. *Memories of a Hundred Years.* 2 vols. New York: Macmillan, 1904.

Hargreaves-Mawdsley, William Norman, comp. *Spain under the Bourbons, 1700 1833: A Collection of Documents.* London: Macmillan, 1973.

———. *Eighteenth Century Spain, 1700–1788: A Political, Diplomatic, and Institutional History.* London: Macmillan, 1979.

Harris, Seymour. *The European Recovery Program.* Cambridge: Harvard University Press, 1948.

Hart, Albert Bushnell. *American History Told by Contemporaries.* 5 vols. New York: Macmillan, 1968.

Hayes, Carlton. *Wartime Mission in Spain, 1942–1945.* New York: Macmillan, 1946.

Herr, Richard. *The Eighteenth-Century Revolution in Spain.* Princeton: Princeton University Press, 1958.

Hilt, Douglas. *The Troubled Trinity: Godoy and the Spanish Monarchs.* Tuscaloosa: University of Alabama Press, 1987.

Hoare, Samuel. *Complacent Dictator.* New York: Knopf, 1947.

Hughes, Emmet John. *Report from Spain.* New York: Henry Holt, 1947.

Hull, Cordell. *The Memoirs of Cordell Hull.* 2 vols. New York: Macmillan, 1948.

Iriye, Akira. *Pacific Estrangement: Japanese and American Expansion, 1897–1911.* Cambridge: Harvard University Press, 1972.

Jefferson, Thomas. *The Writings of Thomas Jefferson.* 10 vols. Collected and edited by Paul Leicester Ford. New York: G. P. Putnam's Sons, 1892–1899.

Kamen, Henry. *The War of Succession in Spain, 1700–1715.* London: Weidenfeld and Nicolson, 1969.

Kennedy, Paul. *The Rise and Fall of the Great Powers: Economic Change and Military Conflict from 1500 to 2000*. New York: Random House, 1987.

Kindelán, Alfredo. *Ejército y Política*. Madrid: Ediciones Ares, 1946.

King, Georgiana. *Heart of Spain*. Cambridge: Harvard University Press, 1941.

La Feber, Walter. *The New Empire: An Interpretation of American Expansion, 1860–1898*. Ithaca, N.Y.: Cornell University Press, 1963.

Langley, Lester. *The Cuban Policy of the United States: A Brief History*. New York: Wiley, 1968.

La Parra López, Emilio. *La Alianza de Godoy con los Revolucionarios: España y Francia a fines del Siglo XVIII*. Madrid: Consejo Superior de Investigaciones Científicas, 1992.

Mackenzie, Alexander Slidell. *A Year in Spain, by a Young American*. 2 vols. London: John Murray, 1831.

———. *Spain Revisited*. 2 vols. New York: Harper and Brothers, 1836.

Mar-Molinero, Clare, and Angel Smith, eds. *Nationalism and the Nation in the Iberian Peninsula*. Oxford: Berg, 1996.

Mason, Gregory. *Remember the* Maine. New York: Henry Holt, 1939.

May, Ernest. *Imperial Democracy: The Emergence of America as a Great Power*. New York: Harcourt, Brace and World, 1961.

———. *American Imperialism: A Speculative Essay*. Chicago: Imprint Publications, 1991.

———. ed. *American Cold War Strategy: Interpreting NSC 68*. Boston: Saint Martin's Press, 1993.

Millis, Walter. *The Martial Spirit*. Cambridge: Riverside Press, 1931.

Muriel, Andrés. *Historia de Carlos IV*. 2 vols. Biblioteca de Autores Españoles. Madrid: Atlas, 1959.

O'Toole, George. *The Spanish War: An American Epic—1898*. New York: Norton, 1984.

Pelotte, Donald. *John Courtney Murray: Theologian in Conflict*. New York: Paulist Press, 1976.

Pérez, Louis. *Cuba between Empires, 1878–1902*. Pittsburgh: University of Pittsburgh Press, 1983.

Pike, Frederick. *Hispanismo, 1898–1936: Spanish Conservatives and Liberals and Their Relations with Spanish America*. Notre Dame: University of Notre Dame Press, 1971.

Prados de la Escosura, Leandro. *De Imperio a Nación: Crecimiento y Atraso Económico en España, 1780–1930*. Madrid: Alianza Editorial, 1988.

Preston, Paul. *Franco: A Biography*. London: HarperCollins, 1993.

Ratcliff, Dillwyn. *Prelude to Franco: Political Aspects of the Dictatorship of General Miguel Primo de Rivera*. New York: Las Americas, 1957.

Rippy, James Fred. *Rivalry of the United States and Great Britain over Latin America, 1808–1830*. New York: Octagon Books, 1972.

Romanones, Alvaro Figueroa y Torres, Conde de. *Sagasta o el Político*. Madrid: Espasa-Calpe, 1930.

Rubottom, Richard, and Carter Murphy. *Spain and the United States Since World War II*. New York: Praeger, 1984.

Shneidman, J. Lee. *Spain and Franco, 1949–1959: Quest for International Acceptance.* New York: Facts on File, 1973.

Spain. Ministerio de Asuntos Exteriores. *Los Convenios con los Estados Unidos de América.* Texto íntegro del discurso pronunciado por el Ministro de Asuntos Exteriores D. Alberto Martín Artajo, en la Sesion Plenaria de las Cortes Españolas, el dia 30 de Noviembre de 1953. Madrid: Oficina de Información Diplomática, 1953.

Spain. Ministerio de Estado. *Spanish Diplomatic Correspondence and Documents, 1896–1900; Presented to the Cortes by the Minister of State.* Translation. Washington, D.C.: Government Printing Office, 1905.

Stanton, Edward. *Hemingway and Spain: A Pursuit.* Seattle: University of Washington Press, 1989.

Stein, Harold, ed. *American Civil-Military Decisions: A Book of Case Studies.* Birmingham: University of Alabama Press, 1963.

Stourzh, Gerald. *Benjamin Franklin and American Foreign Policy.* Chicago: University of Chicago Press, 1954.

Strong, Josiah. *Our Country: Its Possible Future and Its Present Crisis.* New York: The American Home Missionary Society, 1885.

Sumner, William. "The Conquest of the United States by Spain." A lecture before the Phi Beta Kappa Society of Yale University, January 16, 1899.

Tortella Casares, Gabriel. *El Desarrollo de la España Contemporánea: Historia Económica de los Siglos XIX y XX.* 2nd ed. Madrid: Alianza Editorial, 1995.

Traina, Richard. *American Diplomacy and the Spanish Civil War.* Bloomington: Indiana University Press, 1968.

Truman, Harry S. *Memoirs.* 2 vols. Garden City, N.Y.: Doubleday, 1955–1956.

Tucker, Norman. *Americans in Spain: Patriots, Expatriates, and the Early American Hispanists, 1780–1850.* Boston: Atheneum, 1980.

U.S. Department of State. *Foreign Relations of the United States.* FRUS, 1925 vol. 2, 1931 vol. 2, 1945 vol. 2 and 5, 1946 vol. 5, 1947 vols. 2 and 3, 1948 vol. 3, 1949 vol. 4, 1950 vol. 3, 1951 vol. 4, 1958–1960 vol. 7. Washington, D.C.: Government Printing Office.

———. *A Decade of American Foreign Policy: Basic Documents, 1941–1949.* Rev. ed. Washington, D.C.: Government Printing Office, 1985.

———. *The Spanish Government and the Axis.* Documents. Washington, D.C.: Government Printing Office, 1946.

Waciuma, Wanjohi. *Intervention in Spanish Floridas, 1801–1813: A Study in Jeffersonian Foreign Policy.* Boston: Branden Press, 1976.

Wallis, Severn Teackle. *Glimpses of Spain; or, Notes of an Unfinished Tour in 1847.* New York: Harper and Brothers, 1849.

Weeks, William Earl. *John Quincy Adams and American Global Empire.* Lexington: University Press of Kentucky, 1992.

Welles, Sumner. *The Time for Decision.* New York: Harper and Brothers, 1944.

Wharton, Francis, ed. *The Revolutionary Diplomatic Correspondence of the United States.* 6 vols. Washington, D.C.: Government Printing Office, 1889.

Whitaker, Arthur. *The United States and the Independence of Latin America, 1800–1830.* Baltimore, Md.: The Johns Hopkins University Press, 1941.

————. *Spain and Defense of the West: Ally and Liability*. New York: Harper Brothers, 1961.

Williams, Stanley. *The Life of Washington Irving*. 2 vols. New York: Oxford University Press, 1935.

————. *The Spanish Background of American Literature*. 2 vols. New Haven: Yale University Press, 1968.

Wolff, Leon. *Little Brown Brother: How the United States Purchased and Pacified the Philippine Islands at the Century's Turn*. Garden City, N.Y.: Doubleday, 1961.

Yela Utrilla, Juan Francisco. *España Ante la Independencia de los Estados Unidos*. 2nd ed. 2 vols. Madrid: Ediciones Istmo, 1988.

Index

About the Author

RODRIGO BOTERO, an economist and historian, is a former finance minister of Colombia. He has also served the Colombian government in other capacities at home and abroad, including appointments as special adviser to the president on economic affairs and economic counselor at the Colombian Embassy in Washington D.C. Dr. Botero was founder and first executive director of a nongovernmental policy research center located in Bogota (Fedesarrollo), of which he is now a trustee. He was also founder and publisher of *Coyuntura Economica*, a quarterly economics journal, and of *Estrategia*, a journal on contemporary economic, social, and political affairs.